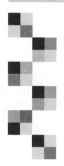

Reengineering .NET

- Bradley Irby

✦ Addison-Wesley

Upper Saddle River, NJ • Boston • Indianapolis • San Francisco
New York • Toronto • Montreal • London • Munich • Paris • Madrid
Capetown • Sydney • Tokyo • Singapore • Mexico City

The publisher offers excellent discounts on this book when ordered in quantity for bulk purchases or special sales, which may include electronic versions and/or custom covers and content particular to your business, training goals, marketing focus, and branding interests. For more information, please contact:

  U.S. Corporate and Government Sales
  (800) 382-3419
  corpsales@pearsontechgroup.com

For sales outside the United States, please contact:

  International Sales
  international@pearsoned.com

Visit us on the Web: informit.com/aw

The Library of Congress cataloging-in-publication data is on file.

ISBN-13: 978-0-321-82145-4
ISBN-10:   0-321-82145-9

Text printed in the United States on recycled paper at
R.R. Donnelley in Crawfordsville, Indiana.
First printing: October 2012

I would like to say thank you to my friends and family for their support and kind words; my children, Max and Lucas, for forgiving me for all those nights when I was writing and couldn't read them a story; and especially my wife, sweet Marcela, for her seemingly unlimited patience, understanding, faith, and encouragement. Many Chuicks!

Contents

Preface

What Is Software Reengineering?

Any developer who has been practicing his craft for more than a few years has been confronted with the task of enhancing an application that is difficult to work with. Navigating the code is difficult, figuring out where to start tracking down a defect is difficult, and making changes is difficult. Everything is difficult with these applications. Enhancements and bug fixes can be time-consuming, risky, and expensive.

One option for these legacy applications is to take them offline for a year or more to rewrite from scratch. Often these applications are so critical to the operation of the business, however, that feature development cannot be stopped for such an extended period of time. Therefore, work on the legacy system continues on, making patches and fixes to try to get through the next release cycle.

There is another option to help these legacy systems—software reengineering.

What Is Old Software?

After a software application is built, it immediately begins to age. Software engineering is a young field, and new ways of building applications are created every day. As new tools are introduced to the industry, if current applications are not retrofitted to use these tools, they become more and more difficult to maintain.

Causes of Software Aging

Software can become old for many reasons. The most obvious is the breathtakingly rapid pace of technology improvement in the world today. New software technology that was developed just a few years ago is already considered old and difficult to maintain.

The rapidity of job changes that is becoming a standard can also add to the deterioration of code. As the original developers pack their bags and move on to other companies, the original intent of much of the code is forgotten, leaving the remaining developers to pick up the pieces and hack together solutions as best they can.

By continually reengineering the system to modern technologies, this dependence on the original architects becomes less crippling. New developers can easily adapt to the system architecture because it is up to date and plenty of information can be found about it on the Web.

Warning Signs

Certain signs can tell when a system reaches the point it needs to be reengineered.

Developer Resistance to Feature Requests

If developers resist the efforts by management or users to enhance an application, it might be because the system is too difficult to work with. Over time, the software can become fragile, causing any feature development to become difficult and frustrating.

Large Bug Fixing Effort Immediately After a Release

If the development team is swamped with defect notices immediately after a new release of the software, it indicates a lack of modern quality tools. Part of the reengineering process involves introducing these automated quality tools so that the defect rate should decrease significantly.

Persistent Quality Problems

Old software can often display its age by the number of defects it contains and the effort necessary to fix them. The older and more fragile software gets, the more difficult it is to fix problems without breaking something else. If you see two defects appear for every one that is fixed, this is a sign that the application needs to be reengineered.

Legacy applications are especially prone to quality problems because they cannot support the new quality assurance approaches of Unit Testing and System Mocking. Without these tools in place, making changes to a system can result in creating a defect in an area seemingly and totally unrelated to the change made.

The Goal and Advantages of Software Reengineering

The goal of software reengineering is to incrementally improve an existing system by injecting modern architecture and software development techniques, while continuing to enhance the system with new features and while never having to take the system offline. This means we can take an existing system and slowly improve on it until it is brought up to modern software development standards without the need for a large, concerted rewrite effort. Throughout the reengineering project, the system is ready for production release. In other words, we can keep the plane in the air while we fix it.

Injecting Modern Architecture

The architecture of a software system is what determines how the many necessary details are built. Trying to use the latest approach to build a new data entry form for an old system is like trying to attach a jet engine to a biplane. You might get it off the ground, but the frame is not going to hold up for long.

The first reaction of most managers when they hear that the system architecture must be updated is to assume the application must be rewritten from scratch. This is not necessarily true. Bringing the architecture up to date can be done incrementally, as long as the new pieces are introduced in the proper order and using the proper steps.

Injecting a new architecture does not have to be a large effort by a team of people. The approaches described here can be introduced slowly by a small team of people (or even a single architect), regardless of the size of the full development team or the number of lines of code. Each step is a standalone element that can be introduced without affecting the rest of the application. Injecting a new architecture and quality measurements can be done without a large budget or dedicated team.

Adding New Features While Never Going Offline

The steps in this book are designed so they do not interfere with other development that might be going on simultaneously. The structures are introduced in such a way that they will have no detrimental effect while they are being added, but when complete can be turned on with a few lines of code. This enables the product manager to continue accepting new feature requests and pushing new versions into production, while in the background, each of these new versions is a little better than the last.

Any enhancement that takes more than a single day by a single developer has been designed to be pushed out in small steps so that the application can continue to work with some of the features converted to the new structure and some still using the old structure.

As each piece of the application is converted to the new design, it becomes much more testable, and the defect rate for the application should decrease dramatically.

Playing Well with Agile Approaches

Many development shops have adopted some sort of Agile development strategy. For those not familiar with this approach, a basic tenet of Agile is short development efforts (measured in days or weeks, and called a Sprint) at the end of which the application is in a potentially releasable state.

Keeping the application in a potentially releasable state is what reengineering is about. Each change made should be complete and self-contained, so that when the code is checked in, the system still runs perfectly but does so in a slightly better way and with higher quality. This is the way the steps in this book are designed. Each can be done within a single sprint and often in a single day. The few reengineering efforts that require more time are designed to have no impact on the system if they are halfway implemented. The system continues to run, just some features run the old way and some run the new way.

Reducing Risk

After years of working with a software system, business users fall into a pattern of how they use it to get their jobs done. Rewriting a system from scratch can lose touch with these undocumented processes, forcing the users to adapt their workflow to the new system.

Reengineering maintains these undocumented business processes that are part of the normal workings of the company. By slowly injecting new architecture into the existing system, these processes are left undisturbed. If introducing some new architecture does disrupt the normal flow of business in some way, there is immediate feedback because the application can be pushed into production on a fast schedule just like normal.

Reducing Cost

Rewriting a system from scratch requires that all of the business logic also be redeveloped from scratch. Legacy systems normally have a large investment of time and knowledge that is literally thrown away and must be recreated for a rewrite.

Reengineering saves that large investment and reuses the existing business logic code, saving significant amounts of time and money. The numbers of tasks that can be skipped with a reengineering project are significant. Fewer requirement documents must be created because the existing system already embodies the requirements. This can save weeks or months of a business analyst's time in researching and documenting all of the user's needs. The business logic to implement those requirements is also already done so there is even more savings.

In 1990, W. M. Ulrich wrote an article for the October issue of *American Programmer* in which he described a commercial system with an estimate of $50 million to rewrite from scratch. The same project was successfully reengineered for a total cost of $12 million. Reengineering can be significantly less expensive than new development.

Who Is this Book For?

This book is intended to help anyone involved in keeping these systems up and running. For technical managers and product managers, it describes the process necessary to improve the reliability of the system—make it faster, easier to maintain, and with fewer defects. For architects and developers, it contains detailed descriptions of the possible choices for the new architecture and the code necessary to implement the key pieces. It contains detailed suggestions on how to incrementally improve the structure and quality of an application by adding modern architecture and automated testing approaches. Following the steps outlined in this book can improve the quality of an application and make it easier and faster to add new features.

Reengineering an existing system is easier, cheaper, and less risky than building an equivalent system from scratch. If you follow the suggestions outlined in this book, you will be able to improve both the speed of development and the resulting quality, all while "keeping the plane in the air."

I hope you find this book a great resource and time saver.

—Bradley Irby
bradirby.com

Acknowledgments

It would have been impossible for me to write this book without the help of many people. First, I would like to thank my technical editors, Joey Ebright and Peter Himschoot, who did an excellent job in making sure my code was clean, correct, and to the point. Their architectural insight and suggestions made this book much better than it could have been had I made the attempt alone. I would also like to thank my editors, Christopher Cleveland and Jeff Riley, for their valuable input on structure and flow of the book. And finally, I would like to thank Joan Murray for having the confidence in me to let me take on this challenge. I hope I get a chance to work with everyone again on another book.

About the Author

Bradley Irby is an accomplished software architect and CTO. During his 25-year professional career, he has overseen the development of highly customized internal and customer-facing applications, including a property management system to manage the repossessed properties for Bank of America, a commercial accounting system for high-net-worth individuals, a property tax prediction system for the County of San Mateo, California, and a distributed reporting system for Chevy's Restaurants. His other work includes projects for General Electric, Kashi, Wells Fargo, HP, and Adidas, in addition to many projects for medium-sized companies and startups such as OpenTable and Prosper.com.

Bradley specializes in software reengineering and software migration, injecting quality and stability into existing legacy systems. Bradley has converted many applications from VB6, ASP Classic, and early .NET versions into more modern applications with current architecture and the latest quality approaches. His recent projects include reengineering a two million-line .NET application to use modern architectures and unit testing, resulting in a near zero defect count. He is an expert at updating applications without having to shut them down or stop feature development. Using a reengineering process Bradley developed, old applications can be updated to improve quality and satisfy existing customers, while also allowing continued feature development to keep pace with competitors and attract new customers.

Bradley manages the San Francisco .NET user group and is a frequent speaker on technical software topics throughout the U.S. He holds a bachelor of Computer Science degree from the University of North Carolina and an MBA from the University of California at Berkeley.

Part I

Target Architecture

1.
Implementing a Service-Oriented Architecture

Before we begin looking at our code and how it needs to change, we need to discuss the overall architecture we are trying to move to. Understanding where we are going will make it much easier to make the correct decisions along the way.

We will implement a service-oriented architecture (SOA). This design describes our software architecture from a high level, explaining how large pieces should interact so the application does not become tightly coupled. This approach permeates the entire book, so understanding the principles here is critical to your projects' success.

An SOA is a way of designing an application to be extendable and easy to maintain. The SOA principles were first formalized by Thomas Erl in 2005 (http://soaprinciples.com/) and have been a popular design choice in recent years. The published principles are designed to apply to large-scale systems that can run on any piece of hardware that is accessible via a network. In the full description, these services can be internal or external to the application or even managed by someone outside of the development team, so service discovery and description of the components are significant pieces of Thomas Erl's SOA description. If you design a service that can be consumed by an outside entity, such as an API for a website or a third-party library to be used by other developers, these are excellent guidelines to follow.

For the purposes of this book, we use only part of the principles presented in Erl's excellent work. We assume that all of the services are internal to the application and that you have knowledge of the services that are built so that any interface definitions are known at build time. In other words, we assume that you have a full understanding and control of all the services that are used in the application while building the code. There is no need to build the code so that it can dynamically adapt to a changing external service. This assumption does not mean we cannot make the services we build available to an outside party; in this book, we just don't to go to the extra effort of advertising the service to the outside world or to the effort of creating an externally available definition of available features. If it is necessary to design and build an externally available service such as a public API, the additional Erl principles can be easily applied to just those instances where needed.

An Overview of the Service-Oriented Architecture

An SOA involves a collection of classes called services that provide various functions for use by the application. These are the basic building blocks of much of our application, so they are used frequently. Services are unassociated with each other and can operate as individual pieces or in concert with each other. Creating individual services improves maintainability of your application because each service can be enhanced or even replaced without affecting the rest of the system. This modularity also promotes decoupling of the pieces, allowing better reuse of the components. (We discuss what we mean by decoupling later in this chapter.)

In general, there are two types of services to build.

- **Application agnostic services**: Agnostic services are those that can provide their services without knowing anything about the application they are used in. There are no business rules specific to the application they are in, no business specific data manipulation, and no references to outside code that requires this type of knowledge.

- An example of an application agnostic service is a class that writes log messages to a text file. This type of class can be used by any type of application, regardless of the business purpose of the app. The methods and properties required from a logger class or service would likely not change between one application and another, so the logger is application-agnostic.

- Another example is a class that interacts with Facebook. This type of class can be built in a general manner so that it can be reused in other applications without any changes. Any data specific to an application can be passed into the Facebook service when necessary.

- Application agnostic services can also be collections of classes, such as a user management system. It is common to have the same user and security information used in the same way from one application to another, such as maintaining the username, password, and any security roles that the logged in user is granted. If this logic is general enough to be used among different applications, then it is application agnostic.

- **Application specific services**: These are services that need to have knowledge of the specific problem domain they work under. Typically, this means they work with data specific to the application or they implement business rules that do not apply to a generic business application. These services can possibly be used elsewhere within the same company, but they are unlikely to be useful in a different environment.

- An example of an application specific service is a class that enforces specific business rules. Assume you are building a sales management system and any potential sale over $100,000 must be approved by the sales manager. This rule is specific to the application it is in, and so any classes that enforce this rule are application specific.

As we build our services, we will make them application agnostic when possible to improve their portability. We will also keep these two types of services in different projects to further enable their reuse. Application agnostic services are not common, but they can be useful when they are encountered, so when working with them, we need to take extra care not to pollute these services with business-specific logic.

Services in an SOA can be described using the basic principles in the following sections.

Understanding Standardized Service Contracts

Each service must have a published and standardized service contract that callers can rely on. A service contract is simply a class that describes what properties and methods a class exposes for use by callers. In our application, we implement service contracts using interfaces. Interfaces are available in either C# or VB.NET (indeed, virtually all languages support interfaces), so this should not limit the choice of language you use in your project.

Service contracts are a fundamental aspect of SOA because they allow the calling code to use the functionality provided by a service without having a direct reference to the actual class that performs the logic. This is called loose coupling, and we discuss it in more detail in the next section.

> **NOTE**
>
> In Chapter 4, "Understanding the Dependency Inversion Principle," you learn how to create and use a service without having a direct reference to it. This is a key part of the architecture we use.

Interfaces

An interface describes just the signatures of methods, properties, or events that an implementing class provides. An interface does not provide any logic to implement these features (in fact, an interface with logic coded inside does not compile).

Creating an Interface

As shown in Listing 1.1, the syntax for creating an interface is slightly different than for creating a class.

LISTING 1.1: Creating an Interface

```
/// <summary>
/// Interfaces only describe the properties,
/// methods, and events that a class exposes for use.
/// Logic to implement these features is not allowed in
/// an interface.
/// </summary>
public interface IExample
{
  /// <summary>
  /// Example of a string property the implementing class
  /// must provide.
  /// </summary>
  string StringProperty { get; set; }

  /// <summary>
  /// Example of a read-only property.
  /// </summary>
  string ReadOnlyStringProperty { get; }

  /// <summary>
  /// Example of a method that accepts two parameters.
  /// </summary>
  int OperateOnTwoNumbers(int pNum1, int pNum2);
}
```

In this example, the interface describes two properties and a method that any class that wants to implement this interface must provide. By definition, any item described in an interface is available to calling code so the permission modifiers of public, private, internal and protected do not apply. The only code that is present in the interface is a description of the items the implementing class must provide. Also, notice the interface name starts with an uppercase "I" followed by the name of the implementing class; this is a naming standard accepted quite widely, so we also use it.

Implementing an Interface

An interface by itself is of little use because it cannot contain any logic. We need to build a class that implements the items that are listed in the interface, as shown in Listing 1.2.

LISTING 1.2: Implementing an Interface

```
/// <summary>
/// An implementing class MUST provide the appropriate
/// items described in the interface or the project will not build.
/// The implementing class can add any additional
/// features deemed appropriate.
/// </summary>
public class Example : IExample
{
   /// <summary>
   /// Implement the StringProperty described in the interface.
   /// </summary>
   public string StringProperty { get; set; }

   /// <summary>
   /// The ReadOnlyStringProperty cannot have a public setter,
   /// but can have a private, protected, or internal setter.
   /// </summary>
   public string ReadOnlyStringProperty { get; internal set; }

   /// <summary>
   /// The implementing class must provide the method signatures
   /// described in the interface, though if no logic is
   /// added to the method, it will still build.
   /// </summary>
   public int OperateOnTwoNumbers(int pNum1, int pNum2)
   {
      return pNum1 + pNum2;
   }

   /// <summary>
   /// Any further customization of the implementing
   /// class is allowed.
   /// </summary>
   public bool MethodNotInTheInterface()
   {
      return true;
   }
}
```

This class implements the interface in Listing 1.2, as you can see in the line containing the class definition. For a class to implement an interface, it must provide all of the items described in that interface. If the implementing class does not implement something defined in the interface, the solution does not build. On the other hand, the class can implement as many additional properties as necessary without affecting the interface.

This allows you to add any additional code necessary to make the class perform the duties it has committed to.

The only requirement that a class implementing an interface must fulfill is to implement all of the signatures of the items the interface describes. Because the interface does not designate how the methods are implemented, we don't have to provide any logic at all as long as the method exists.

In the example shown in Listing 1.3, we decide that the `OperationOnTwo Numbers` method requires no implementation for our purposes, so we simply throw a `NotImplementedException`. If you believe the implementing class does not need to define a method, throwing this exception is preferable to leaving it empty. By throwing an exception, we are sure to encounter the error if the method is called unexpectedly. If we left the implementation blank, the method could be called unknowingly and cause defects that would be difficult to find.

LISTING 1.3: An Example Showing Methods Do Not Need Implementation Logic

```
/// <summary>
/// Implementing a method described in an interface does not
/// require that proper logic be added, only that the method
/// signature is provided.
/// </summary>
public int OperateOnTwoNumbers(int pNum1, int pNum2)
{
    throw new NotImplementedException("OperateOnTwoNumbers");
}
```

Using an Interface

Now that we have defined our interface and implementing class, let's look at how we use the interface in our business logic. The example in Listing 1.4 shows how a class that implements some business logic uses an interface and implementing class. (For now, we create our `Example` class simply using the `new` keyword. Soon, we explore a better way of creating these classes called Service Location.)

LISTING 1.4: Using an Interface

```
/// <summary>
/// This is an example of a class that uses the
/// interface we just created.
/// </summary>
public class BusinessLogic
{
  public int UseInterfaceImplementation()
  {
    //Though we are creating a real Example class, we
    //are assigning it to an IExample variable.
    IExample sampleClass = new Example();

    //We can use the variable reflecting the interface
    //as if it were the real class.
    return sampleClass.OperateOnTwoNumbers(1, 2);
  }
}
```

The important thing to notice here is that though we create the concrete class Example, our variable is defined as the interface, not the class. This means that the only methods and properties available from that variable are the ones in the interface. As shown in Figure 1.1, the MethodNotInTheInterface method is not available.

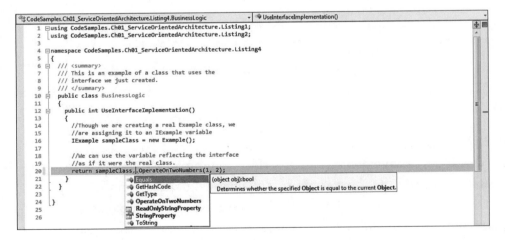

FIGURE 1.1: Methods not defined in the interface are not available.

A powerful and critically important aspect of interfaces is that more than one class can implement an interface at the same time. In addition to the class in Listing 1.2, we can also declare the class that follows in the same project. As shown in Listing 1.5, the implementation of the items in the interface can be completely different from the implementations of the first class as long as they have the proper signatures to satisfy the interface.

LISTING 1.5: A Second Implementation of the Interface

```
/// <summary>
/// This is a second implementation of the IExample interface.
/// It has no relation to the other implementation and can
/// implement completely different logic.
/// </summary>
public class AlternateExample : IExample
{
  /// <summary>
  /// The string property is the same as the previous implementation.
  /// </summary>
  public string StringProperty { get; set; }

  /// <summary>
  /// The ReadOnlyStringProperty will always return the
  /// given value.
  /// </summary>
  public string ReadOnlyStringProperty
  {
    get { return "I'm an Alternate"; }
  }

  /// <summary>
  /// This method operates on the two inputs in a different
  /// way, returning a completely different result than our
  /// previous implementation.
  /// </summary>
  public int OperateOnTwoNumbers(int pNum1, int pNum2)
  {
    return pNum1 * pNum2;
  }
}
```

These are the important features of using interfaces. The reason we need to have these aspects present in our services is explained in detail in later chapters. For now, just take it on faith that there is a good reason for all services to have an associated interface, and your code is much more flexible and easier to use when it implements interfaces.

Understanding Coupling

Coupling refers to the relationship between two pieces of code. Two classes can be tightly coupled or loosely coupled, which is determined by how much knowledge each class has of the other. The more intimate knowledge one class has of another class, the more tightly coupled they are. So what does "intimate knowledge" mean? Consider the example shown in Listing 1.6.

LISTING 1.6: **An Example of Tightly Coupled Classes**

```
/// <summary>
/// This class will retrieve a string from the database and
/// display it on the screen.
/// </summary>
public class ShowDatabaseInfo
{
  /// <summary>
  /// Main driver method
  /// </summary>
  public void GetAndShowData(int recordId)
  {
    ADODB.Recordset data = GetData();
    DisplayForm frm = GetForm();
    ShowDataInForm(frm, data);
  }

  /// <summary>
  /// Open an ADO connection to Microsoft SQL Server,
  /// get the data, and return it.
  /// </summary>
  public ADODB.Recordset GetData()
  {
    var connection = new ADODB.Connection();
    connection.ConnectionString = "my connection string";
    connection.Open();
    var rs = new ADODB.Recordset();

    //The following query is specific to Microsoft SQL Server
    //it will not execute properly on Oracle.
    rs.Open("Microsoft SQL Specific Query", connection);

    rs.ActiveConnection = null;
    return rs;
  }

  /// <summary>
  /// Get the proper form to use for our display
```

```csharp
    /// </summary>
    private DisplayForm GetForm()
    {
      return new DisplayForm();
    }


    /// <summary>
    /// Show the information to the user in the given form.
    /// </summary>
    public void ShowDataInForm(DisplayForm frm, ADODB.Recordset data)
    {
      frm.UserInfo = data;
      frm.Show();
    }
}


/// <summary>
/// Form that displays the information to the user.
/// </summary>
public class DisplayForm : Form
{
  private readonly Label _userFirstNameLbl;
  private readonly Label _userLastNameLbl;
  private ADODB.Recordset _userInfo;

  /// <summary>
  /// Constructor that creates the data display form.
  /// </summary>
  public DisplayForm()
  {
    _userFirstNameLbl = new Label();
    Controls.Add(_userFirstNameLbl);

    _userLastNameLbl = new Label();
    Controls.Add(_userLastNameLbl);
  }


  /// <summary>
  /// Property to assign the data to the proper labels.
  /// </summary>
  public ADODB.Recordset UserInfo
  {
    get { return _userInfo; }
    set
    {
      _userInfo = value;
      _userFirstNameLbl.Text = _userInfo.Fields[0].ToString();
      _userLastNameLbl.Text = _userInfo.Fields[0].ToString();
    }
  }
}
```

In this example, the ShowDatabaseInfo class is tightly coupled to many things. First, let's examine the tight coupling with the DisplayForm. Creating something directly in code creates a tight coupling because it creates a dependency on that specific class. Imagine we had another display form declared, as demonstrated in Listing 1.7.

LISTING 1.7: A DisplayForm Descendant

```
public class DisplayFormDescendant : DisplayForm
{
   //empty class
}
```

Our DisplayFormDescendant adds nothing to the DisplayForm. It behaves in exactly the same way as DisplayForm, and in theory, it is a perfect replacement. However, looking at our ShowDatabaseInfo class again, if the GetForm method tries to create and return a DisplayFormDescendant instead of a DisplayForm, the solution would not build. To make this substitution, we would have to change all the occurrences of DisplayForm to DisplayFormDescendant. This is called a dependency on DisplayForm, and it makes the code brittle.

Another example of tight coupling in this example is with the data access technology Active Data Objects (ADO). If another data access technology was introduced (such as EntityFramework) and we wanted to move to it, we would have to refactor the entire application due to the various dependencies on ADO-related classes. This tight coupling to ADO makes the application brittle because any attempt to change one thing leads to the need for unrelated changes elsewhere.

A more subtle dependency in the example is to Microsoft SQL Server. Because our data query has Microsoft SQL Server-specific details, it is not portable to Oracle. If the application needed to support both Microsoft and Oracle, we would have to maintain two completely separate code lines. This is brittle code.

In the chapters that follow, you learn how to change this tightly coupled brittle code into something that is much easier to update. Interfaces are a key part of this transformation.

Understanding Service Abstraction

Service abstraction refers to how much the internal workings of a class are hidden from outside manipulation. We should make private as many of the service properties and methods as possible to prevent outside callers from manipulating anything in the service that was not intended for use. By hiding this information, we force the application to be more loosely coupled.

Referring back to the example in Listing 1.6, consider the way the ShowDatabaseInfo class and the DisplayForm class interact. ShowDatabaseInfo assigns values directly to the labels exposed by the form.

LISTING 1.8: Assigning Values Directly to Labels

```
/// <summary>
/// Show the information to the user in the given form.
/// </summary>
public void ShowDataInForm(DisplayForm frm, ADODB.Recordset data)
{
  frm.UserFirstNameLbl.Text = data.Fields[0].ToString();
  frm.UserLastNameLbl.Text = data.Fields[0].ToString();
  frm.Show();
}
```

Imagine you wanted to change the form to use a different type of control to display the information, such as a list box. This change in the form, which does not affect the logic in the ShowDatabaseInfo class, would require a code change in that class due to the lack of abstraction in the form.

Introducing a way for these two classes to interact without this tight coupling means we must create an abstraction for the form so it can change as necessary, without requiring corresponding changes to the classes that use it. This idea of service abstraction enables the classes to evolve as necessary. Examine the abstracted code that achieves the same purpose.

LISTING 1.9: An Abstracted Version of Tightly Coupled Classes

```
/// <summary>
/// This class will retrieve a string from the database and
/// display it on the screen.
/// </summary>
public class ShowDatabaseInfoAbstracted
{
```

```csharp
/// <summary>
/// Main driver method
/// </summary>
public void GetAndShowData(int recordId)
{
    ADODB.Recordset data = GetData();
    DisplayFormAbstracted frm = GetForm();
    ShowDataInForm(frm, data);
}

/// <summary>
/// Open an ADO connection to Microsoft SQL Server,
/// get the data, and return it.
/// </summary>
public ADODB.Recordset GetData()
{
    var connection = new ADODB.Connection();
    connection.ConnectionString = "my connection string";
    connection.Open();
    var rs = new ADODB.Recordset();

    //The following query is specific to Microsoft SQL Server.
    //It will not execute properly on Oracle.
    rs.Open("Microsoft SQL Specific Query", connection);

    rs.ActiveConnection = null;
    return rs;
}

/// <summary>
/// Get the proper form to use for our display.
/// </summary>
private DisplayFormAbstracted GetForm()
{
    return new DisplayFormAbstracted();
}

/// <summary>
/// Show the information to the user in the given form.
/// </summary>
public void ShowDataInForm(DisplayFormAbstracted frm, ADODB.
Recordset data)
{
    frm.UserFirstName = data.Fields[0].ToString();
    frm.UserLastName = data.Fields[0].ToString();
    frm.Show();
}
}
```

```csharp
/// <summary>
/// Form that displays the information to the user.
/// </summary>
public class DisplayFormAbstracted : Form
{
  /// <summary>
  /// This is private so it cannot be used by an outside
  /// consumer, thus improving the abstraction.
  /// </summary>
  private Label _userFirstNameLbl;
  private Label _userLastNameLbl;

  /// <summary>
  /// These getters and setters can change as the
  /// display requirements change, but the calling
  /// code will be unaffected.
  /// </summary>
  public string UserFirstName
  {
    get { return _userFirstNameLbl.Text; }
    set { _userFirstNameLbl.Text = value; }
  }

  /// <summary>
  /// These getters and setters can change as the
  /// display requirements change, but the calling
  /// code will be unaffected.
  /// </summary>
  public string UserLastName
  {
    get { return _userLastNameLbl.Text; }
    set { _userLastNameLbl.Text = value; }
  }

  /// <summary>
  /// Constructor that creates the data display form.
  /// </summary>
  public DisplayFormAbstracted()
  {
    _userFirstNameLbl = new Label();
    Controls.Add(_userFirstNameLbl);

    _userLastNameLbl = new Label();
    Controls.Add(_userLastNameLbl);
  }

}
```

The difference between this listing and Listing 1.6 is the definition of the `DisplayFormAbstracted`. It now exposes only the string properties for the user's first name and last name, instead of exposing the entire label. This helps with the abstraction because it removes the need for any consumer of the form to know how the data is being displayed. The `DisplayFormAbstracted` can change to a text box or anything else, and the `ShowDatabaseInfoAbstracted` class does not have to change.

Designing Reusable Services

We design our services to be as reusable as possible so that we can be as efficient in our work as possible. This means the services can be used any-place in the system without fear that code in another location does not make a conflicting request. Preferably, it also means the service can be used in completely different systems, but this depends on the aspects of the service and is sometimes difficult to achieve.

We discuss reusability in more detail as we build the individual services that we need.

Understanding Service Autonomy and Service Composability

The original principles espoused by Thomas Erl in his book, *Service-Oriented Architecture: Concepts, Technology, and Design,*" speak about services as both autonomous and composable. The composability section says, "A service can represent any range of logic from any types of sources, including other services." The section on autonomy says it "...eliminates dependencies on other services, which frees a service from ties that could inhibit its deployment and evolution." This seems to carry the contradictory message that services can and cannot use other services. However, if we examine the two statements, we can see they are not mutually exclusive.

Service composability means a service can use another service whenever the functionality the second service contains is needed. However, we cannot use that secondary service in such a way that it creates a dependency between the two services. We have seen that dependencies are created by referring to another class explicitly or by using properties or methods that are inappropriately exposed. Using Service Location (which is covered in Chapter 4), you learn how to create a service that is autonomous and composable.

Understanding Service Statelessness

Statelessness refers to the storage of variable values internal to the service. If a service is truly stateless, we should be able to call any method or reference any property on the service, and as long as we pass the same parameters, the service should behave in the same way. In other words, no values are stored in the service that cannot be changed by an outside caller and that affect the outcome of an operation.

To understand statelessness, review Listing 1.10, which shows a service that describes the process of buying an item at a store.

LISTING 1.10: A Sample Sales Process with No Refunds

```
/// <summary>
/// Class representing the process of buying an item
/// from a store.
/// </summary>
public class SalesclerkNoRefunds
{
  /// <summary>
  /// Method to call when a customer is buying an item.
  /// </summary>
  public void SellItem(string itemToSell, string nameOfPurchaser)
  {
    var price = GetItemPrice(itemToSell);
    GetPaymentFromCustomer(price);
  }

  /// <summary>
  /// Interacts with the customer to get payment.
  /// </summary>
  private void GetPaymentFromCustomer(double amount)
  {
    //Get the payment from the customer
  }

  /// <summary>
  /// Lookup the price of the item and return it
  /// </summary>
```

```
private double GetItemPrice(string itemToSell)
{
  //Lookup the price of the item and return it.
  return 15.00;
}
}
```

In this sales process, we can purchase an item from any clerk in the store we choose, and we can complete our purchase without any problems. This service has no local variables and no state, so any sales clerk can handle the transaction. However, this process does not allow for returning an item to the store; it supports purchasing items only. Let's enhance the class to add a method for returning an item we previously purchased. Consider the enhanced class and the ReturnItem method, as demonstrated in Listing 1.11.

LISTING 1.11: A Sample Sales Process Allowing for Refunds

```
/// <summary>
/// Class representing the process of buying an item.
/// </summary>
public class SalesclerkWithState
{
  private List<Purchase> _rememberedPurchases;

  public SalesclerkWithState()
  {
    _rememberedPurchases = new List<Purchase>();
  }

  /// <summary>
  /// Method to call when a customer is buying an item.
  /// </summary>
  public void SellItem(string itemToSell, string nameOfPurchaser)
  {
    var purchase = new Purchase();
    purchase.PurchaserName = nameOfPurchaser;
    purchase.SaleDate = DateTime.Today;
    purchase.ItemSold = itemToSell;
    purchase.AmountPaid = GetItemPrice(itemToSell);
    ReceiveOrRefundPayment(purchase.AmountPaid);
    _rememberedPurchases.Add(purchase);
  }

  /// <summary>
  /// Method to call when the customer is returning the item.
  /// </summary>
```

```
public void ReturnItem()
{
  var purchase = RememberItemSoldToCustomer();
  ReceiveOrRefundPayment(-purchase.AmountPaid);
}


/// <summary>
/// Charge the customer credit card for the purchase.
/// </summary>
private Purchase RememberItemSoldToCustomer()
{
  //Recall the customer and how much they paid.
  return _rememberedPurchases[0];
}


/// <summary>
/// Interacts with the customer to get the credit card number.
/// </summary>
private void ReceiveOrRefundPayment(double amount)
{
  //Get the payment from the customer
}


/// <summary>
/// Lookup the price of the item and return it.
/// </summary>
private double GetItemPrice(string itemToSell)
{
  //Lookup the price of the item and return it.
  return 154.00;
}

private class Purchase
{
  public string PurchaserName { get; set; }
  public double AmountPaid { get; set; }
  public DateTime SaleDate { get; set; }
  public string ItemSold { get; set; }
}
}
```

In this class, we introduce the ReturnItem method, but notice that we also introduce state into our service. To allow a customer to return an item, the clerk must know what that customer paid for the item. If we did not do this, someone can buy an item during a sale and then return the item when the sale is over and get full price in return. Therefore, our sales clerk needs to remember every person who purchased something, what was purchased, and for what price. To track this information, we introduce the Purchase class and a list of purchases.

We can now buy and return a purchase at the same store. However, with the current design, we must always talk to the same salesclerk who originally sold the item. Notice that the Purchase class is private representing the idea that only the original salesclerk can access his own memory. If we go to a different salesclerk, he will not remember the purchase and not be able to refund the money. This is the penalty of introducing state into a service. We cannot instantiate two copies of the Salesclerk class and return something randomly between the two. We must couple ourselves to the salesclerk that originally sold us the item.

So far, the only two options in building the service are as follows:

- To be stateless but not contain all the functionality we wish
- To introduce application state and the problems associated with it

We can't get rid of the need for saving the state of the system, but we can solve this problem by having the state stored externally and handing it to the service when necessary. Consider a stateless version of the sales process with refunds, as shown in Listing 1.12.

LISTING 1.12: A Sample StatelessSales Process Allowing for Refunds

```csharp
/// <summary>
/// Class representing the process of buying a shirt.
/// </summary>
public class SalesClerkWithNoState
{
  /// <summary>
  /// Method to call when a customer is buying an item.
  /// </summary>
  public SalesReceipt SellItem(string itemToSell)
  {
    var receipt = new SalesReceipt();
    receipt.SaleDate = DateTime.Today;
    receipt.ItemSold = itemToSell;
    receipt.AmountPaid= GetItemPrice(itemToSell);
    ReceiveorRefundPayment(receipt.AmountPaid);
    return receipt;
  }
}
```

```csharp
/// <summary>
/// Method to call when the customer is returning the item.
/// </summary>
public void ReturnItem(SalesReceipt receipt)
{
  GetReceiptAndItemFromCustomer();
  ReceiveorRefundPayment(-receipt.AmountPaid);
}


/// <summary>
/// Get the necessary items from the customer.
/// </summary>
private void GetReceiptAndItemFromCustomer()
{
  //receive the item and receipt from customer
}


/// <summary>
/// Interacts with the customer to get the credit card number.
/// </summary>
private void ReceiveorRefundPayment(double amount)
{
  //Get the payment from the customer
}


/// <summary>
/// Lookup the price of the item and return it.
/// </summary>
private double GetItemPrice(string itemToSell)
{
  //lookup the price of the item and return it
  return 154.00;
}
}


/// <summary>
/// Reflects information about the purchase.
/// </summary>
public class SalesReceipt
{
  public double AmountPaid { get; set; }
  public DateTime SaleDate { get; set; }
  public string ItemSold { get; set; }
}
```

In this class, we introduce the SalesReceipt class and remove the Purchase class. We made the SalesReceipt class public. We also remove the private list of purchases that we once needed to remember all of the purchases.

By introducing the public idea of a receipt, we transfer the burden of remembering state to the outside caller, making the `SalesClerkWithNoState` conform to the stateless requirement. With the receipt in hand, we are now free to visit any sales clerk we want to return the item, making the transaction much easier to complete and the service much more useful.

We strive to make services as stateless as possible, but quite often, it is necessary to maintain some state in the service. How much state is maintained is dictated by the purpose of the service.

A Service Example

Using all of these principles, let's examine a real-life example. The code in Listing 1.13 is for a `DialogService`. This is a service that is used to show informational messages to the user in a dialog box.

LISTING 1.13: A Sample Service Implementation

```
/// <summary>
/// Interface for a service that displays messages to the user.
/// </summary>
public interface IDialogService
{
  /// <summary>
  /// Show the given message to the user in a dialog
  /// with just an OK button.
  /// </summary>
  void Show(string pUserMessage);

  /// <summary>
  /// Show a message to the user with the specified
  /// window caption and buttons.
  /// </summary>
  DialogResult Show(string pUserMessage, string pCaption,
    MessageBoxButtons pMessageBoxButtons);
}

/// <summary>
/// The dialog service will show a message to the user
/// and accept an appropriate response as requested
/// by the caller.
/// </summary>
public class DialogService : IDialogService
{
  /// <summary>
```

```
/// Show the given message to the user in a dialog
/// with just an OK button.
/// </summary>
public void Show(string pUserMessage)
{
  MessageBox.Show(pUserMessage);
}

/// <summary>
/// Show a message to the user with the specified
/// window caption and buttons.
/// </summary>
public DialogResult Show(string pUserMessage, string pCaption,
  MessageBoxButtons pMessageBoxButtons)
{
  return MessageBox.Show(pUserMessage, pCaption, pMessageBoxButtons);
}
}
```

If we compare this implementation with the principles for creating a service, we get the following:

- **Standardized service contract**: Use an interface so there is a standardized contract that all callers can interact with.

- **Loose coupling**: There are no hard references to any other objects, so this service is not tightly coupled to anything else. (One can make the argument that it is tightly coupled to the System.Windows.Forms class because we use MessageBox to show our message. In this case, coupling is acceptable.)

- **Abstraction**: The method that actually displays the message is internal, so it cannot be accessed by outside methods. The only methods exposed are those specified by the interface.

- **Autonomy and composability**: The service does not use any outside services, so it is autonomous, and there is no restriction on other services using it, so the DialogService is also composable.

- **Statelessness**: The service does not have any internal variables, so it is completely stateless.

We have satisfied all of the criteria for a stateless service, so the DialogService appears to be a good design that does not force tight coupling on the developer using it.

Summary

In this chapter, we reviewed the core of the structure we will move to. This structure is designed from the ground up to improve how the pieces interact, making the components easier to maintain and the entire application of higher quality. Key in this approach is using interfaces on all services. We saw how interfaces can introduce a layer of indirection between code using a service and how the service is constructed. This indirection provides us with the loose coupling and service abstraction that is crucial for an application that can grow over time.

In addition to the discussion of loose coupling and the components that enable it, we looked at how we can better use services by designing them for autonomy and composability. By building the services so they can interact with each other, each business problem we encounter can be solved by combining given services in different ways. To enable this composability, however, services need to be stateless, and we looked at several examples of stateless services and how they are structured.

We now have the necessary background in place to continue with a discussion of application architectures in the next chapter.

2

Understanding Application Architecture

We discussed how a service-oriented architecture (SOA) works and why we chose it. We now address another architectural theory that helps keep the business logic, view logic, and data storage aspects separate and easy to work with.

Working with Architectural Patterns

We work with three patterns in this book: Model-View-Controller (MVC), Model-View-Presenter (MVP), and Model-View-ViewModel (MVVM). Alhough each has its strengths and weaknesses, from a reengineering standpoint, they can be treated similarly. Regardless of which you choose for your target architecture, the techniques described here apply. When there are significant differences that affect the approach we take, we point out how to work with each pattern individually. There isn't a single definition for any of these patterns. If you search the Web, you can find several slightly different descriptions of each, so for convenience, we standardize on the Microsoft interpretation. The definitions we use can be found here:

- **MVC:** http://msdn.microsoft.com/en-us/library/ff649643.aspx
- **MVP:** http://msdn.microsoft.com/en-us/magazine/cc188690.aspx
- **MVVM:** http://msdn.microsoft.com/en-us/magazine/dd419663.aspx

An Overview of Architectural Patterns

These architectural patterns have the same goal to help keep the application structured in such a way that it is easy to maintain and has low coupling. They separate our application into three major sections.

- **Model**: This is the data model and is typically represented by the database and any direct interaction with the database. This includes the queries used to extract the data from the database, classes that represent a row in each table (entity classes), and entity class validation logic to ensure that the data in the database is consistent with the business rules. The validation logic ensures that the data is consistent with business rules before it is stored in the database.

  There is typically only one data model in any given application, though in rare cases, there can be more. For example, it might be necessary to have two data models if you want to access data from a different application and that model must change independently. It might also be convenient to have two models if the application requires data from both MS SQL Server and Oracle.

- **View**: This is the code that displays the data on the screen for use by the user. It includes the code to create the window and add the controls necessary to display data. A significant piece that is *not* in the view is data manipulation and business logic. Changing data is the responsibility of the third piece, the controller, presenter, or view model.

- **Controller / presenter / view model**: The place where the three patterns differ is in this third piece. Depending on which pattern you choose, you have only a controller, only a presenter, or only a view model. The general goal of these pieces is the same in all three patterns, but the specifics and implementation details differ.

  In general, each view has either a controller, presenter, or view model associated with it. This is the section that glues the model and view together and orchestrates the interaction between the two. This is where we put the business logic necessary to decide which rows in the database need to be retrieved and the code to query those rows (using the model) and deliver that data to the view to display to the user. This piece uses the services we described earlier to implement some of the generic business logic, and the logic specific to the requested operation is included here.

> **▪ NOTE**
>
> Though you can use databases, flat files, or nearly anything else for your Model's data storage, we assume you're using a database to make the discussion easier. Implementing other types of data storage does not affect the discussion.

Differences Among MVP, MVC, and MVVM

From a high-level perspective, these three patterns are similar. They strive to separate the user interface (UI) logic from the business logic and data tier. The differences among the patterns are relatively small, but they are significant.

The main driver for many of the differences described in this section is testability. A goal of any application architecture is to make the code as testable as possible. In any application, the UI (Winforms, Windows Presentation Foundation [WPF] or Silverlight, or ASP) is notoriously difficult to test. Testing the UI classes means the UI must be instantiated, which causes many problems with automated test runners. Therefore, we try to move as much of our logic out of the view and into other classes.

> **▪ NOTE**
>
> When we discuss MVP, we specifically discuss the Passive View version of Martin Fowler's Model-View-Presenter pattern. MVP has two versions that differ in how the data model is accessed.
>
> - Passive View: http://martinfowler.com/eaaDev/ PassiveScreen.html
>
> - Supervising Presenter: http://martinfowler.com/eaaDev/ SupervisingPresenter.html

Model Access

One of the differences among these three patterns is access to the data model. In MVC, both the view and the controller have a reference to the model, as illustrated in Figure 2.1 This structure makes it easier to build views because the view can bind to the data model properties directly. However, this means the views are more difficult to reuse outside of the current application because they are bound to a specific data model that might not be used in another application. It also means the binding logic cannot be tested because it resides in the view.

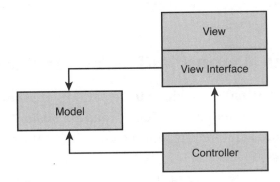

FIGURE 2.1: **Model-View-Controller**

MVP does not allow this reference from the view to the model, so the presenter must take on the responsibilities of binding the data model to the input controls, as illustrated in Figure 2.2. This enhances testability because more code is in the presenter rather than the view; however, implementing binding logic without having direct access to the UI controls can be challenging.

MVVM has a concept of a view model that is a class that holds data and logic specifically for that view. It is analogous to the controller or presenter in that it has logic to control the view and that logic is testable. However the question of whether the view should have access to the model is side-stepped with this pattern due to the binding features in WPF. MVVM is used with XAML-based applications, which provides a new way of binding data that does not need a direct reference to the object containing the data. With this new binding method, we can easily refrain from adding any model references to the view. Figure 2.3 shows the relationships in the MVVM pattern.

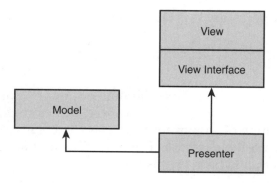

FIGURE 2.2: **Model-View-Presenter (Passive view)**

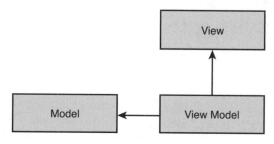

FIGURE 2.3: **Model-View-ViewModel**

View Models

Only the MVVM pattern mentions the existence of a view model, so it would appear that is the only pattern that uses one, but this isn't true. An emerging standard is to also use a view model with MVC and MVP patterns, but using a different interpretation of the term view model.

Before we discuss the differences in the interpretations of view model, let's discuss a common thread that runs through all of them. Whether being used in MVC, MVP, or MVVM, a view model is always used as a container for data necessary to display the view. To illustrate this concept, assume you have a view that manages a user and his security permissions. For the view to display the appropriate data, it needs access to the user entity, a list of security attributes granted to the user, a list of all security attributes that exist, and a system configuration setting of the minimum number of characters required in a password. Listing 2.1 illustrates the view, the controller, and the logic necessary to create the view and display it on the screen.

> **■ NOTE**
>
> In this example, we use a class called a Repository. We discuss repositories in detail in Chapter 12, "Advanced Refactoring to Services," but for now think of a repository as a class that is responsible for all interaction with the database. The only class in a system that contains queries should be the repository.

LISTING 2.1: A Sample View Interface

```
using System.Collections.Generic;

namespace CodeSamples.Ch02_ApplicationArchitecture.Listing01
{
  public class SampleView
  {
    private User User { get; set; }
    private ICollection<UserRole> AvailableRoles { get; set; }
    private int RequiredPasswordChars { get; set; }

    public SampleView (User usr, ICollection<UserRole> roles,
 int passwordLen)
    {
      this.User = usr;
      this.AvailableRoles = roles;
      this.RequiredPasswordChars = passwordLen;
    }

    public void Show()
    {
      //show the view
    }
  }

  public class SampleViewController
  {
    public SampleViewController()
```

```
      {
        var repo = new Repository();
        var usr = repo.GetUserInfo();
        var roles = repo.GetUserRoles();
        var passwordLen = repo.GetPasswordChars();
        var view = new SampleView(usr, roles, passwordLen);
        view.Show();
      }
    }

    public class Repository
    {
      public User GetUserInfo()
      {
        //get user info from DB
        return new User();
      }

      public List<UserRole> GetUserRoles()
      {
        //get user roles from DB
        return new List<UserRole>();
      }

      public int GetPasswordChars()
      {
        //get required password length from dB
        return 6;
      }
    }

    public class User
    {
      //user info goes here
    }

    public class UserRole
    {
      //security role info goes here
    }
}
```

This sample uses the traditional controller approach by creating the view and setting each property appropriately before showing the view. A presenter pattern looks similar. The advantage of this approach is how obvious the information needed is for this view to function. Simply examining the constructor line shows the necessary inputs. The disadvantage of this approach is the amount of refactoring necessary should the list of required inputs change. If we decided to add a new parameter to the constructor line, we would have to search for every occurrence of this class and add the parameter, forcing a rebuild (and possibly redistribution to the end user) of every affected DLL.

Applying the common strategy of the view model that each presentation pattern supports, we would create a new class that would contain the data the view needs to use. This structure looks like Listing 2.2.

LISTING 2.2: **A Sample View Interface with View Model**

```
using System.Collections.Generic;

namespace CodeSamples.Ch02_ApplicationArchitecture.Listing02
{
  public class SampleView
  {
    private SampleViewModel _viewModel;

    public SampleView(SampleViewModel viewModel)
    {
      _viewModel = viewModel;
    }

    public void Show()
    {
      //show the view
    }
  }

  public class SampleViewController
  {
    public SampleViewController()
    {
      var repo = new Repository();
      var vm = new SampleViewModel();
      vm.User = repo.GetUserInfo();
      vm.AvailableRoles = repo.GetUserRoles();
      vm.RequiredPasswordChars = repo.GetPasswordChars();
      var view = new SampleView(vm);
      view.Show();
    }
  }

  public class SampleViewModel
```

```csharp
{
  public User User { get; set; }
  public ICollection<UserRole> AvailableRoles { get; set; }
  public int RequiredPasswordChars { get; set; }
}

public class Repository
{
  public User GetUserInfo()
  {
    //get user info from DB
    return new User();
  }

  public List<UserRole> GetUserRoles()
  {
    //get user roles from DB
    return new List<UserRole>();
  }

  public int GetPasswordChars()
  {
    //get required password length from dB
    return 6;
  }
}


public class User
{
  //user info goes here
}

public class UserRole
{
  //security role info goes here
}

}
```

Listing 2.1 shows an additional class called `SampleViewModel`. This class has a property for every piece of information that the view needs to interact with the user as desired. To create and use the view, we create this view model class and fill it with the appropriate data. Though it is more difficult to see the data the view requires, refactoring to add additional information is simplified.

If we decide that the view requires more information, this pattern avoids the need to edit the constructor line of each view creation. However, we still have to visit the places where the view is used to fill the view model with the appropriate data, so this structure doesn't buy us much.

A common implementation that solves this problem is to push view model population into the view model itself, so the caller needs to create only the view model without needing to know what goes inside of it. Consider the implementation shown in Listing 2.3.

LISTING 2.3: A View Model Using Repository

```csharp
using System.Collections.Generic;

namespace CodeSamples.Ch02_ApplicationArchitecture.Listing03
{
    public class SampleView
    {
        private SampleViewModel _viewModel;

        public SampleView(SampleViewModel viewModel)
        {
            _viewModel = viewModel;
        }

        public void Show()
        {
            //show the view
        }
    }

    public class SampleViewController
    {
        public SampleViewController()
        {
            var repo = new Repository();
            var vm = new SampleViewModel(repo);
            var view = new SampleView(vm);
            view.Show();
        }
    }

    public class SampleViewModel
    {
        public User User { get; set; }
        public ICollection<UserRole> AvailableRoles { get; set; }
```

```csharp
    public int RequiredPasswordChars { get; set; }

    public SampleViewModel(Repository repo)
    {
      this.User = repo.GetUserInfo();
      this.AvailableRoles = repo.GetUserRoles();
      this.RequiredPasswordChars = repo.GetPasswordChars();
    }
  }

  public class Repository
  {
    public User GetUserInfo()
    {
      //get user info from DB
      return new User();
    }

    public List<UserRole> GetUserRoles()
    {
      //get user roles from DB
      return new List<UserRole>();
    }

    public int GetPasswordChars()
    {
      //get required password length from dB
      return 6;
    }
  }

  public class User
  {
    //user info goes here
  }

  public class UserRole
  {
    //security role info goes here
  }

}
```

In this code sample, we pass the Repository to the view model when creating it. This enables us to centralize the code necessary to populate the view model appropriately, and it insulates the controller from the need to know what parameters are necessary for the view model. However, notice that the view model properties are all public, so if there are special circumstances where the controller wishes to replace the default values in the view model, that is possible. When using a view model with the MVC or MVP pattern, this is the view model to use.

In this implementation, the only thing that is needed from the caller is the `Repository` to use. Even this requirement can be removed if we create our `Repository` inside the view model, but this is not a good idea for various reasons we discuss in Chapter 10, "Establishing the Foundation."

Adding the logic for the view model to populate itself introduces the difference among all the interpretations of the responsibilities of a view model. The three presentation patterns disagree on the amount of business logic that should be placed in the view model. For strict MVC or MVP implementations, use the view model just like it is—as a convenient container for view data. The other end of the spectrum is the MVVM pattern, which places all of the business logic necessary for the view into the view model. Most MVC or MVP implementations fall somewhere in the middle.

In summary, though the use of a view model is not in the official description of the MVC or MVP patterns; using a view model with the presentation patterns can be useful and is becoming more commonplace. In this book, we stick with the strict definitions of MVP and MVC, which exclude a view model. However, if you like the pattern and want to use it, your preference does not affect the processes recommended here.

Handling UI Events

Another point of departure among these three patterns is how the UI events are handled. For example, consider a button push. In strict MVC, there is *no* UI event logic in the code behind file for a view; *all* processing happens in the controller. This means that the view has to expose button press events and any other UI events to the controller for processing. The controller has to attach a handler to each event that it considers significant and process that event accordingly.

In MVP, the code behind for the view preprocesses UI events before passing them on to the controller for processing. If a request is strictly

UI-related with no business logic, the view can handle the request and return without involving the presenter.

In MVVM, again this issue is sidestepped due to the capability of XAML-based applications to bind to commands the view model provides.

Let's look at an example of the difference between MVC and MVP. Assume your application is up and running, displaying a grid of data. The user wants to see the details of one of the rows, so he presses the Show Details button to open a dialog window with more detailed data. In our UI, it is also possible to show details by right-clicking the context menu. Listing 2.4 shows an example of the MVC version.

LISTING 2.4: An MVC View Exposing Events to Controller

```
using System;
using System.Windows.Forms;

namespace CodeSamples.Ch02_ApplicatiorArchitecture.Listing04
{
  public class SampleForm : Form
  {
    private DataGrid Grid;
    private Button showDetailsBtn;
    private Button maximizeWindowBtn;
    private ContextMenu mnu;

    public event EventHandler ShowDetailsButtonClicked;
    public event EventHandler MaximizeWindowButtonClicked;
    public event EventHandler ContextMenuItemClicked;

    public SampleForm()
    {
      Grid = new DataGrid();
      showDetailsBtn = new Button();
      maximizeWindowBtn = new Button();
      mnu = new ContextMenu();

      showDetailsBtn.Click += showDetailsBtn_Click;
      maximizeWindowBtn.Click += maximizeWindowBtn_Click;
      var mnuItem = mnu.MenuItems.Add("Details");
      mnuItem.Click += mnuItem_Click;
    }

    void maximizeWindowBtn_Click(object sender, EventArgs e)
    {
      if (MaximizeWindowButtonClicked != null)
        MaximizeWindowButtonClicked(this, e);
```

```csharp
    }

    void mnuItem_Click(object sender, EventArgs e)
    {
       if (ContextMenuItemClicked != null)
ContextMenuItemClicked(this, e);
    }

    void showDetailsBtn_Click(object sender, EventArgs e)
    {
       if (ShowDetailsButtonClicked != null)
ShowDetailsButtonClicked(this, e);
    }

    public void Maximize()
    {
       //maximize window
    }
  }

  public class SampleFormController
  {
    private SampleForm _form;
    public SampleFormController()
    {
      _form = new SampleForm();
      _form.ShowDetailsButtonClicked += _form_ShowDetailsButtonClicked;
      _form.ContextMenuItemClicked += _form_ContextMenuItemClicked;
      _form.MaximizeWindowButtonClicked += _
➥form_MaximizeWindowButtonClicked;
    }

    void _form_MaximizeWindowButtonClicked(object sender, EventArgs e)
    {
      _form.Maximize();
    }

    void _form_ContextMenuItemClicked(object sender, EventArgs e)
    {
      ShowDetailsForm();
    }

    void _form_ShowDetailsButtonClicked(object sender, EventArgs e)
    {
      ShowDetailsForm();
    }

    private void ShowDetailsForm()
    {
```

```
      }
    }
}
```

In MVC, the controller receives the button press event directly and executes the appropriate logic. It also attaches a separate handler to the context menu event. All of these event handlers can call the same method to do the work to actually process the event, but there is still the need to have multiple event handlers. If yet another UI method for viewing details is added (such as a hotkey), the view needs to be updated to expose this additional event handler, and the controller needs to be updated to process the event. Also note that the user request to maximize the window is sent out to the controller, which calls the proper method on the form.

Now consider the equivalent example but in an MVP configuration, as demonstrated in Listing 2.5.

Listing 2.5: An MVP View Exposing Events to Presenter

```csharp
using System;
using System.Windows.Forms;

namespace CodeSamples.Ch02_ApplicationArchitecture.Listing05
{
  public class SampleForm : Form
  {
    private DataGrid Grid;
    private Button showDetailsBtn;
    private Button maximizeWindowBtn;
    private ContextMenu mnu;

    public event EventHandler ViewDetailsRequested;
    public event EventHandler MaximizeWindowButtonClicked;

    public SampleForm()
    {
      Grid = new DataGrid();
      showDetailsBtn = new Button();
      maximizeWindowBtn = new Button();
      mnu = new ContextMenu();

      showDetailsBtn.Click += showDetailsBtn_Click;
      maximizeWindowBtn.Click += maximizeWindowBtn_Click;
      var mnuItem = mnu.MenuItems.Add("Details");
      mnuItem.Click += mnuItem_Click;
```

```
    }

    void maximizeWindowBtn_Click(object sender, EventArgs e)
    {
      //maximize window
    }

    void mnuItem_Click(object sender, EventArgs e)
    {
      if (ViewDetailsRequested != null)
        ViewDetailsRequested(this, e);
    }

    void showDetailsBtn_Click(object sender, EventArgs e)
    {
      if (ViewDetailsRequested != null)
        ViewDetailsRequested(this, e);
    }

  }

  public class SampleFormPresenter
  {
    private SampleForm _form;
    public SampleFormPresenter()
    {
      _form = new SampleForm();
      _form.ViewDetailsRequested += _form_ShowDetailsButtonClicked;
    }

    void _form_ShowDetailsButtonClicked(object sender, EventArgs e)
    {
      ShowDetailsForm();
    }

    private void ShowDetailsForm()
    {

    }
  }
}
```

This MVP example implements an event filtering process in the view to abstract away the various ways for a user to request an action. Instead of the presenter adding event handlers for the button and context menu events, the code behind in the view does that. The view also defines a new event called ViewDetailsRequested. Each of the event handlers in the view subsequently raise the same `ViewDetailsRequested` event, which the presenter creates a handler for. The view filters the individual UI requests into a general action event for the presenter to handle. With this structure, if we add our hotkey to show details only, the view needs updating to handle the additional functionality. The interface and presenter remain unchanged.

Also note in this implementation that the view itself takes care of the window maximize request. Because no business logic is required to fulfill this request, the view performs the requested action without involving the presenter. If the presenter needs to know of the request for some reason, we can always refactor to send this message out to the presenter.

How Do the Patterns Work?

A good way to understand how the different patterns work is to examine the process flow of a typical user request. We take the scenario just presented of a user pressing a button to show more details regarding a particular data row in a grid. The following sequence of actions would result.

1. When the user presses the Show Details button, Windows generates a button push event.
2. Depending on the pattern in use, one of the following would happen. In all patterns, the controller, presenter, or view model receives notification that the user requested an action, as follows:
   a. MVC: The controller receives the event and checks the view to see which data row is current.
   b. MVP: The view receives the event and in response generates a different event for the presenter to consume. This event has the current row information embedded in it and any other relevant information the presenter needs.
   c. MVVM: The advanced binding that is available with XAML-based applications means the button is bound to a button press command in the view model automatically. This same advanced binding enables us to bind a view model property to the data grid so the view model has a pointer to the currently active row.

3. Using the information on the current row, the controller, presenter, or view model makes a request of the data model for additional data.

4. The model (that is, the repository in the model) receives the request for data and issues a query to the database.

5. The raw database data is returned to the model, which does any pre-processing necessary to change the raw data into an entity data class by copying values into the proper entity properties. If you use an Object Relational Mapping tool such as Entity Framework or NHibernate, the ORM does this step.

6. The business entity is returned from the model back to the controller, presenter, or view model.

7. The controller, presenter, or view model can execute any further processing required by the Show Details request. For example if your application displayed financial data, it might get an instance of a StockPriceService and request the current price for the stock the user is interested in, then update the entity class.

8. To show the dialog with the detailed stock data, the controller, presenter, or view model creates another controller (or presenter or view model), which we call the DialogController, gives it the proper information to display and then calls a ShowDialog method on the DialogController.

9. The DialogController creates the proper view, creates the bind data to appropriate text boxes on the view, and shows the view to the user.

This is one of the simplest of all processes. The controller, presenter, or view model can get much more complicated and perform as many duties as the user wishes. However, the basic division of labor should always be maintained.

- The view has only UI logic and no business rules or other logic.
- The model (the data model, not the view model) has only data access, entity class generation logic, and data validation.
- The controller, presenter, or view model has the logic necessary to perform the specific action the user requested.

Which Pattern Should You Choose?

All three of the patterns are good designs, so which you choose for your reengineering project depends on the target UI. If you want to build a browser-based web application, MVC is the best pattern to choose. ASP.NET MVC is designed around the MVC architecture, making new development and reengineering easier and faster.

If you want to reengineer a Winforms application, MVP is the best choice because it simplifies testing by consolidating event handling. Because MVP puts binding logic in the presenter, it also enables more testing because the model binding logic (indeed, any logic) in the view is untestable.

Finally, if you want to reengineer to either WPF or Silverlight, MVVM is the best choice because it takes advantage of the strengths of WPF command binding and other features, greatly enhancing testability of the application.

Summary

In this chapter, we discussed the different options for your target architecture. Though this book makes no distinction among the different architectures, we discussed which are more appropriate for your project depending on the target display you have in mind (web, WPF, or Winforms). We found, however, that the three basic architectures have the same basic idea of separating business logic, display logic, and data model. Keeping these three pieces separate is the key to creating an application that can adapt to the changing requirements of the real world.

In the next chapter, we discuss how to take advantage of the separation of these pieces by creating unit tests.

3

Unit Testing

The primary goal of the architectural patterns we discuss is to break our application into smaller pieces that have fewer references to each other to reduce coupling. This is an advantage because it becomes much easier for a class to evolve if there are fewer hard references to it that must be updated. It also introduces more opportunities for automated testing, or unit testing.

Unit testing is a way of automating much of the quality assurance function of a development department. The goal of unit testing is to isolate classes from the rest of the application so their methods can be tested via code. We write special test methods that exercise the system under test and ensure that it executes proper logic.

Unit tests are a critical part of the reengineering process. If your team does not have a unit-testing framework installed, now is the time to get one.

In this chapter, we touch on the high points of what unit tests are and how to implement them. There are many good books dedicated completely to unit testing; if you are new to the subject, read one (or more). We discuss the topic in as much depth as necessary to provide a continuous narrative. Though you learn the basics of how to create unit tests here, it is recommended that you take your skills to a higher level.

An Example of Unit Testing

Imagine you are writing a method that needs to calculate the payments to be made on a mortgage at a given interest rate. The caller can specify the initial amount of the loan, the number of years over which it is to be paid, and the interest rate. Your job is to write a method that can calculate the payments the borrower needs to make for any given loan configuration.

After you write this method, how do you test it? You can create a data entry screen that gives the user a way of entering the various values and then manually key in test data to cover the many different values for which you know what payments should be created. This approach is wasteful because it requires you to build a data entry screen that is subsequently thrown away and requires someone to manually test the results of the method before each production release of the product just to ensure that no changes are introduced that can break the calculation.

Now imagine writing code that would test the method for us. We can code something similar to the pseudo code in Listing 3.1.

LISTING 3.1: Pseudo Code for Unit Testing

```
mthlyPmt1 = CalcLoanPayment(Principal =1000, Interest=5%, NumMonths=360)
CheckForProperPayments(lst1)

mthlyPmt2 = CalcLoanPayment (Principal =1000, Interest=10%,
NumMonths=360)
CheckForProperPayments(lst2)

mthlyPmt3 = CalcLoanPayment (Principal =1000, Interest=10%,
NumMonths=240)
CheckForProperPayments(lst3)
```

...and more tests go here

If we write code to execute the tests shown previously, then we can run that test code anytime and we can ensure that the method is still working. We can even automate running the tests on each code check-in. This would virtually guarantee that the method is correct for all the scenarios we want to support and that it will never break.

Creating Unit Tests

Before we show a real example of a unit test, we need to look at how to create a unit test project. We will use the unit test project that is built into Visual Studio because it is a robust product that is well integrated into the IDE.

> **⬛ NOTE**
>
> We use the Microsoft Unit Testing framework, but there are many good frameworks available. The ideas we review here are applicable to any of these frameworks.

The Microsoft Unit Testing framework has a special project type to hold the unit tests, so the first thing we must do is add a new project. Right-click the solution in the Solution Explorer and choose **Add > New Project**. Choose a Test Project type and give it an appropriate name and then press **OK**. We use a separate test project for every standard project in the solution. Therefore, as shown in Figure 3.1, we name the test project with the name of the standard project and we append UnitTests to the end.

This creates a new project with a sample test already created and all the necessary references added. The sample test class comes with sample code that is not necessary right now, so to keep things simple, modify your sample test to look like this. This is all that is necessary for your first unit test; it simply ensures that True == True.

LISTING 3.2: A First Simple Test

```
using Microsoft.VisualStudio.TestTools.UnitTesting;

namespace CodeSamples.Ch03_UnitTesting.Listing2
{
  [TestClass]
  public class ExampleUnitTest
  {
    [TestMethod]
    public void ExampleTest()
    {
```

```
        Assert.IsTrue(true);
      }
    }
}
```

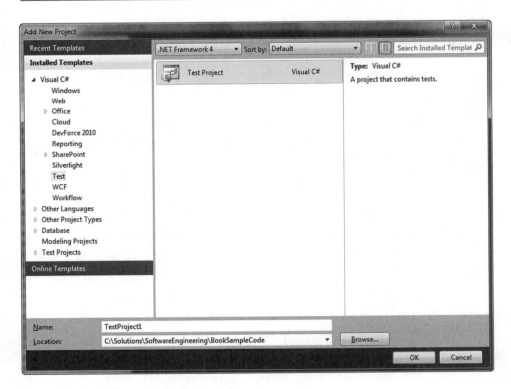

FIGURE 3.1: **Adding a new test project**

To run this test, right-click the name of the class and choose **Run Tests**, as demonstrated in Figure 3.2.

After running the test, the window shown in Figure 3.3 shows that the test passed.

Just so you can see what happens when a test fails, modify your code to make the test fail (see Listing 3.3).

LISTING 3.3: A Failing Test

```csharp
using Microsoft.VisualStudio.TestTools.UnitTesting;

namespace CodeSamples.Ch03_UnitTesting.Listing3
{
  [TestClass]
  public class ExampleFailingUnitTest
  {
    [TestMethod]
    public void ExampleTest()
    {
      Assert.IsTrue(false);
    }
  }
}
```

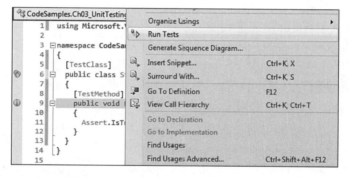

FIGURE 3.2: **Running a test from within the IDE**

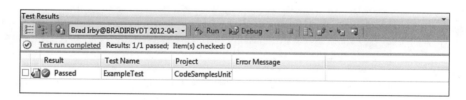

FIGURE 3.3: **Test result screen**

You should see something similar to Figure 3.4.

Now that we know how to create unit test files, let's get back to testing.

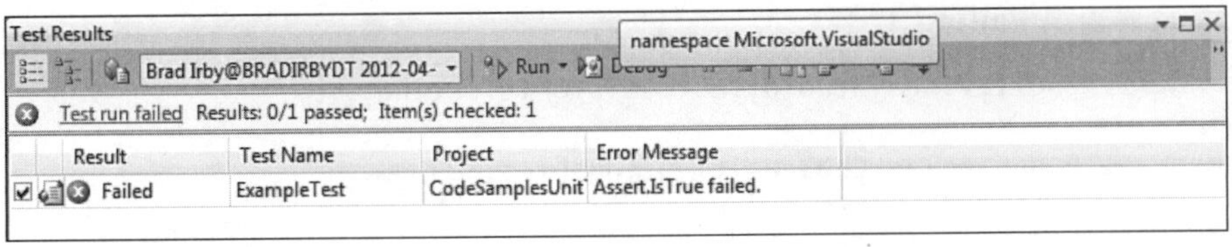

FIGURE 3.4: **Failing test**

Writing a Test

Let's look at an example of a class to be tested and the unit tests we build for it. The method shown in Listing 3.4 continues the previous example where we calculate the monthly payment for a loan.

LISTING 3.4: **A Method Under Test**

```
using System;

namespace CodeSamples.Ch03_UnitTesting.Listing4
{
  public class FinancialFunctions
  {
    /// <summary>
    /// P = (Pv*R) / [1 - (1 + R)^(-n)]
    /// where
    ///     Pv  = Present Value (beginning
    ///           value or amount of loan)
    ///     APR = Annual Percentage Rate
    ///           (one year time period)
    ///     R   = Periodic Interest Rate =
    ///           APR/ # of interest periods per year
    ///     P   = Monthly Payment
    ///     n   = # of interest periods for overall
    ///           time period (i.e., interest
    ///           periods per year * number of years)
    /// </summary>
    /// <param name="pLoanAmount">Original amount of the loan</param>
    /// <param name="pYearlyInterestRate">Yearly interest rate</param>
    /// <param name="pNumMonthlyPayments">Num of mthly payments</param>
    public double CalcLoanPayment(double pLoanAmount,
      double pYearlyInterestRate, int pNumMonthlyPayments)
    {
      var mthlyInterestRate = pYearlyInterestRate / 12;
      var numerator = pLoanAmount * mthlyInterestRate;
```

```
    var denominator = (1 - Math.Pow(1 + mthlyInterestRate,
            -pNumMonthlyPayments));
    var mthlyPayment = Math.Round(numerator / denominator, 2);
    return mthlyPayment;
  }

 }

}
```

We want to create some tests that ensure this method works for all cases that it supports. To begin, we write a test for a scenario that should produce no errors. To check the results, we can use one of the many mortgage rate calculators on the Web or Excel. Using one of these tools, we find that the payment for a $1,000 loan at 10 percent over 30 years should be $8.78 per month. In Listing 3.5, we write the test to pass in these values and Assert that the return value is valid.

LISTING 3.5: A Sample Unit Test

```
using CodeSamples.Ch03_UnitTesting.Listing4;
using Microsoft.VisualStudio.TestTools.UnitTesting;

namespace CodeSamples.Ch03_UnitTesting.Listing5
{
  [TestClass]
  public class FinancialFunctionsUnitTest
  {
    [TestMethod]
    public void CalcLoanPayment_Loan1000Int10Pmt360_
➡ReturnsProperPayment()
    {
      //Arrange
      var ex = new FinancialFunctions();

      //Act
      var pmt = ex.CalcLoanPayment(1000, 10, 360);

      //Assert
      Assert.AreEqual(8.78, pmt);
    }
  }
}
```

Let's take this test one line at a time. The first thing to notice is the TestClass attribute on the class. This is required to tell the unit-testing framework that this class is a test class. Each unit-testing framework has a different attribute, but they all require something similar to decorate test classes. On the test method, there is also an attribute labeling the method as a test; this is called TestMethod.

The name of the class itself is technically unimportant, so we typically name it the same name as the class that is tested and then append UnitTest to the end. The method name here is also technically unimportant because it will never be called by any code. The standard we use for naming unit test methods is to start with the name of the method or property being tested, add the conditions for the specific case being tested, and finally, add the results expected. In this case, we test that the CalcLoanPayment method, when called with a loan amount of $1,000, a yearly interest rate of 10 percent, and 360 monthly payments, it returns the proper payment, so we get the following name. The name should be descriptive enough so when you see a red "fail" indicator next to it in your test runs, you will know the scenario that has failed.

```
CalcLoanPayment_Loan1000Int10Pmt360_ReturnsProperPayment
```

The body of the test method is quite simple. We create a new instance of the class we wish to test and then call the method under test with the appropriate parameters. The only code in this method that we have not seen before is the Assert line. The Assert keyword is where we ensure that the method we test works properly. By using the Assert to test the results of our method, we ensure that our CalcLoanPayment method works properly for the given values. If the return value is what we expect, this test passes; otherwise, it fails.

This type of test structure is called Arrange-Act-Assert. The first step of the test is to arrange the classes so that they reflect the situation we want to test. We then act on the class under test to execute the code we want to test. Finally, we assert that the return value (or the actions taken) are appropriate for our test. When we run this test, we can see that our method returns the wrong value, as shown in Figure 3.5. We find our first bug!

Figure 3.5 shows the expected value and the actual returned value in the error message.

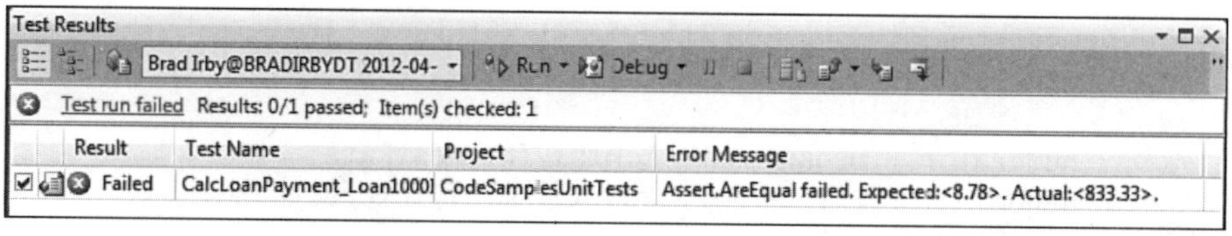

FIGURE 3.5: Failed first test

Upon examination of the code, we can see that the interest rate we pass in is a number between 0 and 100, whereas our code is expecting a number between 0 and 1. We can either change our test or change our code depending on which we think is in error. Because it is common to refer to yearly interest as 10 percent rather than 0.1, we allow users to pass in a number between 0 and 100 so that a 10 for the yearly interest is valid. That means we must update our business logic to accommodate this, as shown in Listing 3.6.

LISTING 3.6: A Fixed Unit Under Test

```
using System;

namespace CodeSamples.Ch03_UnitTesting.Listing6
{
  public class FinancialFunctions
  {
    /// <summary>
    /// P = (Pv*R) / [1 - (1 + R)^(-n)]
    /// where
    ///      Pv  = Present Value (beginning
    ///            value or amount of loan)
    ///      APR = Annual Percentage Rate
    ///            (one year time period)
    ///      R   = Periodic Interest Rate =
    ///            APR/ # of interest periods per year
    ///      P   = Monthly Payment
    ///      n   = # of interest periods for overall
    ///            time period (i.e., interest
    ///            periods per year * number of years)
    /// </summary>
    /// <param name="pLoanAmount">Original amount of the loan</param>
    /// <param name="pYearlyInterestRate">Yearly interest rate</param>
```

```
/// <param name="pNumMonthlyPayments">Num of mthly payments</param>
public double CalcLoanPayment(double pLoanAmount,
   double pYearlyInterestRate, int pNumMonthlyPayments)
{
  //Change the divisor for the yearly interest rate
  var mthlyInterestRate = pYearlyInterestRate / 1200;

  var numerator = pLoanAmount * mthlyInterestRate;
  var denominator = (1 - Math.Pow(1 + mthlyInterestRate,
       -pNumMonthlyPayments));
  var mthlyPayment = Math.Round(numerator / denominator, 2);
  return mthlyPayment;
}

  }
}
```

Running the test again proves that the code now works properly, as shown in Figure 3.6.

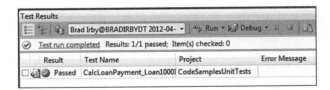

FIGURE 3.6: Fixed system under test

As shown in Listing 3.7, we can now add more methods to test different scenarios and ensure that the return values are valid.

LISTING 3.7: Additional Unit Tests

```
using CodeSamples.Ch03_UnitTesting.Listing4;
using Microsoft.VisualStudio.TestTools.UnitTesting;

namespace CodeSamples.Ch03_UnitTesting.Listing7
{
  [TestClass]
  public class FinancialFunctionsUnitTest
  {
    [TestMethod]
    public void CalcLoanPayment_Loan1000Int10Pmt360_ReturnsPmt()
```

```
    {
      //Arrange
      var ex = new FinancialFunctions();

      //Act
      var pmt = ex.CalcLoanPayment(1000, 10, 360);

      //Assert
      Assert.AreEqual(8.78, pmt);
    }


    [TestMethod]
    public void CalcLoanPayment_Loan1000Int5Pmt360_ReturnsPmt()
    {
      //Arrange
      var ex = new FinancialFunctions();

      //Act
      var pmt = ex.CalcLoanPayment(1000, 15, 360);

      //Assert
      Assert.AreEqual(12.64, pmt);
    }

    [TestMethod]
    public void CalcLoanPayment_Loan1000Int10Pmt12_ReturnsPmt()
    {
      //Arrange
      var ex = new FinancialFunctions();

      //Act
      var pmt = ex.CalcLoanPayment(1000, 10, 12);

      //Assert
      Assert.AreEqual(87.92, pmt);
    }

  }
}
```

All of these tests should pass, as shown in Figure 3.7.

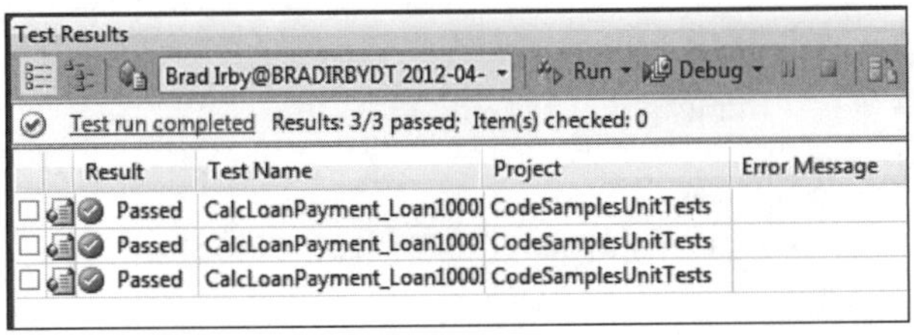

FIGURE 3.7: Successfully running unit tests

Detecting Exceptions

When writing your tests, be sure to include tests for invalid values. For instance, what happens if we pass a negative number to our method as an interest rate? This is a condition that should not be allowed, so we should throw an exception. Normally if an exception is thrown in the business logic, we want that treated as a test failure, but in this case, it should cause the test to succeed. To do this, we use the ExpectedException attribute.

Update the business logic to look like Listing 3.8.

LISTING 3.8: A Method That Throws an Exception

```
using System;

namespace CodeSamples.Ch03_UnitTesting.Listing8
{
  public class FinancialFunctions
  {
    /// <summary>
    /// P = (Pv*R) / [1 - (1 + R)^(-n)]
    /// where
    ///     Pv  = Present Value (beginning
    ///           value or amount of loan)
    ///     APR = Annual Percentage Rate
    ///           (one year time period)
    ///     R   = Periodic Interest Rate =
    ///           APR/ # of interest periods per year
    ///     P   = Monthly Payment
    ///     n   = # of interest periods for overall
    ///           time period (i.e., interest
    ///           periods per year * number of years)
    /// </summary>
    /// <param name="pLoanAmount">Original amount of the loan</param>
    /// <param name="pYearlyInterestRate">Yearly interest rate</param>
```

```
/// <param name="pNumMonthlyPayments">Num of mthly payments</param>
/// <returns></returns>
public double CalcLoanPayment(double pLoanAmount,
  double pYearlyInterestRate, int pNumMonthlyPayments)
{
  //start code change ********************************
  if (pYearlyInterestRate < 0)
    throw new ArgumentException(
      "pYearlyInterestRate cannot be negative");
  //end code change ********************************

  var mthlyInterestRate = pYearlyInterestRate / 1200;
  var numerator = pLoanAmount * mthlyInterestRate;
  var denominator = (1 - Math.Pow(1 + mthlyInterestRate,
      -pNumMonthlyPayments));
  var mthlyPayment = Math.Round(numerator / denominator, 2);
  return mthlyPayment;
}

}

}
```

With this business logic, we can write a test like this to ensure the exception is thrown. Listing 3.9 shows the new test added to the top of our existing tests.

LISTING 3.9: Testing a Method That Throws an Exception

```
using System;
using CodeSamples.Ch03_UnitTesting.Listing8;
using Microsoft.VisualStudio.TestTools.UnitTesting;

namespace CodeSamples.Ch03_UnitTesting.Listing9
{
  [TestClass]
  public class FinancialFunctionsUnitTest
  {
    [TestMethod]
    [ExpectedException(typeof(ArgumentException))]
    public void CalcLoanPayment_Loan1000IntNeg10Pmt12_Throws()
    {
      //Arrange
      var ex = new FinancialFunctions();

      //Act
      ex.CalcLoanPayment(1000, -10, 12);
    }
```

```
[TestMethod]
public void CalcLoanPayment_Loan1000Int10Pmt360_ReturnsPmt()
{
  //Arrange
  var ex = new FinancialFunctions();

  //Act
  var pmt = ex.CalcLoanPayment(1000, 10, 360);

  //Assert
  Assert.AreEqual(8.78, pmt);
}


[TestMethod]
public void CalcLoanPayment_Loan1000Int5Pmt360_ReturnsPmt()
{
  //Arrange
  var ex = new FinancialFunctions();

  //Act
  var pmt = ex.CalcLoanPayment(1000, 15, 360);

  //Assert
  Assert.AreEqual(12.64, pmt);
}

[TestMethod]
public void CalcLoanPayment_Loan1000Int10Pmt12_ReturnsPmt()
{
  //Arrange
  var ex = new FinancialFunctions();

  //Act
  var pmt = ex.CalcLoanPayment(1000, 10, 12);

  //Assert
  Assert.AreEqual(87.92, pmt);
}

  }
}
```

In the first test, note the ExpectedException attribute just after the TestMethod attribute. Another item to note is the lack of an Assert statement. The Assert is not needed because execution of the test stops when the exception is thrown. If the exception is not thrown, the test fails due to the ExpectedException attribute.

This test should run as shown in Figure 3.8.

	Result	Test Name	Project	Error Message
☐	Passed	CalcLoanPayment_Loan1000I	CodeSamplesUnitTests	
☐	Passed	CalcLoanPayment_Loan1000I	CodeSamplesUnitTests	
☐	Passed	CalcLoanPayment_Loan1000I	CodeSamplesUnitTests	
☐	Passed	CalcLoanPayment_Loan1000I	CodeSamplesUnitTests	

Test Results

Brad Irby@BRADIRBYDT 2012-04- Run ▾ Debug ▾

Test run completed   Results: 4/4 passed   Item(s) checked: 0

FIGURE 3.8: All four tests now pass.

Understanding the Power of Assert

The power of a unit test comes from the Assert keyword. There are many things that can be asserted aside from just true or false. We can test the equality of two items, whether they are null, or many other things, as shown in Figure 3.9. Of course the Assert.IsTrue is the most powerful because we can write any code we want to test a value and see whether that value is correct.

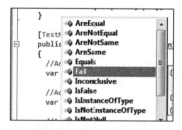

FIGURE 3.9: The many options of Assert

Comparing Unit Tests to Integration Tests

So far in this discussion, we have looked at unit tests, but there is another type of test called an integration test. A unit test can be loosely defined as a test that does not use any external resources such as the hard drive, a database, or the Web. It is completely self-sufficient for the resources it needs. In other words, it does not need to access anything but memory to execute the test, which should make a unit test fast to run. A unit test should also be repeatable, meaning that we can run the same test multiple times and always receive the same result. If a test relies on an external condition to pass and we do not have control of that external condition, it is not a unit test.

An integration test, on the other hand, uses external resources such as a database or a web service. These tests are often larger than unit tests because there are more moving pieces involved. For example, an integration test can ensure that a method can read several rows out of the database, process them properly by updating the data in the class representing the data row, and then save those rows back to the database. A unit test, on the other hand, assumes that the database read and write are working properly and it tests only that the given data was updated properly.

Integration tests are an important part of a full testing strategy, but we treat them separately because they are usually much more resource-intensive than unit tests. By using the outside resources, integration tests also normally take much longer. Unit tests for a project should run to completion in just a minute or two, but it's not uncommon to see integration test suites that run for an hour or more. The integration tests can be more thorough than a unit test, but the time commitment is so much greater that it is normally not possible to run integration tests just before a check-in like we do for unit tests. Therefore, integration tests are normally scheduled to be run once or twice a day.

Using the InternalsVisibleTo Attribute

A problem that plagues unit test writing is adding the proper references to the test project to allow access to the methods we want to test. The point of having unit tests is to exercise code and make sure it runs properly. However in a well-designed class, there are several methods that should be private to the class so they cannot be accessed by outside code. This presents a problem because this also limits the capability of our test to access the method.

One solution is to make public all methods that we test, but this can lead to problems later when internal methods are used inappropriately, making a class unstable. Imagine a new developer coming aboard who is unaware a certain method was made public simply to test it. He might think all public methods are available for use and then use this method, potentially introducing serious defects into the code.

Another solution is to always place the test classes in the same project as the live code. If we do this and set the methods to Internal, then we get past the problem; however, now the test code gets compiled into the same DLL as the live code, which causes the files to be bloated.

The .NET framework has addressed this problem with the `Internals VisibleTo` project attribute. By adding this to the AssemblyInfo.cs file, we can expose an internal property or method only to a specific project in the solution. This enables the test class to access any methods that are necessary while still maintaining the proper encapsulation for the business logic.

Figure 3.10 shows where you can find the `AssemblyInfo.cs` file.

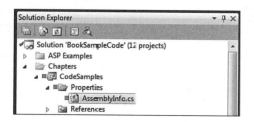

FIGURE 3.10: AssemblyInfo.cs File Location

Listing 3.10 shows what the `InternalsVisibleTo` attribute looks like. See the last line of the listing for an example.

LISTING 3.10: An InternalsVisibleTo Example

```
using System.Reflection;
using System.Runtime.CompilerServices;
using System.Runtime.InteropServices;

// General Information about an assembly is controlled through the
➥following
// set of attributes. Change these attribute values to modify the
➥information
// associated with an assembly.
[assembly: AssemblyTitle("CodeSamples")]
[assembly: AssemblyDescription("")]
```

```
[assembly: AssemblyConfiguration("")]
[assembly: AssemblyCompany("Reengineering .NET")]
[assembly: AssemblyProduct("CodeSamples")]
[assembly: AssemblyCopyright("Copyright © Brad Irby")]
[assembly: AssemblyTrademark("")]
[assembly: AssemblyCulture("")]

// Setting ComVisible to false makes the types in this assembly not
➡visible
// to COM components. If you need to access a type in this assembly from
// COM, set the ComVisible attribute to true on that type.
[assembly: ComVisible(false)]

// The following GUID is for the ID of the typelib if
// this project is exposed to COM.
[assembly: Guid("693b33bf-7738-42b0-b743-ed05a8d28d8e")]

// Version information for an assembly consists of the following four
➡values:
//
//      Major Version
//      Minor Version
//      Build Number
//      Revision
//
// You can specify all the values or you can default the
// Build and Revision Numbers
// by using the '*' as shown below:
// [assembly: AssemblyVersion("1.0.*")]
[assembly: AssemblyVersion("1.0.0.0")]
[assembly: AssemblyFileVersion("1.0.0.0")]

[assembly: InternalsVisibleTo("CodeSampleUnitTests")]
```

The string is the project name you want to grant use of internal methods to (that is, the test project). This line should be added to the `AssemblyInfo.cs` file in the live-code project that contains the logic to be tested. Listing 3.11 shows an example of a private method that is marked `Internal` to allow access by the test.

LISTING 3.11: A Sample Internal Method

```
namespace CodeSamples.Ch03_UnitTesting.Listing11
{
  public class SampleInternalMethod
  {
    /// <summary>
```

```
    /// Sample method with the internal setting
    /// </summary>
    internal void InternalMethod(string pMessage)
    {
      //code goes here
    }


  }
}
```

Understanding Test Driven Development

Our discussion of unit testing would not be complete without addressing the Test Driven Development (TDD) movement. TDD has recently become popular as a way of building high-quality software by writing unit tests before writing the production code. Extreme TDD practitioners write the first test before coding a single line of business logic, in which case the test "fails" because the application won't build.

The assumption in TDD is that the developer should know the requirements for the code (or they shouldn't be writing code yet), so these requirements should be enforced via unit tests and the business logic written to satisfy the tests. Then the cycle repeats where another unit test is written and the production code is updated to make the test pass.

This approach has advantages when building new code, but when reengineering an existing system, TDD is a difficult approach to use. Because we are taking an existing code base and trying to enhance it with new architecture, it is impossible to write the test before writing the code. Also, because most systems that require reengineering are in such a state due to tight coupling, adding unit tests to this code is difficult or impossible. For these reasons, we do not take a TDD approach to our tests.

Learning More About Unit Testing

This chapter provides a brief introduction to unit testing, intended to give enough background so anyone who is not familiar with this process can continue reading the book and understand what is discussed. There are many books on the market that do an excellent job of explaining this topic in more detail. For example, *Software Testing with Visual Studio 2010* by Jeff Levinson is an excellent choice for .NET-focused examples. Also, *The Art of Unit Testing* by Roy Osherove is thorough. If you are new to unit testing, it is well worth the time to read one of these books.

Summary

This chapter introduced methods of ensuring the quality of your application in an automated fashion. By creating unit tests, we are able to write code that tests code, introducing dramatic improvements in quality because we can prove that code is working as it should be. Unit tests also enable us to thoroughly test code more often because these tests are now available at the push of a button.

This chapter discussed how to create your first unit tests, how to structure the tests to properly exercise your application, and how to detect exceptions that your code might generate in response to error conditions. We discussed the important distinction between integration tests and unit tests, and what that difference means to developers and to the build master. Finally, we introduced some Visual Studio-specific features of unit testing that can make your test-writing life much easier.

In the next chapter on the Dependency Inversion Principle, we begin to delve into automated ways of creating services and other objects so consumers can be insulated from the details of how to create those services.

■ 4 ■

Understanding the Dependency Inversion Principle

In this chapter, we discuss the cornerstone of the architecture we work with throughout this book—The Dependency Inversion Principle (also known as Inversion of Control, or IoC). Applying this principle is the first step toward breaking the tight coupling of the application and making it easier to enhance and test.

The goal of Dependency Inversion is to break the tight coupling in software that causes code to be rigid and fragile. Before we talk about how the Dependency Inversion Principle helps us remove the tight coupling from the application, let's discuss what tight coupling is and why it makes an application fragile.

Understanding Tight Coupling

Classes in applications can be split into two broad groups—the high-level components and the low-level components. Low-level components perform the work of the system, such as updating a database, verifying user-entered information, and reading from a configuration file. The low-level components are the worker-bees of the system, and they know the intimate details of the domain in which the application is working.

High-level components focus on the management of low-level and possibly other high-level components. High-level components tend to be more abstract and have less knowledge of the domain. When tracing the logic flow of an application, you encounter the high-level components first, which create and manage the other components that are necessary to make the application work.

In legacy applications, you encounter one of two situations. Most commonly, you find that the high-level and low-level components are combined into the same class. Combining these components obviously results in tight coupling because there is no way to separate the two from each other.

You also find that the high-level components create the low-level components to assist in performing a certain function. Due to this, the high-level components necessarily have knowledge of the lower-level components and what they are capable of doing. In other words, the high-level components are dependent on the low-level components. This dependency is called *tight coupling*.

Tight coupling makes an application difficult to manage and update. Imagine that you have a high-level class called SalesRegistrationService that registers a sale made by a salesperson. To get its job done, the SalesRegistrationService must make use of the functionality contained in the low-level classes called SecurityService and Repository. The Sales RegistrationService creates an instance of the SecurityService and Repository to call the appropriate methods to achieve the goal. The SecurityService also creates an instance of the Repository to retrieve necessary information from the database. Listing 4.1 shows an example.

LISTING 4.1: A Tightly Coupled SalesRegistrationService

```csharp
using System;

namespace CodeSamples.Ch04_DependencyInjectionPrinciple.Listing01
{
    /// <summary>
    /// Sample of a main driver program.
    /// </summary>
    public class Program
    {
        public Program()
```

```
    {
      var salesRegSvc = new SaleRegistrationService();
      salesRegSvc.CompleteSale("username", Guid.NewGuid(), 4);
    }
  }

  /// <summary>
  /// Service that registers a sale of a product
  /// </summary>
  public class SaleRegistrationService
  {
    /// <summary>
    /// Method called when a salesperson makes a sale
    /// </summary>
    public string CompleteSale(string salespersonUserName, Guid
productId,
      int quantity)
    {
      //Sale of some products is restricted.
      //Ensure this salesperson is allowed to sell this product.
      var security = new SecurityService();
      if (!security.CanUserSellProduct(salespersonUserName, productId))
        return "Error - No permission to sell this product";

      //make sure there is enough product on hand
      var repo = new Repository();
      var canRemoveFromInventory = repo.RemoveFromInventory(productId,
quantity);
      if (!canRemoveFromInventory)
        return "Error - not enough of that product in inventory";

      repo.FinalizeSale(salespersonUserName, productId, quantity);
      return "success";
    }
  }

  /// <summary>
  /// Class that provides all access to security
  /// </summary>
  public class SecurityService
  {
    /// <summary>
    /// Decide if the given username has access
    /// to the requested object.
    /// </summary>
    public bool CanUserSellProduct(string username, Guid productId)
    {
      //super user can do anything
      if (username == "SuperSalesPerson") return true;
```

```
      var repo = new Repository();
      if (!repo.IsUserActive(username)) return false;
      return (repo.DoesUserHavePermission(username, productId));
   }
 }

 /// <summary>
 /// Repository class that controls all interaction
 /// with the database.
 /// </summary>
 public class Repository
 {
   public bool RemoveFromInventory(Guid productId, int quantity)
   {
     //Query the DB to see if there is enough inventory
     //for this transaction.
     return true;
   }

   public void FinalizeSale(string salesPersonName, Guid productId, int
quantity)
     {
     //Finalize the sale by saving info to the database
     //for who sold the product and how many of them.
     }

   public bool IsUserActive(string username)
   {
     //Query the DB to see if this user is active.
     return true;
   }

   public bool DoesUserHavePermission(string username, Guid productId)
   {
     //Query the DB to see if this user has
     //sufficient permissions.
     return true;
   }
 }
}
```

All three of these classes are tightly coupled. The SalesRegistrationService is tightly coupled to the SecurityService, and the SecurityService is tightly coupled to the Repository. We see this in the way the different classes are instantiated. When the SalesRegistrationService needs the SecurityService, it must create the SecurityService directly via a call to "new." If the SecurityService was in a different namespace, this would result in a Using clause to include the namespace with the SalesRegistrationService, which is tight coupling. The same example is between the SalesRegistrationService and the Repository, and between the SecurityService and the Repository.

To demonstrate how tight coupling makes maintenance more difficult, imagine that we implement federated security in our application so that the permissions information comes from a web service somewhere. However, the URL of the web service is different for each customer using the application, so we should pass in the web service URL on the constructor line to the SecurityService. Now the SecurityService looks like Listing 4.2.

LISTING 4.2: **Using Federated Security with SecurityService**

```
/// <summary>
/// Class that provides all access to security.
/// </summary>
public class SecurityService
{
  private string _federatedSecurityLRL;
  public SecurityService(string federatedSecurityURL)
  {
    _federatedSecurityURL = federatedSecurityURL;
  }
  /// <summary>
  /// Decide if the given username has access
  /// to the requested object.
  /// </summary>
  public bool CanUserSellProduct(string username, Guid productId)
  {
    //Super user can do anything.
    if (username == "SuperSalesPerson") return true;

    var permissionsString = GetUserPermissionsFromURL(_
➥federatedSecurityURL);
    if (permissionsString.Contains("Inactive")) return false;

    var repo = new Repository();
    return (repo.DoesUserHavePermission(username, productId));
  }
```

This satisfies the requirement but what will this refactoring do to the SalesRegistrationService? We now need to pass in a URL string to the SecurityService when we create it. Where do we get the URL? We can enhance the SecurityService so that it has the logic to go find the URL, but that should not be the responsibility of the SecurityService.

The only other option is to have the string passed in by the caller, the SalesRegistrationService. However, this moves the problem up the chain. So a simple refactoring to add a string parameter to the SecurityService results in a refactoring of both classes.

Listing 4.3 shows the impact that refactoring of the SecurityService has on the rest of the code.

LISTING 4.3: The Impact of Refactoring SecurityService

```csharp
using System;

namespace CodeSamples.Ch04_DependencyInjectionPrinciple.Listing03
{
    /// <summary>
    /// Sample of a main driver program.
    /// </summary>
    public class Program
    {
        public Program()
        {
            var salesRegSvc = new SaleRegistrationService();
            salesRegSvc.CompleteSale("username", Guid.NewGuid(), 4);
        }
    }
    /// <summary>
    /// Service that registers a sale of a product.
    /// </summary>
    public class SaleRegistrationService
    {
        /// <summary>
        /// Method called when a salesperson makes a sale
        /// </summary>
        public string CompleteSale(string salespersonUserName, Guid productId,
            int quantity)
        {
            //Sale of some products is restricted.
            //Ensure this salesperson is allowed to sell this product.
            var security = new SecurityService("federated security URL");
            if (!security.CanUserSellProduct(salespersonUserName, productId))
                return "Error - No permission to sell this product";

            //Make sure there is enough product on hand.
            var repo = new Repository();
            var canRemoveFromInventory = repo.RemoveFromInventory(productId,
quantity);
```

```
      if (!canRemoveFromInventory)
        return "Error - not enough of that product in inventory";

      repo.FinalizeSale(salespersonUserName, productId, quantity);
      return "success";
    }
  }


  /// <summary>
  /// Class that provides all access to security.
  /// </summary>
  public class SecurityService
  {
    private string _federatedSecurityURL;
    public SecurityService(string federatedSecurityURL)
    {
      _federatedSecurityURL = federatedSecurityURL;
    }
    /// <summary>
    /// Decide if the given username has access
    /// to the requested object.
    /// </summary>
    public bool CanUserSellProduct(string username, Guid productId)
    {
      //Super user can do anything.
      if (username == "SuperSalesPerson") return true;

      var permissionsString = GetUserPermissionsFromURL(_
➥federatedSecurityURL);
      if (permissionsString.Contains("Inactive")) return false;

      var repo = new Repository();
      return (repo.DoesUserHavePermission(username, productId));
    }


    /// <summary>
    /// Retrieve a permissions string from the external registration
➥site.
    /// </summary>
    /// <param name="url"></param>
    /// <returns></returns>
    private string GetUserPermissionsFromURL(string url)
    {
      //Use federated security URL to get permission string.
      return "permissions go here";
    }
  }
```

```
/// <summary>
/// Repository class that controls all interaction
/// with the database.
/// </summary>
public class Repository
{
    public bool RemoveFromInventory(Guid productId, int quantity)
    {
        //Query the DB to see if there is enough inventory
        //for this transaction.
        return true;
    }

    public void FinalizeSale(string salesPersonName, Guid productId, int quantity)
    {
        //Finalize the sale by saving info to the database
        //for who sold the product and how many of them.
    }

    public bool IsUserActive(string username)
    {
        //Query the DB to see if this user is active.
        return true;
    }

    public bool DoesUserHavePermission(string username, Guid productId)
    {
        //Query the DB to see if this user has
        //sufficient permissions.
        return true;
    }
}
```

Implementing the Abstract Factory Pattern

The way out of this predicament is to implement the Abstract Factory Pattern. A Factory is a class whose sole responsibility is to create other things when requested. Creating a factory class does not remove the need to create supporting objects in the example, but at least it centralizes the code so we only have to maintain it in one place. If the constructor for anything changes, there is only one place we have to go to update the code.

The Factory we create looks like Listing 4.4.

LISTING 4.4: Example of Abstract Factory Pattern

```
/// <summary>
/// Abstract factory class to create services.
/// </summary>
public static class ObjectFactory
{
  /// <summary>
  /// This property will be set at application startup
  /// or user login when it is known what URL to use.
  /// </summary>
  public static string SecurityURL { get; set; }

  public static SecurityService CreateSecurityService()
  {
    return new SecurityService(SecurityURL);
  }

  public static Repository CreateRepository()
  {
    return new Repository();
  }
}
```

In this code, we create the ObjectFactory class, which creates either the SecurityService or the Repository when requested. This is a step in the right direction because it enables us to remove the security URL string from the SaleRegistrationService. This string is needed only to create the PermissionProvider, and now that the factory takes care of that, we don't need it. Removing it from the SaleRegistrationService simplifies the constructor and the logic.

Notice that we make the factory a static class. This is necessary so we can set the SecurityURL in one place at application startup to make it available for use wherever necessary. The alternative is to require each class that needs the SaleRegistrationService or SecurityService to know the proper value for this URL, which defeats the purpose of the factory. Because the factory is used throughout the system, making it a static class also makes it easier to access and use.

> **■ NOTE**
>
> There are many problems with creating static classes in the applications, so creating static classes is normally not a good idea. We do it here only as an interim step toward the goal architecture.

We can now refactor the other classes to use the factory, as shown in Listing 4.5.

LISTING 4.5: Refactoring to Use the ObjectFactory

```
using System;

namespace CodeSamples.Ch04_DependencyInjectionPrinciple.Listing05
{
  /// <summary>
  /// Sample of a main driver program.
  /// </summary>
  public class Program
  {
    public Program()
    {
      var salesRegSvc = new SaleRegistrationService();
      salesRegSvc.CompleteSale("username", Guid.NewGuid(), 4);
    }
  }
  /// <summary>
  /// Service that registers a sale of a product.
  /// </summary>
  public class SaleRegistrationService
  {
    /// <summary>
    /// Method called when a salesperson makes a sale.
    /// </summary>
    public string CompleteSale(string salespersonUserName, Guid
➥productId,
      int quantity)
    {
      //Sale of some products is restricted.
      //Ensure this salesperson is allowed to sell this product.
      var security = ObjectFactory.CreateSecurityService();
      if (!security.CanUserSellProduct(salespersonUserName, productId))
        return "Error - No permission to sell this product";

      //Make sure there is enough product on hand.
      // *** The following line was updated to use the ObjectFactory.
```

```csharp
      var repo = ObjectFactory.CreateRepository();
      var canRemoveFromInventory = repo.RemoveFromInventory(productId,
quantity);
      if (!canRemoveFromInventory)
        return "Error - not enough of that product in inventory";

      repo.FinalizeSale(salespersonUserName, productId, quantity);
      return "success";
    }
  }


  /// <summary>
  /// Class that provides all access to security.
  /// </summary>
  public class SecurityService
  {
    private string _federatedSecurityURL;
    public SecurityService(string federatedSecurityURL)
    {
      _federatedSecurityURL = federatedSecurityURL;
    }
    /// <summary>
    /// Decide if the given username has access
    /// to the requested object.
    /// </summary>
    public bool CanUserSellProduct(string username, Guid productId)
    {
      //super user can do anything
      if (username == "SuperSalesPerson") return true;

      var permissionsString = GetUserPermissionsFromURL
(_federatedSecurityURL);
      if (permissionsString.Contains('Inactive")) return false;

      // *** The following line was updated to use the ObjectFactory.
      var repo = ObjectFactory.CreateRepository();
      return (repo.DoesUserHavePermission(username, productId));
    }

    /// <summary>
    /// Retrieve a permissions string from the external registration
site.
    /// </summary>
    private string GetUserPermissionsFromURL(string URL)
    {
      //Use federated security URL to get permission string.
      return "permissions go here";
    }
  }
```

```csharp
/// <summary>
/// Repository class that controls all interaction
/// with the database.
/// </summary>
public class Repository
{
  public bool RemoveFromInventory(Guid productId, int quantity)
  {
    //Query the DB to see if there is enough inventory
    //for this transaction.
    return true;
  }

  public void FinalizeSale(string salesPersonName, Guid productId, int
➥quantity)
  {
    //Finalize the sale by saving info to the database
    //for who sold the product and how many of them.
  }

  public bool IsUserActive(string username)
  {
    //Query the DB to see if this user is active.
    return true;
  }

  public bool DoesUserHavePermission(string username, Guid productId)
  {
    //Query the DB to see if this user has
    //sufficient permissions.
    return true;
  }
}

/// <summary>
/// Abstract factory class to create services.
/// </summary>
public static class ObjectFactory
{
  /// <summary>
  /// This property will be set at application startup
  /// or user login when it is known what URL to use.
  /// </summary>
  public static string SecurityURL { get; set; }

  public static SecurityService CreateSecurityService()
  {
    return new SecurityService(SecurityURL);
  }
```

```
    public static Repository CreateRepository()
    {
        return new Repository();
    }
  }
}
```

Introducing Interfaces

The code has improved quite a bit so far. It goes from a tightly coupled structure where each class has to know the details of how to create its dependencies, to a structure where the knowledge is delegated to a central class so the individual classes that use a service are relieved of the responsibility. However, we are still tightly coupled to the services used. By declaring variables of the respective types, the SalesRegistrationService creates a tight coupling with the SecurityService and the Repository. We must remove the references to make the structure loosely coupled, but we still need the references to execute the business logic.

To achieve this, we need to introduce interfaces to the classes. An *interface* is a list of methods and properties that an implementing class conforms to, which is like a contract. The interface describes what a class can do, and it's up to the class to have the corresponding logic. The advantage is that more than one class can implement an interface, making the classes interchangeable.

> ### ■ NOTE
>
> If you are unfamiliar with interfaces and how they work, please review that now. Interfaces are critical to the architecture we use, so you should be comfortable with them. You can find a review of interfaces in any C# programming book (*The C# Programming Language* by Anders Hejlsberg is a good choice), or on MSDN at http://msdn.microsoft.com/en-us/library/ms173156.aspx.

As shown in Listing 4.6, we have an AlternateSecurityService class that stores permissions by keeping a local file with permissions listed, but still has the same methods and properties.

LISTING 4.6: Using an Alternate to SecurityService

```csharp
using System;

namespace CodeSamples.Ch04_DependencyInjectionPrinciple.Listing06
{
  public class AlternateSecurityService
  {
    private string _filename;
    public AlternateSecurityService(string pFilename)
    {
      _filename = pFilename;
    }

    public bool CanUserSellProduct(string username, Guid productId)
    {
      //Use local file to decide if user has permission.
      return true;
    }
  }

}
```

In theory, the provider should be interchangeable with the other providers because it performs the same job but in a different manner. However if we use this provider, we get a build error because we cannot assign an `AlternateSecurityService` to a `SalesRegistrationService` variable. To use the `AlternateSecurityService`, we must change the code in the `SalesRegistrationService` to use it instead. This is another example of tight coupling.

Now let's introduce an interface for the security services and the repository, as shown in Listing 4.7.

LISTING 4.7: Introducing Interfaces for the Services

```csharp
using System;

namespace CodeSamples.Ch04_DependencyInjectionPrinciple.Listing07
{
  public interface ISecurityService
  {
    bool CanUserSellProduct(string username, Guid productId);
  }

  public interface IRepository
  {
```

```
      bool RemoveFromInventory(Guid productId, int quantity);
      void FinalizeSale(string salesPersonName, Guid productId, int
   quantity);
      bool IsUserActive(string username);
      bool DoesUserHavePermission(string username, Guid productId);
   }

}
```

Our interfaces are simple, and both security services implement ISecurityService. If we design the rest of the code correctly, these two objects can be interchangeable. Let's refactor the factory to look like what's shown in Listing 4.8.

LISTING 4.8: Refactoring Object Factory to Return Interfaces

```
/// <summary>
/// Abstract factory class to create services
/// </summary>
public static class ObjectFactory
{
  /// <summary>
  /// This property will be set at application startup
  /// or user login when it is known what URL to use.
  /// </summary>
  public static string SecurityURL { get; set; }

  // *** This method now returns an interface.
  public static ISecurityService CreateSecurityService()
  {
    return new SecurityService(SecurityURL);
  }

  // *** This method now returns an interface.
  public static IRepository CreateRepository()
  {
    return new Repository();
  }
}
```

Notice that the factory now returns an interface, not a concrete object. By returning the interface, the factory enables the SecurityService to lose its tight coupling with the Repository, and the SalesRegistrationService is no longer tightly coupled with the SecurityService. Now they both use an interface for the services they need but do not know (and do not care) what concrete object performs the duties.

With this structure, we can swap out the SecurityService and instead use the AlternateSecurityService by refactoring the object factory. No other code needs to be rebuilt.

> **■ NOTE**
>
> Extracting interfaces is a common task when reengineering a legacy system. This is easily done with Visual Studio 2012 by right-clicking on the class name and choosing **Refactor > Extract Interface**.

Creating Unit Tests

We reengineer the classes to be loosely coupled by using a factory and interfaces. The architecture is beginning to look similar to the final goal, but we are not done yet because the current structure does not support unit tests very well.

Let's create some unit tests for the SalesRegistrationService. There are many things we need to verify in this class, but let's test security first. We need to test what happens if the sales person is one of three possibilities:

- SuperSalesPerson (who can sell anything)
- NormalSalesPerson (who has permission to sell the product)
- NormalSalesPerson (who does *not* have permission to sell the product)

The current logic has the SalesRegistrationService calling the SecurityService to check permissions. The SecurityService calls the Repository to get the access rights for the user from the database. This means that we need a fully configured database available to test the method. We must configure this database to have the appropriate rights for the various test user accounts we will use and then maintain this database so that the tests do not break. This requirement makes the unit test fragile because making a seemingly unrelated change in the database will break this test.

In the previous section, we refactor the code so that any class can be used as a SecurityService as long as it implements the proper interface. Using this interface, we can create some special test security services that return values we want. For example, we can create a TestObjectFactory that creates a TestSecurityService, which returns the specific value we want. As shown in Listing 4.9, we can then use conditional compilation to load this permission provider instead of the real one.

LISTING 4.9: Testing SecurityService and Object Factory

```
    /// <summary>
    /// Abstract factory class to create services
    /// </summary>
    public static class ObjectFactory
    {
      /// <summary>
      /// This property will be set at application startup
      /// or user login when it is known what URL to use.
      /// </summary>
      public static string SecurityURL { get; set; }

      // *** This now can return a test class if in debug mode.
      public static ISecurityService CreateSecurityService()
      {
#if Debug
        return new TestSecurityService(SecurityURL);
#else
        return new SecurityService(SecurityURL);
#endif
      }

      public static IRepository CreateRepository()
      {
        return new Repository();
      }
    }

  public class TestSecurityService : ISecurityService
    {
      public TestSecurityService(string pFilename)
      {
        //Don't need to save anything for the test service.
      }
```

```
  public bool CanUserSellProduct(string username, Guid productId)
  {
    //Always return false for test purposes.
    return true;
  }
}
```

However, this method is clumsy and fragile. It might work when we want to test what happens when the permissions provider returns true, but how do we test when the permissions provider returns false? We would need to recode the test factory to create a test permissions provider that returns false. This approach gets unmanageable very quickly. What we need is a factory where we can decide at runtime what object is created. With this approach, we do not have to change any production code to run tests, we don't have to have conditional compilation statements, and we still get full control during unit tests. For this, we turn to service location.

Understanding Service Location

Service location is a way of creating a factory that can be configured at runtime to create different objects depending on the situation (either test or live). You can program it to return your live production objects when the application is running in production, but change what objects are delivered during a unit test so you can thoroughly test all the logic paths. Furthermore, you can do all of this without changing any code in your production system.

Before discussing service location, however, we need to discuss the idea of Inversion of Control Containers.

Inversion of Control Containers

Inversion of Control containers (also known as dependency injection containers) are classes that enable the user to register a certain class as a proxy for another. When a caller asks the container for the proxy class, the container will return the class to which the proxy is registered. In other words, we register with the container that whenever we request the interface IClass1, the container should create and return the concrete class Class1. It is a factory for any type of object you want it to create.

> ### ■ NOTE
>
> In all the examples, we use an IoC container called *Unity*. This container is part of the Prism package that is released by the Microsoft Patterns and Practices group. You can download the code and libraries from http://unity.codeplex.com/.
>
> There are other containers that are freely available on the Web, which are very good. If you have a favorite container, it should work just as well for your reengineering project, though some of the examples in this book might need to be updated to suit your containers' syntax.

Listing 4.10 shows how we set up a container.

LISTING 4.10: Registering a Class with Unity

```
using Microsoft.Practices.Unity;

namespace CodeSamples.Ch04_DependencyInjectionPrinciple.Listing10
{
  /// <summary>
  /// Interface for the class that does the real work.
  /// </summary>
  public interface IExampleClass
  {
    void DoWork();
  }

  /// <summary>
  /// Concrete implementation of the worker class.
  /// </summary>
  public class ExampleClass : IExampleClass
  {
    public void DoWork()
    {
      //Do work here.
    }
  }


  public class IoCContainerExample
  {
    public void ExampleUsage()
    {
      //Create the container so we can register our classes.
      var container = new UnityContainer();
```

```
    //This is how we register our class with the container.
    //This tells the container that when a caller requests
    //an IExampleClass, the container should create and
    //return an ExampleClass.
    container.RegisterType<IExampleClass, ExampleClass>();

    //This is how we get an instance of the ExampleClass.
    //We request an instance of the IExampleClass and
    //the container creates and returns an Exam-pleClass which
    //implements the IExampleClass interface.
    var instance = container.Resolve<IExampleClass>();
  }

  }
}
```

In this example, we have our concrete class and the associated interface. In the ExampleUsage method, we create the container where we register the types. We next register the interface and the concrete class together, indicating that when a caller requests an IExampleClass, the container should create and return an ExampleClass. A requirement of this registration is that the second class be castable as the first. In other words, if ExampleClass did not implement the IExampleClass interface, this RegisterType statement would not build. Finally in the example, we can ask the container for an instance of the ExampleClass by resolving the interface. This statement tells the container to create an ExampleClass and return it to the caller. We can then use the class for any purpose.

So let's take the example and make it a bit more complicated. Assume the ExampleClass has a dependency on a DependencyClass, as shown in Listing 4.11.

LISTING 4.11: An Example Class Using Another Class

```
using Microsoft.Practices.Unity;

namespace CodeSamples.Ch04_DependencyInjectionPrinciple.Listing11
{
  /// <summary>
  /// Interface for the class that does the real work.
  /// </summary>
  public interface IExampleClass
  {
    void DoWork();
  }
```

```csharp
/// <summary>
/// Concrete implementation of the worker class.
/// </summary>
public class ExampleClass : IExampleClass
{
  public void DoWork()
  {
    //Do work using another class.
    var dependencyClass = new DependencyClass();
    dependencyClass.DoDependencyWork();
  }
}


public interface IDependencyClass
{
  void DoDependencyWork();
}


public class DependencyClass : IDependencyClass
{
  public void DoDependencyWork()
  {
    //do work
  }
}


public class IoCContainerExample
{
  public void ExampleUsage()
  {
    var container = new UnityContainer();
    container.RegisterType<IExampleClass, ExampleClass>();
    var instance = container.Resolve<IExampleClass>();
  }

}
}
```

With this structure, the ExampleClass is tightly coupled with the DependencyClass because we must "new it up" in the DoWork method. As in the example, though, the container can act as a factory and create objects so that we do not have this tight coupling. The problem is getting the container into the ExampleClass so it can be used. This is where we create the ServiceLocator.

Service Locator

Remember, when we create the factory, we make it static so it is easier to use and setup. If we combine the idea of a static factory with the power of the container to build objects via a reference, we have a ServiceLocator. The ServiceLocator is a factory that uses the IoC container to register and resolve instances of objects. If we implement a bare-bones ServiceLocator and refactor the example to use it, it would look like Listing 4.12.

> ### ■ NOTE
>
> You might think that you can make a static variable that exposes the IoC container instead of using the ServiceLocator, but we enhance the ServiceLocator later, so keeping it in the static class is a better way to go.

LISTING 4.12: A Simple Service Locator

```
using Microsoft.Practices.Unity;

namespace CodeSamples.Ch04_DependencyInjectionPrinciple.Listing12
{
  /// <summary>
  /// Interface for the class that does the real work.
  /// </summary>
  public interface IExampleClass
  {
    void DoWork();
  }

  /// <summary>
  /// Concrete implementation of the worker class
  /// </summary>
  public class ExampleClass : IExampleClass
  {
    public void DoWork()
    {
      //*** We are now using the ServiceLocator to resolve our
➥dependency.
      var dependencyClass = ServiceLocator.Resolve<IDependencyClass>();
      dependencyClass.DoDependencyWork();
    }
  }
```

```csharp
public interface IDependencyClass
{
  void DoDependencyWork();
}

public class DependencyClass : IDependencyClass
{
  public void DoDependencyWork()
  {
    //do work
  }
}

public class IoCContainerExample
{
  public void ExampleUsage()
  {
    //*** We are now using the ServiceLocator to get
    //our example class.
    var instance = ServiceLocator.Resolve<IExampleClass>();
  }

}

public static class ServiceLocator
{
  private static UnityContainer _container;

  static ServiceLocator()
  {
    //Create our container.
    _container = new UnityContainer();

    //Set up all class registrations so they can be resolved
    //in code later.
    _container.RegisterType<IExampleClass, ExampleClass>();
    _container.RegisterType<IDependencyClass, DependencyClass>();
  }

  public static TProxyType Resolve<TProxyType>()
  {
    return _container.Resolve<TProxyType>();
  }
}
}
```

Let's take these classes one by one. The DependencyClass and its interface have not changed. The ExampleClass, however, uses the ServiceLocator to resolve an instance of the DependencyClass via the interface. Notice that there is not a reference in the ExampleClass to the concrete DependencyClass; there are only references to the interface. We removed the tight coupling between the ExampleClass and the DependencyClass.

Now look at the IocContainerExample class and notice there are no references to the concrete ExampleClass anymore. These have all been removed and replaced with ServiceLocator calls, so now we have also removed the tight coupling between the IoCContainerExample and the ExampleClass. Using the ServiceLocator, we are now able to remove the tight coupling among all three classes we are using.

A Real World Example

Now that we have the ServiceLocator in place, let's return to the original example with the SecurityService and Repository and see whether the new structure can handle something more reminiscent of the real world. Using these classes, the code now looks like Listing 4.13.

LISTING 4.13: A Service Locator Example

```csharp
using System;
using Microsoft.Practices.Unity;

namespace CodeSamples.Ch04_DependencyInjectionPrinciple.Listing13
{
  /// <summary>
  /// Sample of a main driver program.
  /// </summary>
  public class Program
  {
    public Program()
    {
      var salesRegSvc = ServiceLocator.Resolve<ISaleRegistrationService>
  ();
      salesRegSvc.CompleteSale("username", Guid.NewGuid(), 4);
    }
  }

  public interface ISaleRegistrationService
  {
    /// <summary>
    /// Method called when a salesperson makes a sale.
    /// </summary>
```

```csharp
      string CompleteSale(string salespersonUserName, Guid productId,
                                     int quantity);
   }


   /// <summary>
   /// Service that registers a sale of a product.
   /// </summary>
   public class SaleRegistrationService : ISaleRegistrationService
   {
      /// <summary>
      /// Method called when a salesperson makes a sale.
      /// </summary>
      public string CompleteSale(string salespersonUserName, Guid
productId,
         int quantity)
      {
         //Sale of some products is restricted.
         //Ensure this salesperson is allowed to sell this product.
         var security = ServiceLocator.Resolve<ISecurityService>();
         if (!security.CanUserSellProduct(salespersonUserName, productId))
            return "Error - No permission to sell this product";

         //Make sure there is enough product on hand.
         var repo = ServiceLocator.Resolve<IRepository>();
         var canRemoveFromInventory = repo.RemoveFromInventory(productId,
quantity);
         if (!canRemoveFromInventory)
            return "Error - not enough of that product in inventory";

         repo.FinalizeSale(salespersonUserName, productId, quantity);
         return "success";
      }
   }

   public interface ISecurityService
   {
      bool CanUserSellProduct(string username, Guid productId);
   }


   /// <summary>
   /// Class that provides all access to security.
   /// </summary>
   public class SecurityService : ISecurityService
   {
      private string _federatedSecurityURL;
      public SecurityService(string federatedSecurityURL)
      {
         _federatedSecurityURL = federatedSecurityURL;
      }
```

```csharp
    /// <summary>
    /// Decide if the given username has access
    /// to the requested object.
    /// </summary>
    public bool CanUserSellProduct(string username, Guid productId)
    {
      //Super user can do anything.
      if (username == "SuperSalesPerson") return true;

      var permissionsString = GetUserPermissionsFromURL(_
➥federatedSecurityURL);
      if (permissionsString.Contains("Inactive")) return false;

      var repo = ServiceLocator.Resolve<IRepository>();
      return (repo.DoesUserHavePermission(username, productId));
    }

    /// <summary>
    /// Retrieve a permissions string from the external registration
➥site.
    /// </summary>
    private string GetUserPermissionsFromURL(string URL)
    {
      //Use federated security URL to get permission string.
      return "permissions go here";
    }
  }


  public interface IRepository
  {
    bool RemoveFromInventory(Guid productId, int quantity);
    void FinalizeSale(string salesPersonName, Guid productId, int
➥quantity);
    bool IsUserActive(string username);
    bool DoesUserHavePermission(string username, Guid productId);
  }

  /// <summary>
  /// Repository class that controls all interaction
  /// with the database.
  /// </summary>
  public class Repository : IRepository
  {
    public bool RemoveFromInventory(Guid productId, int quantity)
    {
      //Query the DB to see if there is enough inventory
      //for this transaction.
      return true;
    }
```

```
    public void FinalizeSale(string salesPersonName, Guid productId, int
 ➥quantity)
    {
      //Finalize the sale by saving info to the database
      //for who sold the product and how many of them.
    }

    public bool IsUserActive(string username)
    {
      //Query the DB to see if this user is active.
      return true;
    }

    public bool DoesUserHavePermission(string username, Guid productId)
    {
      //Query the DB to see if this user has
      //sufficient permissions.
      return true;
    }
  }

  public static class ServiceLocator
  {
    private static UnityContainer _container;

    static ServiceLocator()
    {
      //Create our container
      _container = new UnityContainer();

      //Set up all class registrations so they can be resolved
      //in code later.
      _container.RegisterType<IRepository, Repository>();
      _container.RegisterType<ISecurityService, SecurityService>();
      _container.RegisterType<ISaleRegistrationService,
 SaleRegistrationService>();
    }

    public static TProxyType Resolve<TProxyType>()
    {
      return _container.Resolve<TProxyType>();
    }
  }


}
```

Our SecurityService is refactored to use the ServiceLocator and has no reference to the concrete Repository class. Even the SalesRegistrationService is refactored to use the ServiceLocator, so it has no references to the other concrete classes.

Now the code will build, but there is a runtime error. When the Unity container tries to create the SecurityService, it finds a string parameter on the constructor line. The container does not know how to resolve this string parameter, and the creation will fail.

This situation can happen frequently in code where a class needs to perform some setup when it is created. The container is flexible enough to handle this, though, with the RegisterInstance method. Consider the adjustment to the constructor of the ServiceLocator demonstrated in Listing 4.14.

LISTING 4.14: **Using RegisterInstance with Unity**

```
public static class ServiceLocator
{
  private static UnityContainer _container;

  static ServiceLocator()
  {
    _container = new UnityContainer();
    _container.RegisterType<IRepository, Repository>();

    //If a class needs setup logic, it can be created and the
    //instanced registered with the container.
    var securitySvc = new SecurityService("security URL goes here");
    _container.RegisterInstance<ISecurityService>(securitySvc);
  }

  public static TProxyType Resolve<TProxyType>()
  {
    return _container.Resolve<TProxyType>();
  }
}
```

In this snippet, we manually create a new SecurityService and perform any setup that is necessary. We then register the specific instance of this class with the RegisterInstance method. Now any code that requests an ISecurityService gets the same SecurityService instance that we just set up. RegisterInstance makes the class a *singleton* as long as it is resolved via the ServiceLocator. In other words, if all instances of the SecurityService are created via the ServiceLocator, this class is a singleton. However, it is possible for code to "new up" a SecurityService by hand instead.

> **NOTE**
>
> If you are unfamiliar with the singleton pattern, please review that now. We use singletons frequently in the structure. There are many pages on the Web with excellent descriptions of this including Wikipedia (http://en.wikipedia.org/wiki/Singleton_pattern) and MSDN (http://msdn.microsoft.com/en-us/library/ff650316.aspx). Keep in mind, however, that these examples do not use dependency injection and, therefore, implement the singleton using a static class. The dependency injection container enables us to have a singleton pattern available but not pay the price of adding a static class.

Speaking of singletons, it would be nice if the Repository was also a singleton. There is no need to create multiple versions of that service because it carries no state. A small refactoring of the registration makes the Repository a singleton, as demonstrated in Listing 4.15.

LISTING 4.15: Registering a Singleton

```
public static class ServiceLocator
{
  private static UnityContainer _container;

  static ServiceLocator()
  {
    _container = new UnityContainer();

    //By adding the parameter in the RegisterType call,
    //we have made the Repository a singleton.
    _container.RegisterType<IRepository, Repository>(
      new ContainerControlledLifetimeManager());

    //If a class needs setup logic, it can be created and the
    //instanced registered with the container.
    var securitySvc = new SecurityService("security URL goes here");
    _container.RegisterInstance<ISecurityService>(securitySvc);
  }
```

```
public static TProxyType Resolve<TProxyType>()
{
  return _container.Resolve<TProxyType>();
}
}
```

By adding the previous parameter to the `RegisterType` method, we turn the `Repository` into a singleton. The first call to the `ServiceLocator` to resolve an `IRepository` results in the `Repository` being created. All subsequent calls to `Resolve` return the `Repository` created in the first call. This is the definition of a singleton.

OnDemand Service Properties

A shortcut to using the `ServiceLocator` discussed often in this book is the `OnDemand` service property. This is a convenient way of resolving a class automatically without being concerned for how the creation happens. Listing 4.16 shows an example of this.

LISTING 4.16: **The OnDemand Service Property**

```
/// <summary>
/// Service that registers a sale of a product.
/// </summary>
public class SaleRegistrationService
{
  protected ISecurityService SecuritySvc
  {
    get
    {
      return _securitySvc ?? (_securitySvc =
        ServiceLocator.Resolve<ISecurityService>());
    }
  }

  private ISecurityService _securitySvc;


  /// <summary>
  /// Method called when a salesperson makes a sale.
  /// </summary>
  public string CompleteSale(string salespersonUserName, Guid
➥productId,
    int quantity)
```

```
    {
        //Sale of some products is restricted.
        //Ensure this salesperson is allowed to sell this product.
        if (!SecuritySvc.CanUserSellProduct(salespersonUserName,
➥productId))
            return "Error - No permission to sell this product";

        //Make sure there is enough product on hand.
        var repo = ServiceLocator.Resolve<IRepository>();
        var canRemoveFromInventory = repo.RemoveFromInventory(productId,
➥quantity);
        if (!canRemoveFromInventory)
            return "Error - not enough of that product in inventory";

        repo.FinalizeSale(salespersonUserName, productId, quantity);
        return "success";
    }
}
```

If you look at the definition of the SecuritySvc property, you see
the getter first checks whether the _securitySvc variable is initialized
and if so, returns that value. If the _securitySvc variable is null, a new
ISecurityService instance is resolved via the ServiceLocator and that value
is returned. Therefore, if you use the SecuritySvc property in your class,
you are guaranteed to have a SecurityService available and waiting. There
is nothing you need to do in your code to resolve this service; simply use
this property.

This structure also has the advantage of not creating a reference to
the service if it is not used. It is common when using a ServiceLocator to
resolve all dependencies on object creation. This is a waste of resources if
one of those dependencies is used only in a single method and that method
is never called. By using the OnDemand service property pattern, you create
only the services that are necessary and only when they are necessary.

These properties are so convenient, resource wise, and easy to use that
we often put them in parent classes for all the children to use. If a particular child class never needs a given service, it never creates one, and so no
resources are wasted. If that same child class needs to be refactored to use a
new service, that OnDemand property is readily available. Listing 4.17 shows
an example of this.

LISTING 4.17: **OnDemand Service Properties in Base Classes**

```csharp
public class BaseBusinessClass
{
  protected ISecurityService SecuritySvc
  {
    get
    {
      return _securitySvc ?? (_securitySvc =
        ServiceLocator.Resolve<ISecurityService>());
    }
  }

  private ISecurityService _securitySvc;

  protected IRepository RepositorySvc
  {
    get
    {
      return _repositorySvc ?? (_repositorySvc =
        ServiceLocator.Resolve<IRepository>());
    }
  }

  private IRepository _repositorySvc;

}

/// <summary>
/// Service that registers a sale of a product.
/// </summary>
public class SaleRegistrationService : BaseBusinessClass
{

  /// <summary>
  /// Method called when a salesperson makes a sale.
  /// </summary>
  public string CompleteSale(string salespersonUserName, Guid
➥productId,
      int quantity)
  {
    //Sale of some products is restricted.
    //Ensure this salesperson is allowed to sell this product.
    if (!SecuritySvc.CanUserSellProduct(salespersonUserName,
➥productId))
        return "Error - No permission to sell this product";

    //Make sure there is enough product on hand.
    var canRemoveFromInventory = RepositorySvc
```

```
.RemoveFromInventory(productId, quantity);
    if (!canRemoveFromInventory)
      return "Error - not enough of that product in inventory";

    RepositorySvc.FinalizeSale(salespersonUserName, productId,
➥quantity);
      return "success";
  }
}
```

In this example, we do not have to declare local variables for the services; we just use the properties declared on the base class. This makes development faster when referencing a service because you don't need to worry about calling the ServiceLocator to initialize the property.

> **■. NOTE**
>
> Using this code construct is not a requirement for reengineering the application. It is convenient to use because it simplifies the process of resolving a service, and when a team learns new technologies it is usually a good idea to simplify things as much as possible.

Unit Testing Advantages

Using service location also has advantages when it comes to unit testing. This topic is so important that we have dedicated Chapter 3, "Unit Testing," and Chapter 5, "Using Test Doubles with Unit Tests," to it, but let's look at an example now.

In the production code, we register the various services along with their interfaces—SecurityService, for example. Code that needs to use the SecurityService resolves the interface through the ServiceLocator without knowing which concrete class is returned. In other words, the ServiceLocator returns a real SecurityService, which the calling code does not know. The calling code knows that it received a reference to something that implements the ISecurityService interface.

Now imagine in a unit test where we replace that SecurityService in the container with a TestSecurityService that also implements the

ISecurityService interface. The calling code never knows the difference and uses the TestSecurityService just like normal. Using this approach, we can make the TestSecurityService return any value we want, or even throw an exception, and test how the calling code handles the different scenarios. ServiceLocation can open up a whole new world of testing possibilities. We talk more about this topic in Chapter 5.

Final Tweaks

With the ServiceLocator, we have the cornerstone of the architecture almost in place. Now we can create virtually any class we need, where we need it, with a single call to the Resolve method of the ServiceLocator. The only requirement is that the class must implement an interface that we can use to resolve an instance of the class, and all tight coupling to that class can be eliminated from the application.

When it comes down to daily use, the previous ServiceLocator needs some enhancement to serve our needs. In real code, the Setup method is typically moved to a separate class called the BootStrapper. The BootStrapper configures the container as necessary in preparation for the ServiceLocator to provide access to it.

The ServiceLocator also needs a little enhancement to make it more convenient to use. Listing 4.18 shows the production version of the ServiceLocator.

LISTING 4.18: **A Live Service Locator and a Sample Bootstrapper**

```
using System;
using Microsoft.Practices.Unity;

namespace CodeSamples.Ch04_DependencyInjectionPrinciple.Listing18
{
  /// <summary>
  /// Provides locator services for client code that
  /// needs access to those services.
  /// </summary>
  public class ServiceLocator
  {
    /// <summary>
    /// Unity Container that can resolve required items.
    /// This is set in the Bootstrapper.
    /// </summary>
    /// <remarks>
```

```
/// Make getter private so others don't try to use it
/// to register stuff.  Force them to resolve using
/// the Resolve method.
/// Getter is internal to give access to testing code
/// </remarks>
public static IUnityContainer Container { internal get; set; }


/// <summary>
/// Create and return an instance of the class registered to T.
/// </summary>
public static T Resolve<T>()
{
  return Container.Resolve<T>();
}


/// <summary>
/// Create and return an instance of the class registered to T
/// that was registered with the given name.
/// </summary>
public static T Resolve<T>(string pName)
{
  return Container.Resolve<T>(pName);
}


/// <summary>
/// Create and return an instance of the class registered to T.
/// </summary>
public static object Resolve(Type T)
{
  return Container.Resolve(T);
}


/// <summary>
/// Register the given object with the proxy object T.
/// </summary>
public static void RegisterInstance<T>(T pObject)
{
  Container.RegisterInstance<T>(pObject);
}


/// <summary>
/// Register the given object with the proxy object T
/// and label it with the given occurrence name.
/// </summary>
public static void RegisterInstance<T>(
  string pOccurranceName, T pObject)
{
  Container.RegisterInstance<T>(pOccurranceName, pObject);
}
```

```csharp
/// <summary>
/// Register the given proxy type to create and return a class
/// of the given type.
/// </summary>
public static void RegisterType<T, U>() where U : T
{
  Container.RegisterType<T, U>();
}

/// <summary>
/// Register the given proxy type to create and return a class
/// of the given type.  Name this instance so that this particular
/// one can be accessed by callers.
/// </summary>
public static void RegisterType<T, U>(LifetimeManager
pLifetimeManager)
    where U : T
  {
    Container.RegisterType<T, U>(pLifetimeManager);
  }
}


public class BootStrapperExample
{

  /// <summary>
  /// This is the entry point into our custom bootstrapper
  /// and is called by the base.
  /// </summary>
  protected BootStrapperExample()
  {
    ServiceLocator.Container = new UnityContainer();

    RegisterControlsAndControllers();
    RegisterServices();
  }

  /// <summary>
  /// Registers all services for the application.
  /// </summary>
  protected void RegisterServices()
  {
    ServiceLocator.RegisterType<IRepository, Repository>(
      new ContainerControlledLifetimeManager());
  }
```

```
        /// <summary>
        /// Registers the views and controllers.
        /// </summary>
        protected void RegisterControlsAndControllers()
        {
          //Registering controls and controllers will go here.
        }

    }


    public interface IRepository
    {
      //Method signatures go here.
    }

    public class Repository : IRepository
    {
      //Methods go here.
    }
}
```

There are a few changes we make to this ServiceLocator, but it essentially works the same as the bare-bones version. We add some convenience methods to enable additional ways of registering classes, and we also make the getter for the container internal so no outside processes are tempted to alter the container by hand. Making this internal enables us to get access to the property for unit testing purposes.

We include a sample of a BootStrapper to complete the example, but this is not the production version of one. Included in the code for this book is a project that fully implements the BootStrapper and ServiceLocator.

Using Dependency Injection

Even though we do not use it in the reengineering project, this chapter is not complete without a discussion of dependency injection. Dependency injection is another way of implementing dependency inversion. Service location and dependency injection are similar because they both use an IoC container to create and return an object that is registered with a proxy object. These two approaches differ in how they deliver the newly created object to the caller.

In service location, we have a static class that provides access to the IoC container so that any process in the application can resolve the objects it needs. Dependency injection approaches this problem from a different direction and injects the dependencies into the object via constructor parameters.

Let's take a look at a simple example of some tightly coupled code that we can convert to dependency injection, as demonstrated in Listing 4.19.

LISTING 4.19: Tightly Coupled Code

```csharp
namespace CodeSamples.Ch04_DependencyInjectionPrinciple.Listing19
{
  public class Program
  {
    public Program()
    {
      var parent = new ParentClass();
      parent.DoSomething();
    }
  }

  public interface IParentClass
  {
    void DoSomething();
  }

  public class ParentClass:IParentClass
  {
    public void DoSomething()
    {
      var dep = new DependencyClass();
      dep.DoSomethingElse();
    }
  }

  public interface IDependencyClass
  {
    void DoSomethingElse();
  }
  public class DependencyClass : IDependencyClass
  {
    public void DoSomethingElse()
    {
      //do the actual work
    }
  }

}
```

This is the starting point—a tightly coupled application that has several levels of services that are needed to perform the necessary work. In this example, the dependency is created within the ParentClass by "newing up" the DependencyClass, thus causing the tight coupling. Dependency injection works by injecting the dependency into the parent class on the constructor line. Using Unity, dependency injection would look like Listing 4.20.

LISTING 4.20: A Dependency Injection Example

```
using Microsoft.Practices.Unity;

namespace CodeSamples.Ch04_DependencyInjectionPrinciple.Listing20
{
  public class Program
  {
    public Program()
    {
      var container = new UnityContainer();
      container.RegisterType<IParentClass, ParentClass>();
      container.RegisterType<IDependencyClass, DependencyClass>();

      var parent = container.Resolve<IParentClass>();
      parent.DoSomething();
    }
  }

  public interface IParentClass
  {
    void DoSomething();
  }

  public class ParentClass : IParentClass
  {
    private IDependencyClass _dependency;

    public ParentClass(IDependencyClass dependencyClass)
    {
      _dependency = dependencyClass;
    }

    public void DoSomething()
    {
      _dependency.DoSomethingElse();
    }
  }
```

```
public interface IDependencyClass
{
  void DoSomethingElse();
}
public class DependencyClass : IDependencyClass
{
  public void DoSomethingElse()
  {
    //do the actual work
  }
}

}
```

Examine the constructor lines for the ParentClass. On this constructor line, notice that the dependencies for the class are passed in instead of resolved within the class. The constructor then saves off the services that are given to it so they can be used later. Notice the constructor line specifies the interface for the object they need, which is not the name of the concrete class.

Let's examine this code from the Program class to see how the object creation works. After registering all of the classes, we use the IoC container to resolve an instance of the ParentClass. Unity scans the constructor line of the class to see what parameters are required to create the class, where it encounters the IDependencyClass reference. Unity then looks through its registrations trying to find entries for this interface. If it is not found, Unity throws an exception.

When Unity finds the registration for this interface, it creates the object registered by again examining the constructor line and resolving any dependencies. This process continues until all dependencies are resolved for the main class requested, all the dependencies, and all of their dependencies. The depth of this recursion tree is limited only by the resources of the local machine.

In dependency injection, it is easy to add a new service to a class by putting it on the constructor line. Assume both the DependencyClass and the ParentClass needed access to a repository to do their work. We add this interface to the constructor lines, as shown in Listing 4.21.

LISTING 4.21: Three-Level Dependency Injection

```csharp
using Microsoft.Practices.Unity;

namespace CodeSamples.Ch04_DependencyInjectionPrinciple.Listing21
{
  public class Program
  {
    public Program()
    {
      var container = new UnityContainer();
      container.RegisterType<IParentClass, ParentClass>();
      container.RegisterType<IDependencyClass, DependencyClass>();
      container.RegisterType<IRepository, Repository>();

      var parent = container.Resolve<IParentClass>();
      parent.DoSomething();
    }
  }

  public interface IParentClass
  {
    void DoSomething();
  }

  public class ParentClass : IParentClass
  {
    private IDependencyClass _dependency;
    private IRepository _repo;

    public ParentClass(IDependencyClass dependencyClass,
      IRepository repo)
    {
      _dependency = dependencyClass;
      _repo = repo;
    }

    public void DoSomething()
    {
      _dependency.DoSomethingElse();
      var data = _repo.GetData();
    }
  }

  public interface IDependencyClass
  {
    void DoSomethingElse();
  }
  public class DependencyClass : IDependencyClass
  {
```

```
    private IRepository _repo;
    public DependencyClass(IRepository repo)
    {
      _repo = repo;
    }
    public void DoSomethingElse()
    {
      //do the actual work
      var data = _repo.GetData();
    }
  }

  public interface IRepository
  {
    string GetData();
  }

  public class Repository : IRepository
  {
    public string  GetData()
    {
      return "data";
    }
  }
}
```

If you look at the differences between the previous two listings, you see that the only real change is to add the IRepository parameter to the constructor line, and then use that injected service. We do not have to introduce any tight coupling on the repository.

So we see that dependency injection and service location both achieve the same goal of removing the tight coupling among the necessary classes. They also both perform the implementation using the same IoC container and interfaces. Where they differ is in the timing of the calls to the IoC container to resolve the services that are needed. Service location delays the resolution calls until the service is needed where dependency injection creates and injects the dependencies at object creation time.

Why Is Service Location Better for Reengineering?

When building an application from scratch, both service location and dependency injection are excellent patterns to use. If you create each class with the idea of injecting dependencies in mind, dependency injection works very well. If you rather use a common service locator, that pattern works as well.

However, if you reengineer an existing application, you have no control of the classes that have already been built. Often the class creation hierarchy can be many levels deep, so to create an object via the container, you have to register virtually all classes in the application at once. To register all of these means that you have also added interfaces to them all and converted the code that now uses the instances to instead use the interfaces.

Let's look at an example. Let's say we reengineer an application that is architected in the original, tightly coupled way that we described at the beginning of this chapter. Listing 4.22 presents the code for reference.

LISTING 4.22: Tightly Coupled Code

```
using System;

namespace CodeSamples.Ch04_DependencyInjectionPrinciple.Listing22
{
  /// <summary>
  /// Sample of a main driver program.
  /// </summary>
  public class Program
  {
    public Program()
    {
      var salesRegSvc = new SaleRegistrationService();
      salesRegSvc.CompleteSale("username", Guid.NewGuid(), 4);
    }
  }

  /// <summary>
  /// Service that registers a sale of a product.
  /// </summary>
  public class SaleRegistrationService
  {
    /// <summary>
    /// Method called when a salesperson makes a sale.
    /// </summary>
    public string CompleteSale(string salespersonUserName, Guid
➥productId,
      int quantity)
    {
      //Sale of some products is restricted.
      //Ensure this salesperson is allowed to sell this product.
```

```
      var security = new SecurityService();
      if (!security.CanUserSellProduct(salespersonUserName, productId))
        return "Error - No permission to sell this product";

      //Make sure there is enough product on hand.
      var repo = new Repository();
      var canRemoveFromInventory = repo.RemoveFromInventory(productId,
➥quantity);
      if (!canRemoveFromInventory)
        return "Error - not enough of that product in inventory";

      repo.FinalizeSale(salespersonUserName, productId, quantity);
      return "success";
    }
  }

  /// <summary>
  /// Class that provides all access to security.
  /// </summary>
  public class SecurityService
  {
    /// <summary>
    /// Decide if the given username has access
    /// to the requested object.
    /// </summary>
    public bool CanUserSellProduct(string username, Guid productId)
    {
      //Super user can do anything.
      if (username == "SuperSalesPerson") return true;
      var repo = new Repository();
      if (!repo.IsUserActive(username)) return false;
      return (repo.DoesUserHavePermission(username, productId));
    }
  }

  /// <summary>
  /// Repository class that controls all interaction
  /// with the database.
  /// </summary>
  public class Repository
  {
    public bool RemoveFromInventory(Guid productId, int quantity)
    {
      //Query the DB to see if there is enough inventory
      //for this transaction.
      return true;
    }
```

```
    public void FinalizeSale(string salesPersonName, Guid productId, int
➥quantity)
    {
      //Finalize the sale by saving info to the database
      //for who sold the product and how many of them.
    }

    public bool IsUserActive(string username)
    {
      //Query the DB to see if this user is active.
      return true;
    }

    public bool DoesUserHavePermission(string username, Guid productId)
    {
      //Query the DB to see if this user has
      //sufficient permissions.
      return true;
    }
  }
}
```

To resolve the Repository via dependency injection, we have to:

- Create an interface for the Repository so it can be added to the con-
  structor line of the SecurityService and the SaleRegistrationService.
- Create an interface for the SecurityService so it can be resolved by
  the SaleRegistrationService.
- Create an interface for the SaleRegistrationService so it can be
  resolved by the program.
- Register all classes and interfaces with the container.
- Refactor SalesRegistrationService and SecurityService to have their
  dependencies injected on the constructor line.
- Convert the SecurityService to use the interface IRepository instead
  of the concrete class Repository.
- Convert the SaleRegistrationService to use IRepository.
- Update the rest of the application to accommodate the constructors
  which had to change to accept dependency injection.
  - Changing the constructor means some other class, ClassX, which
    uses the SecurityService and which used to be able to create it

easily, must now also create a Repository in order to pass to the SecurityService. Remember that ClassX has not yet been converted to use the IoC container, so we can either convert that also (which starts the process all over again) or create the Repository by hand.

You can see how trying to adapt an existing application for dependency injection is a long, tough road that often ends up being an all or nothing effort. Making all of these changes at once to an application that you want to continue to be available throughout your upgrades is not wise.

Now let's see how we can convert this application using service location instead of dependency injection:

1. Start with just the Repository because it is one of the lower levels of the hierarchy, and it has no constructor parameters. Create an interface for this class. Note that we do not have to convert all classes at once, we have to create only one interface.
2. Register just the Repository with the ServiceLocator. Nothing else is necessary at this point.
3. Choose a class to convert to using the ServiceLocator to resolve the Repository. We do not have to convert everything at once. In that class, replace calls to new Repository with a call to ServiceLocator. Resolve<IRepository>.
4. We're done.

Now we can test and check in this code, and we've chipped away at the mountain of tight coupling that is the application.

Service location also fits into the project plans better than dependency injection. For example, assume you need to replace a tightly coupled SecurityService with a more advanced version that uses federated security. First, develop and test the new SecurityService to your satisfaction. When you are ready to implement, search through the application and replace all new SecurityService() calls with ServiceLocator calls. Test the application to make sure everything still works exactly as it did before (because you changed no business logic at this point except how you get a reference to the class you need).

Now replace the old SecurityService with the new SecurityService and test again. The SecurityService is replaced with minimal impact on the existing system. Achieving the same goal with dependency injection takes more work and has a much larger impact on the legacy code.

Another example is in unit testing. Let's assume the current application works fine but we want to introduce unit tests. We can't test the class because it relies on so many other classes that cannot be run under a test harness. Go through the class and replace any "new" calls with ServiceLocator calls, creating interfaces as necessary and registering them with the container along the way. In this fashion, we can remove all the dependencies on concrete objects and replace them with interfaces. The class is now testable because for the tests we can register dummy classes for the interfaces instead of the real classes. (For a full discussion of this topic, see Chapter 5.)

In general, service location enables us to proceed much more slowly and cautiously than dependency injection when converting an existing application to a new architecture. We can convert only select pieces and only when appropriate, so that the application never needs to be taken offline but is incrementally upgraded and improved. It also enables us to introduce unit testing on just the critical projects at first, providing a way to prove the theory that unit testing can improve quality and decrease testing time.

Summary

This chapter is one of the most critical chapters in the book. In these pages, we described the cornerstone of any modern software architecture, Dependency Inversion.

We began the chapter looking at a typical legacy application and how it is tightly coupled. We then introduced a factory pattern to help calling code be insulated from the difficulty of creating necessary objects, but this still left the application tightly coupled. Introducing interfaces helped break the dependencies on the concrete implementations of the different services, but we were still left with tight coupling between the consuming class and the factory, and between the factory and the individual implementations.

Finally, by introducing service location and the Bootstrapper, we were able to break the tight coupling between the factory (service locator) and the concrete implementations.

By using dependency inversion and service location, we are able to create applications that are much more flexible and easier to update, while at the same time making them easier to test.

In the next chapter, we examine the topic of unit tests much more closely to demonstrate why implementing a service location architecture can dramatically improve the quality of your application.

■ 5 ■
Using Test Doubles with Unit Tests

We now introduce a significant piece of the unit testing approach—test doubles. Using test doubles is a way of creating a class whose behavior can be changed at runtime. These classes can be used to unit test our code much more thoroughly than we could have otherwise. Let's look at the details of how these classes help write unit tests.

How Do Test Doubles Work?

Test doubles work by replacing real classes with an imitation class that can be created at runtime, not design time. Using this imitation class, we can change the behavior to perform any action or return any values that we want for a test. In this way, we can simulate many different situations happening to the business logic without having to go to the trouble to set up the actual circumstances.

> **▪ NOTE**
>
> A requirement for test doubles is to use interfaces. It is possible to create a test double for a class without an interface, but it severely limits the capabilities of the double and the test. Interfaces are used in many other ways in this book, so the lesson to be learned is to put interfaces on all of your services and many other classes.

What Need Do Test Doubles Satisfy?

A good example of a place where doubles are useful is when implementing a repository. We discussed the repository in the previous chapter, and we talk more about the Repository Pattern in Chapter 12, "Advanced Refactoring to Services." The Repository Pattern is used quite often because it removes the tight coupling with a particular database, allowing easier development and easy replacement of the backend data store.

The code in Listing 5.1 is a typical example of a Repository Pattern. Our business logic uses the repository to retrieve a user from the database, make a change to it, and then save it back to the database.

LISTING 5.1: A Repository Example

```
using System;
using System.Data.SqlClient;
using Microsoft.Practices.Unity;

namespace CodeSamples.Ch05_ClassMocking.Listing01
{
  public class MockingExample
  {
    public void UpdateUserData()
    {
      var repo = ServiceLocator.Resolve<IRepository>();
      var user = repo.GetUserData(1);
      user.Name = "New Name";
      repo.SaveUserData(user);
    }
  }

  public class User
  {
```

```csharp
    public int Id { get; internal set; }
    public string Name { get; set; }
}

public interface IRepository
{
  User GetUserData(int pUserId);
  void SaveUserData(User pUser);
}

public class Repository : IRepository
{
  private string _connectionString = "connStringGoesHere";

  public User GetUserData(int pUserId)
  {
    var qryString = "select * from User where id = @id";
    var conn = new SqlConnection(_connectionString);
    var cmd = new SqlCommand(qryString, conn);
    cmd.Parameters.AddWithValue("@id", pUserId);
    try
    {
      conn.Open();
      var reader = cmd.ExecuteReader();
      reader.Read();
      var usr = new User
      {
        Id = (int)reader[0],
        Name = reader[1].ToString()
      };
      reader.Close();
      return usr;
    }
    catch (Exception)
    {
      //do something with the exception
    }
    return null;
  }

  public void SaveUserData(User pUser)
  {
    var qryString = "Update user set name = @username where id = @id";
    var conn = new SqlConnection(_connectionString);
    var cmd = new SqlCommand(qryString, conn);
    cmd.Parameters.AddWithValue("@id", pUser.Id);
    cmd.Parameters.AddWithValue("@username", pUser.Name);
    try
    {
```

```
      conn.Open();
      cmd.ExecuteNonQuery();
    }
    catch (Exception)
    {
      //do something with the exception
    }
  }
}

public static class ServiceLocator
{
  private static UnityContainer _container;

  static ServiceLocator()
  {
    _container = new UnityContainer();
    _container.RegisterInstance<IUnityContainer>(_container);
    _container.RegisterType<IRepository, Repository>();
  }

  public static TProxyType Resolve<TProxyType>()
  {
    return _container.Resolve<TProxyType>();
  }
}
```

If we wanted to write a unit test for the UpdateUserData method, it would look like Listing 5.2.

LISTING 5.2: A Sample Unit Test

```
[TestClass]
public class MockingExampleTestClass
{
  [TestMethod]
  public void UpdateUserData_WhenCalled_SetsNewName()
  {
    var mockExample = new MockingExample();
    mockExample.UpdateUserData();
    var repo = ServiceLocator.Resolve<IRepository>();
    var user = repo.GetUserData(1);
    Assert.AreEqual("New Name", user.Name);
  }

}
```

The important thing to notice in this test is that the user information comes from the database and is saved back to the database. Even the test must access the database to assert that the proper changes have been made. When a live database is accessed, it changes a unit test into an integration test and also introduces a lot of dependencies, not to mention execution time. This one simple test now makes an active and up-to-date database required for a successful run. This is how tests become brittle.

Creating a Stub

To break the dependency on the database, we write a test double for the repository. This particular type of test double is called a *stub*. Listing 5.3 shows an example of a stub and how one is used.

> **▪▄ NOTE**
>
> We include the test code and business logic in the same code file here only for brevity and convenience. Your code should be put into the proper files and projects, and tests should have appropriate using clauses to access the code to test.

LISTING 5.3: A Repository Stub

```
using System;
using System.Data.SqlClient;
using Microsoft.Practices.Unity;
using Microsoft.VisualStudio.TestTools UnitTesting;

namespace CodeSamples.Ch05_ClassMocking.Listing03
{
  public class MockingExample
  {
    public void UpdateUserData()
    {
      var repo = ServiceLocator.Resolve<IRepository>();
      var user = repo.GetUserData(1);
      user.Name = "New Name";
      repo.SaveUserData(user);
    }
  }
```

```csharp
public class User
{
  public int Id { get; internal set; }
  public string Name { get; set; }
  public DateTime LastUpdateDate { get; set; }
  public DateTime CreateDate { get; set; }

  public User()
  {
    CreateDate = DateTime.Now;
    LastUpdateDate = DateTime.Now;
  }
}

public interface IRepository
{
  User GetUserData(int pUserId);
  void SaveUserData(User pUser);
}

public class Repository : IRepository
{
  private string _connectionString = "connStringGoesHere";

  public User GetUserData(int pUserId)
  {
    var qryString = "select * from User where id = @id";
    var conn = new SqlConnection(_connectionString);
    var cmd = new SqlCommand(qryString, conn);
    cmd.Parameters.AddWithValue("@id", pUserId);
    try
    {
      conn.Open();
      var reader = cmd.ExecuteReader();
      reader.Read();
      var usr = new User
      {
        Id = (int)reader[0],
        Name = reader[1].ToString(),
        CreateDate = DateTime.Parse(reader[2].ToString()),
        LastUpdateDate = DateTime.Parse(reader[3].ToString())
      };
      reader.Close();
      return usr;
    }
    catch (Exception)
    {
      //do something with the exception
    }
```

```
        return null;
    }

    public void SaveUserData(User pUser)
    {
      var qryString = "Update user set name = @username where id = @id";
      var conn = new SqlConnection(_connectionString);
      var cmd = new SqlCommand(qryString, conn);
      pUser.LastUpdateDate = DateTime.Now;
      cmd.Parameters.AddWithValue("@id", pUser.Id);
      cmd.Parameters.AddWithValue("@username", pUser.Name);
      cmd.Parameters.AddWithValue("@CreateDate", pUser.CreateDate);
      cmd.Parameters.AddWithValue("@LastUpdateDate", pUser.
➥LastUpdateDate);
      try
      {
        conn.Open();
        cmd.ExecuteNonQuery();
      }
      catch (Exception)
      {
        //do something with the exception
      }
    }
  }


  public class RepositoryStub : IRepository
  {
    public User StubUser{get;set;}

    public User GetUserData(int pUserId)
    {
      //Replace code to read from the database
      //and just return a new User.
      if (StubUser == null)
      {
        StubUser = new User();
        StubUser.Id = 1;
        StubUser.Name = "Brad Irby";
      }
      return StubUser;
    }

    public void SaveUserData(User pUser)
    {
      //do nothing in this stub
    }
  }
```

```csharp
public static class ServiceLocator
{
    private static UnityContainer _container;

    static ServiceLocator()
    {
        _container = new UnityContainer();
        _container.RegisterInstance<IUnityContainer>(_container);
        _container.RegisterType<IRepository, Repository>();
    }

    public static TProxyType Resolve<TProxyType>()
    {
        return _container.Resolve<TProxyType>();
    }
}

[TestClass]
public class MockingExampleTestClass
{
    [TestMethod]
    public void UpdateUserData_WhenCalled_SetsNewName()
    {
        //Arrange
        var container = ServiceLocator.Resolve<IUnityContainer>();
        var stubRepo = new RepositoryStub();
        container.RegisterInstance<IRepository>(stubRepo);
        var mockExample = new MockingExample();

        //Act
        mockExample.UpdateUserData();

        //Assert
        var repo = ServiceLocator.Resolve<IRepository>();
        var user = repo.GetUserData(1);
        Assert.AreEqual("New Name", user.Name);
    }

}
}
```

In this listing, notice that two classes implement IRepository—the real repository and the RepositoryStub. By implementing that interface, the RepositoryStub can be used as a replacement for the real Repository. Our stub, however, is hardcoded to return a User value without accessing the database, breaking the dependency on the database.

To use the new `RepositoryStub`, we need to replace the real repository in the `ServiceLocator`. To do that, we get a copy of the `Unity` container that the service locator uses and we register an instance of the `RepositoryStub` as the appropriate class to return when calling code requests an `IRepository`. Now, if any class anywhere in the system requests an `IRepository` from the `ServiceLocator`, it receives a copy of our stub `IRepository` instead of a real repository.

> ■ **NOTE**
>
> Some Dependency Injection containers do not replace an existing registration with a new one. We use Unity, which behaves appropriately for this example, but if you use a different container, you must replace the logic with something sufficient to replace the existing `IRepository` registration.

This stub approach works for this one test, but if we write another test that operates in a different way, we are faced with writing another stub that does something different. What we need is a stub whose behavior can be modified at runtime to suit the needs of a particular test. To do this, we turn to our mocking library, Moq.

> ■ **NOTE**
>
> The Moq library is available from Google at http://code.google.com/p/moq/. There are other mocking frameworks on the market that are also good, so if you prefer to use another one, the approaches outlined here work just as well with your framework. Microsoft Research has a framework called Moles that is an excellent alternative. With Visual Studio 2012, Moles will be replaced with a library called Fakes that should also be an attractive alternative.

Distinguishing Between Mocks and Stubs

Before we go to further, we need to distinguish a difference between two types of test doubles (mocks and stubs). Mocks and stubs are both used extensively to replace services for unit testing and are similar in the way they are created and behave. The difference lies in the functionality they replace.

Mocks are used for behavior verification. In other words, if you need to verify that a particular method was called a certain number of times, use a mock. Mocks also verify that methods are called in a certain order or not at all.

Stubs are used to replace behavior in a service. If a method needs to return a specific value when called during a test, use a stub. If you need to ensure that a method is called with the correct parameters, use a stub.

Let's take the current example with the repository. To verify that the GetUserData and SaveUserData are called once each and in that order, use a mock. To replace the GetUserData method to return some predictable data, use a stub.

Fortunately for us, the technical distinction between mocks and stubs is insignificant because the mocking framework we use can create objects that perform both mocking and stubbing activities. When creating a test double, we can count the number of times a method is called and also replace a method to perform some activity, all in the same object.

Our library (Moq) refers to the objects it creates as mocks, but keep in mind that these objects can be used as either mocks or stubs. For the remainder of this book, referring to a mock, we mean a class generated by Moq, not a class that is used exclusively for behavior verification.

Creating a Mock

Getting back to the example, using the same repository and test that we outlined previously, we now convert that test to use a mock created by Moq instead of the repository stub. Listing 5.4 demonstrates how the code looks.

LISTING 5.4: A Repository Mock

```
using System;
using System.Data.SqlClient;
using Microsoft.Practices.Unity;
using Microsoft.VisualStudio.TestTools.UnitTesting;
using Moq;
```

```csharp
namespace CodeSamples.Ch05_ClassMocking.Listing04
{
  public class MockingExample
  {
    public void UpdateUserData()
    {
      var repo = ServiceLocator.Resolve<IRepository>();
      var user = repo.GetUserData(1);
      user.Name = "New Name";
      repo.SaveUserData(user);
    }
  }

  public class User
  {
    public int Id { get; internal set; }
    public string Name { get; set; }
  }

  public interface IRepository
  {
    User GetUserData(int pUserId);
    void SaveUserData(User pUser);
  }

  public class Repository : IRepositcry
  {
    private string _connectionString = "connStringGoesHere";

    public User GetUserData(int pUserId)
    {
      var qryString = "select * from User where id = @id";
      var conn = new SqlConnection(_connectionString);
      var cmd = new SqlCommand(qryString, conn);
      cmd.Parameters.AddWithValue("@id", pUserId);
      try
      {
        conn.Open();
        var reader = cmd.ExecuteReader();
        reader.Read();
        var usr = new User
        {
          Id = (int)reader[0],
          Name = reader[1].ToString()
        };
        reader.Close();
        return usr;
      }
      catch (Exception)
```

```
      {
        //do something with the exception
      }
      return null;
    }

    public void SaveUserData(User pUser)
    {
      var qryString = "Update user set name = @username where id = @id";
      var conn = new SqlConnection(_connectionString);
      var cmd = new SqlCommand(qryString, conn);
      cmd.Parameters.AddWithValue("@id", pUser.Id);
      cmd.Parameters.AddWithValue("@username", pUser.Name);
      try
      {
        conn.Open();
        cmd.ExecuteNonQuery();
      }
      catch (Exception)
      {
        //do something with the exception
      }
    }
}


public static class ServiceLocator
{
  private static UnityContainer _container;

  static ServiceLocator()
  {
    _container = new UnityContainer();
    _container.RegisterInstance<IUnityContainer>(_container);
    _container.RegisterType<IRepository, Repository>();
  }

  public static TProxyType Resolve<TProxyType>()
  {
    return _container.Resolve<TProxyType>();
  }
}

[TestClass]
public class MockingExampleTestClass
{
  [TestMethod]
  public void UpdateUserData_WhenCalled_SetsNewName()
  {
```

```
//Arrange - section 1
var mockRepo = new Mock<IRepository>();
var container = ServiceLocator.Resolve<IUnityContainer>();
container.RegisterInstance<IRepository>(mockRepo.Object);

//Arrange - section 2
var user = new User { Id = 1, Name = "ReplaceMe" };
mockRepo.Setup(mr => mr.GetUserData(1)).Returns(user);

//Act
var mockExample = new MockingExample();
mockExample.UpdateUserData();

//Assert
Assert.AreEqual("New Name", user.Name);
    }
  }
}
```

In this listing, you should notice that the RepositoryStub class is gone. We no longer need that hard-coded class because we are going to use the mocking library to create a mock class at runtime.

Let's take a detailed look at the test. The first line of the Arrange - section 1 section creates a new Mock class of type IRepository using the mocking library. This line creates a new class that can mock any method or property on the given interface. We delve into how to use the mock class in just a few paragraphs, but for now let's concentrate on one of the properties of the mock class. The mock has a property called Object, which returns a class that implements the IRepository interface. This new object can be used in place of any IRepository class anywhere in the application.

By default, this new class does nothing; it has a GetUserData method and a SaveUserData method, but there is no code in either of these methods, so if called, the GetUserData returns a null, and the SaveUserData does nothing. Later, we customize these two methods to do what we need them to do.

The Arrange - section 2 area is where we set up the mock to satisfy the needs of the current test. We first create a new User object to use for the test and we initialize the values as appropriate. We then tell the mock repository that anytime any logic anywhere in the application calls the GetUserData method with a parameter of 1, it should return the user that we created by hand. We can use this setup approach to change the logic of any method that is available on the interface.

Finally, in the Act section, we create an instance of the class we test and call the UpdateUserData method just like we did before. We Assert that the name has been changed appropriately, and our test is complete.

Using mocking, we can replace critical services in our application and make them testable with a minimum of effort or custom code.

A Second Mocking Example

As a second example, let's continue to work with the repository, but now let's test that the newly updated User object is actually saved back to the database. (In Listing 5.5, all the classes are the same so for brevity, we show only the new test.)

LISTING 5.5: **An Additional Repository Test**

```
[TestMethod]
public void UpdateUserData_WhenCalled_SavesNewDataToDB()
{
  //Arrange - section 1
  var mockRepo = new Mock<IRepository>();
  var container = ServiceLocator.Resolve<IUnityContainer>();
  container.RegisterInstance<IRepository>(mockRepo.Object);

  //Arrange - section 2
  var user = new User { Id = 1, Name = "ReplaceMe" };
  mockRepo.Setup(mr => mr.GetUserData(1)).Returns(user);

  //Act
  var mockExample = new MockingExample();
  mockExample.UpdateUserData();

  //Assert
  mockRepo.Verify(mr => mr.SaveUserData(user), Times.Once());
}
```

Nearly the entire test is the same except for the end. The assert call has been replaced with a method call on the mock repository. This method call asserts that the SaveUserData was called exactly one time with the parameter user. If the method is not called or called more than once, this Verify call causes the test to fail. Also, if the SaveUserData method is called with any parameter other than the user we created, the test fails.

One facet of this test is that we assume the SaveUserData method works as designed. We do not test the database to make sure the data arrived, only that the method was called. Testing that SaveUserData actually updates the database is not appropriate here. That test should be put in an Integration test project and run separately.

A Third Mocking Example

The Moq library offers many other options that can make your tests more generic. In the previous example, the test looked for a specific parameter to the SaveUserData method. If we need something more generic, we can Verify that the SaveUserData method is called with any User parameter, not just the one we created (see Listing 5.6).

LISTING 5.6: **Using Generic Verify Parameters**

```
[TestClass]
public class MockingExampleTestClass
{
  private Mock<IRepository> _mockRepo;

  [TestInitialize]
  public void TestInitialize()
  {
    _mockRepo = new Mock<IRepository>();
    var container = ServiceLocator.Resolve<IUnityContainer>();
    container.RegisterInstance<IRepository>(_mockRepo.Object);

  }

  [TestMethod]
  public void UpdateUserData_WhenCalled_SetsNewName()
  {
    //Arrange
    var user = new User { Id = 1, Name = "ReplaceMe" };
    _mockRepo.Setup(mr => mr.GetUserData(1)).Returns(user);

    //Act
    var mockExample = new MockingExample();
    mockExample.UpdateUserData();

    //Assert
    Assert.AreEqual("New Name", user.Name);
  }

  [TestMethod]
  public void UpdateUserData_WhenCalled_SavesNewDataToDB()
  {
    //Arrange
```

```
        var user = new User { Id = 1, Name = "ReplaceMe" };
        _mockRepo.Setup(mr => mr.GetUserData(It.IsAny<int>()))
          .Returns(user);

        //Act
        var mockExample = new MockingExample();
        mockExample.UpdateUserData();

        //Assert
        _mockRepo.Verify(mr => mr.SaveUserData(It.IsAny<User>()),
➥Times.Once());
    }
  }
```

In this listing, we replace the User parameter in the Verify method with
a static class called **It**. This class is specific to Moq (though other frameworks have similar ideas) and can take the place of any type necessary.
By using this parameter, we make our Verify statement pass regardless
of what parameter is passed in, as long as that parameter is of type User. I
made a similar substitution in the GetUserData method, where I allow any
integer to be passed in, not just a 1.

We also simplify our test setup using the TestInitialize attribute on a
new method. This TestInitialize method is run once for every test in the
test fixture and provides an easy, central place to do any necessary setup
for each test.

One cautionary note: It is common to overuse the TestInitialize method
by adding setup tasks that are appropriate only for a small subset of the
tests contained in the fixture. This makes the tests brittle because the environment arranged by the TestInitialize method is used for all tests in
the fixture. It also implies that anything in the TestInitialize method is
required for all tests in the fixture, which can be misleading for developers
working with the test fixture for the first time. It is best to put only setup
code in the TestInitialize that is required for all tests in the fixture.

Using Mocking System Services

With all the power that comes with the mocking framework Moq, there
are some things it cannot do. Mocking of static methods and classes is

not possible with Moq, which is one reason we try to avoid creating static classes. However, when using built-in .NET tools or external libraries, we don't have a choice of whether to create the classes as statics or not. To address this problem, Microsoft has released a mocking framework called Shims that is able to mock static classes, static methods, system classes, and much more.

> **■ NOTE**
>
> Shims are part of the Fakes framework that is available starting with Visual Studio 2012. There is a similar framework called Moles and Pex that can be downloaded for Visual Studio 2010.

To create a Mock for a static class (Microsoft calls these Shims), we must do a little setup first. In this example, we create a Shim for the DateTime static class, which lives in the System assembly. Open the References folder of your Visual Studio test project and right-click the System assembly. Choose **Add Moles Assembly** (see Figure 5.1).

Clicking this option adds a new folder to your project called Fakes and includes several new files in that folder. It also adds two new library references: System.4.0.0.0.Fakes and MsCorlib.4.0.0.0.Fakes. These two new libraries are what allow the Shims in the Fakes framework to function.

To use our new Shims, we must create a ShimsContext class. This class manages the lifetime of the Shim, ensuring that it does not stay around in memory. If we did not limit the lifespan of the Shim, it would replace the DateTime class for all of our tests.

Let's examine how to use this new Shim. In the previous examples, we used a User object that had to be saved to a database. The CreateDate property on a new User should be set to DateTime.Now when the object is created, but this is difficult to test because the value of DateTime.Now might change between the time the property was set and the time the value was asserted. See Listing 5.7.

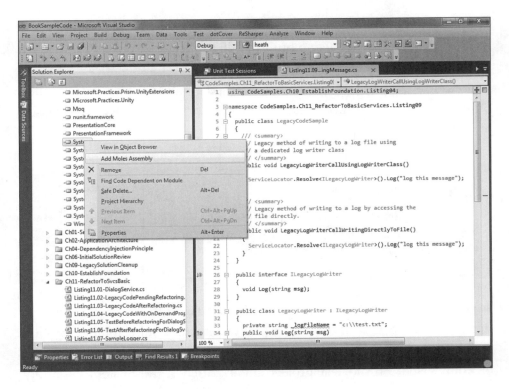

FIGURE 5.1: **Choosing the Add Moles Assembly option**

LISTING 5.7:　A Flawed Test to Check CreateDate

```
[TestMethod]
public void Constructor_WhenCreated_SetsCreateDate()
{
    //this test could fail if the system clock has
//changed since the object was created
    var usr = new User();
    Assert.AreEqual(DateTime.Now, usr.CreateDate);
}
```

Using the Shims, however, we can redefine what is returned by the
DateTime.Now method and force the User class to be created with a specific
value in the CreateDate property. See Listing 5.8.

LISTING 5.8: Using a Shim to Test CreateDate

```
[TestMethod]
public void Constructor_WhenCreated_SetsCreateDate()
{
```

```
// Must create a ShimsContext to run under
using (ShimsContext.Create())
{
  // redefine DateTime.Now to return July 29, 1970
  var expectedDate = new DateTime(1970, 7, 29);
  ShimDateTime.NowGet = () => expectedDate;

  //this test no longer can fail
  var usr = new User();
  Assert.AreEqual(expectedDate, usr.CreateDate);

}
}
```

In this test, we redefine what the Getter of the DateTime.Now property returns, even though it is a static method on the base class. Using this approach, we can replace built-in .NET methods with our own versions, creating any testing scenario we wish.

Learning More About Test Doubles

Using test doubles is a critical tool for a reengineering project, and we do not have enough room here to do justice to this rich testing tool. I recommend you spend some time learning Moq (or your mocking tool of choice) to be able to fully use the power of mocks in your tests. There is an excellent tutorial on Moq that should quickly get you on the road to productivity at http://code.google.com/p/moq/wiki/QuickStart.

Summary

In this chapter, we discussed how to dramatically improve the quality of your application by introducing unit tests. Test doubles, mocking, and stubs are all powerful tools that can enable a developer to fully test aspects of an application before it ever gets in front of QA.

All the procedures and techniques presented in this chapter are highly dependent on the architectures that were presented in earlier chapters. Without dependency inversion, service location, interfaces, and an SOA, the quality that is available via unit testing is not possible.

In the next chapter, we begin the project of reengineering a legacy system by doing an initial solution review to determine where to start and get a rough idea of how much work is involved.

Part II
Reengineering

6

Initial Solution Review

The first step when planning how to reengineer a legacy system is to understand the state of the current system. In the zeal to begin working or with the pressure from a client to start making changes as soon as possible, it is easy to skip this step. However, doing so can hinder your ability to make the decisions you are required to make throughout the project.

It is important to get a feel for the code before beginning the project because you have to make many decisions throughout the reengineering process that depend on the quality and structure of the legacy system. Unless you have a generous deadline or a small code base, there will be insufficient time to fully research the repercussions of each decision you have to make, so you must rely on your intuition.

When doing this initial review, the best place to start is the most basic unit of the legacy system. In C, this is the `Main` method. In C#, it is the `Program` class. Other languages have similar entry points. Look for the main entry point and trace through the code from there. The following section provides a list of specific things to look for points to keep in mind while doing this initial review.

Analyzing the Code

This section provides you with several questions that should be answered in this phase. Go through the list of ideas and then scan through the code to see how they are implemented. Make note of whether they are implemented the same way everywhere or whether each idea is implemented in unique ways in each situation. Standardization is a key component to a quick and smooth reengineering project, so if the same idea is implemented in different ways, it is a sign that you should increase your time estimates.

For example, one of the primary things to look for is how data access is achieved. Open five different data entry forms at random in the code and scan through the code with the database access questions in mind. It is not necessary to build a complete list of method calls or a stack trace for each question. However, creating a list of the classes that are involved in each one of the processes can be helpful later when trying to estimate the impact of a given refactoring task. This is particularly true for larger systems (more than 50 Visual Studio projects) because it is easy to lose track of which classes are involved.

By answering these questions, you can better predict refactoring problems before they happen. These are just sample questions to start the process. As you investigate these, you should note any other problems that you notice and need to keep in mind during the project.

Basic Architecture

Ask yourself the following questions:

- How does a new business process get launched? Is there a central place where requests to start a new process are handled? If there is a central place where these operations are handled, it makes it much easier to refactor the application. Having a similar process launch logic dispersed throughout the application makes centralizing the architecture more difficult.

- Does each business process have a UI associated with it, or can a process be started and executed completely in the background? Processes that are in the background exclusively are candidates for a multithreaded launch approach. If you find a process that has no UI associated with it, take extra care to determine whether the process is ever launched asynchronously. If so, these methods can take longer to reengineer.

- Are there external links that can start a business process, and how does that work? Allowing external processes to launch activities in the legacy system makes it difficult to trace the series of activities necessary to complete an action.

- Are there any processes that need to be aware of others using the system? For example, is there a need to lock certain data so only a single person can edit it at a time. Ideally these restrictions can be removed during the reengineering process

- How are data entry forms created and displayed? How are they destroyed? Creating and destroying data entry forms should be done in a central place. If it is not, refactoring to a central process can be time-consuming. Having these activities scattered about the legacy code can also make it difficult to determine a pattern for launching the processes in a generic way.

- If an error occurs that is not handled by the local code, what happens to it? How are errors handled and displayed to the user? Logging errors for later analysis is important, and if errors are handled in many different places, it makes this task more difficult.

- If the legacy language supports generic classes, how many are there, and what do they do? Generics are a powerful tool, but a bit abstract. If they are used, examining whether they are used well can give insight into the overall skill of the original architect.

Code Structure

Ask yourself the following questions:

- Is there very much inheritance in the object model? Extensive inheritance in the object model can make the lower level objects fragile since changing something seemingly insignificant in a parent class can affect the lower level classes.

- How tall are the inheritance trees for forms? For data objects? Inheritance in forms is particularly troublesome because the view designer in Visual Studio can have difficulty rendering the view in design mode. Often only one or two levels of inherited forms can cause the view designer to fail.

- Is there any recursion, and is it necessary? Recursive methods are difficult to debug and use effectively. If there is a lot of recursion, add time to your project timeline.

- How many static classes are there? Static classes are difficult to reengineer into our target architecture, so having many static classes in the legacy system is an indicator that the time should be extended.

Database Access

Ask yourself the following questions:

- Does each data entry form get data in its own way, or is there a pattern?

- Where are database connections managed? Are they shared?

- How are new database rows created? Creating new database records is often a problem. An especially troublesome use case is when the user creates a new row and then cancels that creation. Understanding how this is currently done is important to understanding the general flow of data in the application.

- Where does data validation happen? Is this in each UI form or centralized? Often data validation is sporadic and manual. Knowing where data validation is currently done can assist in the plan to reengineer to a central validation engine that can be managed more easily.

- Does data validation use a given pattern (such as Microsoft Validation Application Block), a third-party library, or is it home grown?

Data Structures

Ask yourself the following questions:

- Is the data itself structured properly in the database or flat file?
- If the data is not structured effectively, is it required to change the structure during the reengineering, or should it be left for after the first version? The direction you decide to go in response to this question can affect much of your project plan. It's best to make this decision before the reengineering work begins.
- Is there a single primary key for each data row, or is the key composed of multiple fields? Compound keys make it difficult to reengineer table structures and should be a sign that time needs to be added to the plan.
- Is it possible to change a component of the primary key? If so, this process can be complicated; how is it handled? If this possibility exists, it would be best to remove it during the reengineering process.
- Is the legacy code using an Object Relational Mapper (ORM)? Using an ORM is a good sign that it will be easier to remove the tight coupling of the system.
- If the system does not use an ORM, is there a data model? Is there a base class that business entities descend from, and what properties and methods are contained in this base class? Having a base class that business entities descend from can make managing these entities in a generic way much easier.

External Interfaces

Ask yourself the following questions:

- Does the code import or export any data to or from other systems?
- Is there data validation for this external data? Where does this data validation happen?
- Are the external interfaces real-time or batch?
- Where do the external systems reside (Web, local network, or local machine)?

- If the goal is to reengineer for the Web, where does the code assume that resources are on the local network? This can be difficult to find, but often these assumptions are made during data access.

Application Controls Versus Form Controls

Ask yourself the following questions:

- Some controls (such as toolbar buttons, menu items, and so on) apply to the entire system, and others are specific to the currently active form.
- Are these two ideas separated, or do they overlap?
- Is code for handling an application level process (such as File > Open) handled in a central place or in the individual forms?

Analyzing the General Code Structure

In general, any code base can be divided into two very broad categories: the core (or central architecture) and the supporting code. The core code is the main driver of the system, typically controlling how user requests are handled, how new windows are displayed, and providing data when requested. Well designed core code tends to be called from many locations in the system and should handle things in a generic way. The core should be unaware of the current state of the system and can normally fulfill its duties without knowledge of the current state.

In legacy systems, you rarely find a good separation between the core and supporting code. The core operations are intermingled with the UI and other components so that it is difficult to pull the two apart. Such a free-form structure is difficult to work with because it requires a lot more research into all the different ways the core code is implemented before you can start reengineering that core.

For example, creating and displaying a new window is a function that should be implemented in the core. A core process receives a request for a specific window via some sort of UI component: a menu item, button, and so on. The core creates that window and displays it to the user without knowing the purpose of the window or the reason it is needed. It is unnecessary for the core to understand why that window is requested, just that some process requires it. This is the ideal situation but is rarely found in systems that need to be reengineered.

Most systems have a main window that provides a "home" for all operations. It is a single window that hosts the main toolbar and menu and any other data entry forms that are displayed. This is called the shell. Often, in the shell you find code that creates and displays other windows to perform certain tasks. Open the code for those secondary windows to see whether they, in turn, create and display even more windows, or if they somehow send requests back to the shell (or another component) for processing.

■ NOTE

Keep in mind that we are trying to get a general impression of the system in this phase. We need to get an idea of what kind of code base we are working with without spending too much valuable time in analysis. By necessity, we must make some judgments on the code quality without a full inspection of all components. It often goes against an engineer's tendencies to make these snap judgments, but when getting started with an unfamiliar code base, it must be done. (This is one of the most frustrating parts of a reengineering project.)

It is best to decide on a time-box (a limited number of hours to spend) for this step. A good time-box is one to three days, depending on the size of the system. A particularly large solution with about 150 projects and 2MM lines of code might need three days; work with the lead developer who is already familiar with the system.

If the secondary level of windows has code that creates and displays more windows, this is an indicator that you will have trouble extracting an architectural pattern later (and so should increase your time estimate). Creating a good set of core code requires planning and diligence by the original designer. If you find the core code is localized in just a few classes, it is a sign that the system was well planned when first implemented. Spreading the core functions out in many different areas is an easy way to get a specific task done, but it creates structural problems, so it is an indicator that the system was not well architected.

Working with a system where the core code is spread out among the different modules affects your reengineering by making it difficult to identify an overall pattern for creating and displaying the windows. Identifying such a pattern is necessary because when the reengineering effort is complete, we should have a small set of central classes that are responsible for creation of all windows, setting those windows up properly, and displaying them to the user. If this central code is strewn throughout the application, the path to centralize the logic becomes much longer and more difficult.

Managing Language Migration

Reengineering from one language into another is a difficult task. It might be necessary to rewrite instead of reengineer the application if the legacy code is not in the .NET family. To make this decision, look at the legacy code language and see whether it is possible to make method calls into .NET. During the course of reengineering, we try to change only one piece at a time so that the system continues to function throughout the project. To do this, we must always have a connection between the legacy system and the new code, which is normally done via method calls to DLLs. Most languages have a facility for defining a way of calling an entry point to a DLL. If not, it is either because it's not possible or it is too much trouble to do so and you must rewrite the application in .NET.

Note that making method calls among different .NET languages takes no special effort. Calling a C# method from VB.NET, for example, is no different from calling another VB.NET function or subroutine. The VB.NET code creates the given class in the normal way and calls the method.

> ■ **NOTE**
>
> Moving from one development paradigm to an entirely different approach via a reengineering effort is difficult. For example, trying to move from a functional programming approach to object-oriented by reengineering the existing code is an exercise in futility. You must use the legacy code as a functional specification and rewrite the code from scratch. Unfortunately, sometimes "you can't get there from here."

Removing Dead Code

Removing dead code from the legacy system helps simplify the reengineering process by limiting the code that must be examined and converted. If the legacy system is in a .NET language such as C# or VB.NET, dead code removal can be done either as a concerted effort at the beginning or throughout the reengineering process as the dead code is encountered. The dead code detection tools in Visual Studio make this identification and removal process easy.

When migrating from a language that is not .NET, such as VB6 into C# or VB.NET, removing any dead code is more difficult. Depending on the development environment of the legacy system, identifying the dead code can be a difficult task, but it is worth the time to identify as much as possible. Dead code not only costs us time in the conversion process, but it can also disguise the structure of a system by implying that certain features exist when they are unused.

When searching for and removing this dead code, it is best to do it in the legacy environment where a clean build and test process is already established. Trying to identify dead code as it is being reengineered from the legacy language has the potential for creating many problems.

Using Global Variables

A specific thing to note when converting from a legacy language is global variables. In the days when COBOL was the dominant language, it was common to use global variables for nearly everything. Global variables are an easy way to get around architectural problems that prevent modules from sharing information, but they make a system difficult to understand because they introduce tight coupling of all components that use the data. When a variable can be updated from any part of the code, it is also difficult to trace the logic flow when debugging. Having a lot of global variables can make your reengineering project take longer than necessary.

If it is possible to replace the global variables, it is best to do so, but this is not required. An easy refactoring that can help the conversion go faster is to refactor the individual method calls to have the global variables passed in. In other words, ignore the fact that the method has access to the global variable and pass that data to the method in the parameters so that the method can treat it as locally scoped. This helps significantly later when using an automated conversion utility and when creating unit tests.

For example, examine the code in Listing 6.1.

LISTING 6.1: A Global Variable Example

```
namespace CodeSamples.Ch06_InitialSolutionReview.Listing01
{

  public static class GlobalVarExample
  {
    //Assume this variable was declared as a global variable
    //somewhere in the legacy application.
    public static string GlobalVar = "value goes here";
  }

  public class BusinessLogic
  {
    public void DoWork()
    {
      //Call a method that needs the global variable to function.
      DoWorkNeedingGlobalVar();
    }

    public void DoWorkNeedingGlobalVar()
    {
      //Use the global variable to do some work.
      var x = GlobalVarExample.GlobalVar + "!";
    }
  }
}
```

Using global variables is not valid in C#, so our sample listing uses a static class to demonstrate the same principle. In this example, a BusinessLogic class calls a method that uses a global variable. Reengineering and creating tests for the DoWorkNeedingGlobalVar method is difficult due to the use of the global variable. We need access to the GlobalVarExample class, and we need to change the GlobalVar string.

Now consider this slightly refactored code in Listing 6.2.

LISTING 6.2: Refactored Code That Uses the Local Variable

```
namespace CodeSamples.Ch06_InitialSolutionReview.Listing02
{

  public static class GlobalVarExample
  {
    //Assume this variable was declared as a global variable
    //somewhere in the legacy application.
    public static string GlobalVar = "value goes here";
  }

  public class BusinessLogic
  {
    public void DoWork()
    {
      //Call a method that needs the global variable to function.
      DoWorkNeedingGlobalVar(GlobalVarExample.GlobalVar);
    }

    public void DoWorkNeedingGlobalVar(string globalVar)
    {
      //Use the global variable to do some work.
      var x = globalVar + "!";
    }
  }
}
```

In this example, we pass in the global variable to the method instead of using the global version. Note that the results of this refactoring are functionally identical to the previous version, so little more than cursory testing is required. However, this small refactoring makes the method much easier to move to your target language, and it's easier to unit test because we do not have to have access to the global variable.

For methods that alter the global variable, the refactoring is more complex depending on the legacy language. Often for methods that alter the global variable, it is easier to deal with the variable as it is rather than refactoring. However, if your situation requires a refactoring to pass in the global variable, there is a way to do it in C#, and this same technique might be adaptable to your legacy system. As shown in Listing 6.3, you can use an out parameter in the method call to pass the altered value back to the caller.

LISTING 6.3: Refactored Update Global Variable Using an out Parameter

```
namespace CodeSamples.Ch06_InitialSolutionReview.Listing03
{
  public static class GlobalVarExample
  {
    //Assume this variable was declared as a global variable
    //somewhere in the legacy application.
    public static string GlobalVar = "value goes here";
  }

  public class BusinessLogic
  {
    public void DoWork()
    {
      //Call a method that needs the global variable to function.
      DoWorkNeedingGlobalVar(GlobalVarExample.GlobalVar,
        out GlobalVarExample.GlobalVar);
    }

    public void DoWorkNeedingGlobalVar(string globalVar,
      out string updatedGlobalVar)
    {
      //Use the global variable to do some work.
      updatedGlobalVar = globalVar + "!";
    }
  }
}
```

If forced to refactor the method to update the incoming variable, we can do so by passing it in twice. Ideally we would simply label the globalVar parameter as an out parameter, but trying to use an out parameter before it is initialized results in a build error. To get around this, we pass in the global variable twice, once to be used within the body of the method and once to act as a conduit for passing the new value out. In the previous code, note that the GlobalVarExample.GlobalVar is used for both incoming parameters in the DoWorkNeedingGlobalVar method.

This C# solution is far from ideal and should be removed as soon as possible, but if you must refactor a method to pass in an editable global variable, this gets the job done.

Executing these refactorings is fairly easy even if you do not have modern refactoring tools at your disposal. Simply change the signature of the method by adding the extra parameter and build the code. Fixing the build again is easily accomplished by adding this global variable to all function calls where the build breaks.

Converting Code: It's Not All or Nothing

Keep in mind when you are doing the initial solution review that a reengineering project does not require converting all of the legacy code. A possible option for some of the code is to leave it in the legacy language and call those routines from the reengineered code.

There might be sections of code that are overly complicated and difficult to reproduce. If these sections are also unlikely to change, then you should consider leaving that code in the original language and wrapping it with a .NET wrapper. A wrapper is a .NET class that has an appropriate set of public methods and properties that reflect the functionality of the legacy class. Each of the methods and properties simply hands off processing to the underlying legacy methods. Using this approach, you have full control over the external interface that your new code uses, but you do not have to rewrite code unnecessarily.

Wrapping existing code also provides a way to unit test the code in the way you would like. The unit tests call the appropriate methods on the wrapper, which passes those calls to the wrapped class, and any necessary assertions are made. From the outside, your wrapper class looks just like any other .NET class.

To find code that can be wrapped, look for seams where the complicated piece can be broken out from the existing logic. A seam is a convenient location to separate one class into two. Using the seam to separate the module into two pieces is best if done in the legacy system before beginning the reengineering effort. With this approach, it is possible to ensure that the two pieces can stand alone and can be wrapped.

Wrapping legacy code is a particularly valuable alternative if you have a tight deadline for the initial system conversion but are allowed additional time later for further enhancements. In this case, successfully wrapping legacy components can buy you valuable time to dedicate to other issues that cannot be solved so quickly.

A specific instance where wrapping works well is when you have an ActiveX control that is unlikely to change and is working well. Wrap it for now and address the conversion problem later. Keep in mind, though, that this can affect the installation of your application on the end-user machine. The supporting runtime for the language the component was written in must be installed on the user's computer. This is not an insurmountable problem, but it does make the installation process more difficult.

Using an Automated Code Conversion Utility

When considering the timeline for converting legacy code to your modern infrastructure, it is tempting to plan to use an automated code conversion utility. There are several on the market (both free and paid) that claim to be able to convert from one language to another with minimal cleanup required afterward. In reality, it all depends on what language you convert from.

Many reengineering projects start with VB6. It was a popular language and was used to produce quality business systems, so this type of conversion effort is common. Unfortunately, converting from VB6 to .NET is a difficult process. Because VB6 was not object-oriented, the basic paradigm used in designing systems was different. Procedural code is time-consuming to convert into object-oriented code because you must reexamine the basics of how the system operates to pick out the appropriate objects and their behavior. This is not a task appropriate for an automated tool.

However, there is still a place for the automated tools in a VB6 reengineering project. Much of the business logic that is implemented in VB6 will not change, so the specific methods used to implement that logic can be brought into the new codebase as a start for the new code. For example, the code sample in Listing 6.2 to demonstrate refactoring out global variables is a good candidate for the language converter because the function is completely self-contained.

If you want to try to use a code converter to get a step up on the project, first upgrade the legacy system source language to the latest version. For example, if converting from VB6 into VB.NET, first make sure you have the latest version of Visual Studio 6. The online translation utilities assume you are on the latest version of the source language and can produce inaccurate translations if this is not the case. Trying to save time or money by skipping this step can cost you much more later as you try to fix the converted code.

After you are sure your code is in the latest version, the next step is some basic cleanup of the legacy code. Make the legacy code as easy as possible for an automated translator to process. If you declare multiple variables on the same line, break them out into separate lines. Also change any dynamically typed variables into strongly typed declarations. This is especially important if you are migrating to C# where variables are strongly typed (you can use the `dynamic` keyword in C# in order to duplicate the loosely typed variables in the source language if it is difficult or inconvenient to make the legacy variables strongly typed). If using VB, set the `option explicit` option in the legacy code and make sure it builds.

After the compiler has been updated and the small refactoring done in the legacy system, create the appropriate classes in the new language and translate each method in the VB6 that is required to implement the given piece of logic. Put these methods through a converter one by one and clean up the code. Note that though this sounds simple, it is sometimes so much work cleaning up the resulting code that it becomes impractical. I suggest trying this process on about ten different methods to see if it helps in your situation. If not, you may be forced to rewrite those methods.

■ NOTE

If you are moving from VB6 to .NET, there is an excellent article by Dennis Hayes in *.NET Developer's Journal* at http://tinyurl.com/7xttoqj.

Using Data Access Technologies

Data access technologies have changed dramatically in the last few years. There are many more possibilities for persisting data than ever before, and that data can be used in different ways. Understanding how the legacy application stores its data is critical to the reengineering effort because that data access method is most likely to change significantly during the process.

There are two main tasks that need to be accomplished.

- Detecting the Data Model
- Detecting the Data Access Pattern

Detecting the Data Model

A *data model* (or Business Model, or simply model) is a collection of business entities that encapsulate the logic of the application. A *business entity* is a class that has properties reflecting the information that is stored in the database (or whatever data persistence technology is being used).

For example, let's assume your application has the concept of a person, and that person's data needs to be tracked. You might have a class somewhere in the legacy code that looks similar to that shown in Listing 6.4.

LISTING 6.4: A Sample Business Entity

```
namespace CodeSamples.Ch06_InitialSolutionReview.Listing03
{
  public class Person
  {
    public string Id { get; set; }
    public string Name { get; set; }
    public string Address1 { get; set; }
    public string Address2 { get; set; }
    public string City { get; set; }
    public string State { get; set; }
    public string Zip { get; set; }

  }

}
```

This Person class is a business entity (we call them entities). Typically, each entity has properties that reflect the columns or fields in the database table where they are saved. If your legacy application uses a flat file for data storage, the entity class has all the properties that are stored in the file.

When the data is read from the disk (either from a flat file or a database), these entity classes are created and populated from that data. You will probably see code similar to that shown in Listing 6.5.

LISTING 6.5: Code to Fill the Business Entity

```
using System;
using ADODB;

namespace CodeSamples.Ch06_InitialSolutionReview.Listing05
{
  public class Person
  {
    public string Id { get; set; }
    public string Name { get; set; }
    public string ManagerName { get; set; }
  }

  public class Repository
  {
    public Person LoadFromDatabase(string personId, ADODB.Connection
►conn)
    {

      var cmd = new ADODB.Command();
      cmd.ActiveConnection = conn;
      cmd.CommandType = CommandTypeEnum.adCmdText;
      cmd.CommandText = "SELECT Id, Name, ManagerName WHERE PersonNumber
►= "
 + personId;

      object dummy = Type.Missing;
      var rs = cmd.Execute(out dummy, ref dummy, 0);
      if (!rs.EOF)
      {
        var person = new Person();
        person.Id = rs.Fields["Id"].ToString();
        person.Name = rs.Fields["Name"].ToString();
        person.ManagerName = rs.Fields["ManagerName"].ToString();
        rs.Close();
        return person;
```

```
        }
        rs.Close();
        return null;
    }


  }
}
```

This code retrieves the raw data out of a database and copies it into the class to be used by the rest of the system. There is matching code somewhere that saves the entity by copying the current values back into an Update query and executing that command.

If you see code that is similar to that shown here, a data model exists. This is a good sign because it means you can much more easily change the database as necessary to reflect the new needs of the business. It should indicate that the application uses these data objects for updating data and not touch the database directly. An application that makes changes directly to ADO objects is much more difficult to update and work with.

There are many reasons for converting to business entities rather than using raw data like ADO, but we will save that technical discussion for Chapter 12, "Advanced Refactoring to Services," where I go over how to do the conversion. At this point, you just need to understand what technology is used and how it works so that you can plan how to upgrade it.

Detecting the Data Access Pattern

One of the patterns we look at in detail later in the book is called the Repository pattern. This is a way of accessing data in a safe, extendable, and convenient manner. You should look to see whether a repository is already being used. Note that if you did not find a data model in the previous step, a repository is not likely either.

To determine whether your application uses a repository, scan through the solution looking for methods that read data from the disk. These can be database reads or flat file reads, but somehow data needs to get from long-term storage into the application.

For example, in the code snippet from Listing 6.5, the data access methods involve the ADO.Command and ADO.Recordset keywords. If you search for these, you should find them either scattered about the application or centralized in one place. If most or all of these calls are in a single class or project, and that project seems to fill the data needs for all of the application, then there is a repository in place. If database or flat file reads are scattered about the application wherever the data is consumed, there is no repository.

If the legacy application does not have a repository, it is best to refactor it to use the Repository Pattern for data storage. This makes the refactoring process easier in the destination language. However, this refactoring is rarely easy, and so this is typically left for the main refactoring effort in the new language. Depending on the size of your application, if you estimate that refactoring the existing application to use a repository will take less than 1 percent of the total reengineering time, then you should do it in the legacy code. Otherwise, plan to reengineer the converted code.

Summary

This chapter walked you through the steps necessary for reviewing a solution that needs to be reengineered. We discussed how to analyze the solutions basic architecture, code and data structures, external interfaces, and application controls. We presented techniques on how to address the problem of working with global variables during the reengineering process, while simultaneously planning for the removal of them. Finally, we presented techniques on how to recognize the different types of data access models and how to convert them to something more in line with our service-oriented architecture (SOA).

In the next chapter, we continue the planning process by analyzing the legacy application and trying to put a time estimate on the different conversion processes.

■ 7 ■
Planning the Project

Managing a reengineering project is a bit different than managing other types of development projects. A reengineering project combines the hardest parts of building from scratch and enhancing an existing system because not only must the architect manage the target structure, but he must also ensure that the changes necessary to get to that architecture do not break the current application.

In this chapter, we discuss the differences between managing a regular development project and managing a reengineering project.

Managing Expectations

The most important aspect about planning and managing a reengineering project is to manage the expectations of management and customers. Managers accustomed to building applications from scratch, or those accustomed to adding features to an existing system, expect a certain pace of feature development that is not possible in a reengineering project. This is due to the need for the reengineering developers to introduce underlying architectural elements that are not visible to those who do not develop the system. Because these enhancements cannot be seen by the user, it is difficult to demonstrate to management the progress that is being made.

For example, adding a dependency injection container is not a feature that is often requested by users but does make the system much easier to work with and enhances it later while also opening the door to higher quality. This is a dramatic improvement in the structure of the system, but there is no evidence of this improvement to the user community or to management. Managers who expect to see the difference in the application might get concerned at this apparent lack of progress.

The only way to address this potential pitfall is to set realistic expectations from the beginning, informing management that the part of the team that works on reengineering the architecture is making significant progress even though that progress might not visible. Their work pays off later in the form of much faster feature turnaround and higher quality. Failing to set these expectations can result in management getting frustrated with the "lack of progress" and killing the project.

Creating the Reengineering Team

When planning the staffing of the team, it works well to think of two separate teams working together on the same project. There is initially a team that does only reengineering work while the rest of the team continues building features in the normal fashion. Over time, these two teams slowly begin sharing responsibilities as the reengineering part of the team moves back into feature development and the feature part of the team begins reengineering existing code. Near the middle of the project, the teams merge back into one team with everyone participating in feature development and reengineering of the remaining legacy code.

Initially, the reengineering part of the team should consist of the architect and one senior developer because the early part of a reengineering effort does not require many developers. In fact, adding more people can complicate the effort.

Let's examine, chapter by chapter, what the planning and staffing requirements are for our project.

Identifying Development Tools and the Build Process

The basic infrastructure to support the development process should be put in place before any changes to the legacy system are made. This includes introducing a source control system if it doesn't already exist, a defect tracking application, a continuous integration build server, and the various tools for developers. These tools are part of a well-designed development process for any project, not just a reengineering project, so they should be introduced before the reengineering officially starts.

Identifying the tools to use and getting them installed does not require a large team, but it is wise to get input from as many team members as possible to encourage adoption of the chosen technology. The team selecting the tools should endeavor to change the current workflow processes as little as possible. This makes it easier for the team to adapt and reduces the risk of rejection of any of the new tools.

The technical challenges of installation and configuration of these tools are minimal, and the actual implementation tasks should take only a few days. Identifying which tools to use can be a more difficult decision and can often take several weeks. The most time-consuming and difficult part of these early changes, though, can be getting the team to change its process.

Each team, whether big or small, performs or struggles at its own pace and work pattern. When introducing the new tools, these patterns need to be considered and integrated into the team. There is a distinct danger of the new processes and tools being rejected by the team if these processes are not introduced properly and with sufficient explanation of the benefits.

In addition to the difficulties of getting the team to accept the new processes, introducing one or all of the items suggested in this section can also cost a team a significant amount of time to integrate into its normal development routines. There will be missteps and forgotten processes along the way, so the project manager or architect must be patient and let the team adapt to the new ideas.

Introducing Source Control

Introducing source control for the first time to a team, though technically a trivial task, can often become monumental due to the dramatically different work processes that must be adopted to use source control effectively. This is such a fundamental part of the workflow of a well functioning development team, any team not using source control already probably does not have the proper workflow in place, so forcing through the changes necessary to use it can be difficult.

For example, we had a client whose developers used `RemoteDesktop` to control the server where the web application runs and updates live code as needed on the server. The developers had to work on the same code files at the same time, occasionally overwriting each other's work in the process. This might be viewed as a downside of working in a team environment in which everyone has to accept the fact that they would sometimes lose work.

We suggested using a central source control server for the code, enabling each developer to work on his own machine so that changes did not conflict. This suggestion was resisted because it required each developer to have the database loaded on his local machine, and updates to the database structures would then be more difficult. There was also resistance to the idea of forbidding access to the live code on the server because "how can we debug the application?"

We got the team to adopt the practice of using source control by introducing it in a phased approach. We first left the existing work process (everyone updating the server) in place, but checked changes into source control from the server. This gave the team versioning so developers could retrieve previous versions of code if necessary, but it did not disrupt their current workflow.

We had one influential developer check out the code to his local desktop and develop it there, checking code into source control in the normal process. He quickly saw the advantage of not competing with the other developers for source files, and he was able to finish his development tasks more quickly. He then spread the word among the team of how the source control process made his job easier, and the rest of the team was much more open to adopting the new workflow.

If your team does not already have source control in place, you will probably have to invest a lot of time fixing the workflow before the technical part of reengineering the system can begin. Don't underestimate the time and effort necessary for this task.

Introducing Defect Tracking

Introducing a defect tracking system is typically quite easy because development teams are probably tracking their defects in some manual way already. The additional workflow step needed to enter the data into a system does not typically affect the overall process or productivity.

Resistance to introducing defect tracking might come from team members who assume they will be measured by the number of defects that are attributed to them. They see defect tracking as a way for management to measure the quality of each individual developer and a way to use this information for disciplinary measures.

Though the data collected by a defect tracking system can certainly be used for this purpose, it is bad for morale to do so. It can result in a lot of wasted effort trying to decide who was responsible for a given defect, which also makes team members defensive.

When introducing a defect tracking system, take great pains to let the team know that the statistics will be used to measure only *team* performance, not *individual* performance, and that these measurements will be used to help the team perform better, not to discipline anyone. This message must be repeated frequently and publicly by both the team leader and upper management to instill confidence in the team.

Installing and Using a Continuous Integration (CI) Server

A continuous integration server (CI server) is a piece of software that automatically builds the application every time new code is checked in. The CI server receives a notification that new code has been checked in by a developer and then pulls the latest code set and tries to build it. If the application does not build, an error message is sent to the entire team indicating which check-in broke the build.

If the build is successful, the CI server then runs all unit tests associated with the code. If any of the tests fail, the build is considered broken, and again, an email is sent to all team members with the name of the person whose check-in broke the build. Running these tests is a critical part of a mature build process.

Installing and using a CI server is rarely resisted by a skilled development team. CI servers can change the way a team operates because introducing a breaking change becomes much more obvious and public than it was before. As a result, the less skilled and less conscientious developers resist this change the most.

The most difficult part of introducing a CI server is getting the team to consider a broken build a high priority problem. It is common for the team to ignore broken builds when the CI server is first introduced. The team lead should set an example by personally walking around and following up with the team member who submitted the breaking change to ensure it is fixed promptly.

Another way of assisting in adoption is to begin counting the number of broken builds during a sprint and review this number at the sprint review meeting. It is best to initially track broken builds by the team in general, not by individual developer. Only if the team continues to ignore the build breaks should this number be tracked by person.

One result of introducing a CI server is to put some mild pressure on developers to produce higher quality code. As it becomes socially unacceptable among the team to break the build, developers who neglect to run unit tests before a check-in (running the risk of breaking the build) will be encouraged to adopt the new practices, improving the quality of the code.

For more information on CI servers and the build process, Martin Fowler has an excellent article at http://martinfowler.com/articles/continuousIntegration.html.

Cleaning Up Legacy Solutions

The legacy solution cleanup should be done after the source control system is in place (if source control is not in place, that is the top priority), but can be done in parallel with the other tasks described in Chapter 8,

"Identifying Development Tools and the Build Process." The cleanup effort can involve the entire development team or a subset, depending on the project timeline. Getting the entire team involved in the legacy solution cleanup is often a good way of introducing the reengineering idea and showing the development team that changes are being made for the better.

Planning for the legacy solution cleanup phase should be done by the technical lead but executed by all the team members. Before beginning to make legacy code changes, the technical lead should educate the existing developers about the types of cleanup actions that are undertaken. Because these developers continue building features in the legacy system while the reengineering is underway, a lack of education can result in a never-ending cycle of cleanup.

A phased approach is often successful where the development team is presented with a few new practices followed by a cleanup effort. When that is complete, another effort is presented and undertaken. Remember, the goal here is not only to clean up the legacy solution, but also to teach the development team how to write better code. It takes time for people to change their habits.

Establishing the Foundation

Establishing the foundation is done by the architect and senior developer while the rest of the team cleans up the legacy system. Introducing the dependency injection container, service locator, and other infrastructure elements does not affect the legacy system until they are incorporated into that code, so having them in the solution presents no potential problems or defects. These initial elements involve few files and classes, so having many developers working to get them in can be counterproductive. It is best to have the architect and senior developer work together, and then present the final result to the rest of the team for instructional purposes.

If you use all the utilities and versions recommended in this book, implementing the foundation should take less than a week regardless of the size of the application. If you wish to replace some things (that is, use a different dependency injection container or updated version of the libraries), this part might take longer.

This phase is where training the team becomes most important. Care should be taken to ensure that all team members understand the new patterns and accept the need for the change. If the project moves along too quickly without proper training, team members get confused and disoriented by the new patterns, and they cannot contribute fully. This can result in some members of the team rejecting the new patterns and continuing to develop in the old patterns, making the reengineering effort more difficult and time-consuming.

Refactoring to Use Basic Services

Refactoring to use the basic services is not technically difficult, but it can take a lot of time. It requires reviewing the existing legacy code and implementing the new patterns that make the application easier to use and update.

Because this phase involves the first updates to the legacy code, the architect should stay closely involved with the code changes. The core team should consist of just a few of the most experienced developers, possibly two or three in addition to the architect. This enables the architect to ensure that team members implement the new features appropriately. It also gives the architect and team the chance to make any changes to the patterns that might be required. These initial team members become the evangelists and instructors for the rest of the development team, so they need to understand the advantages of the new technology.

This is also the phase where the rest of the development team is pulled into the reengineering process. The core team takes each service and refactors some of the existing legacy code to use it. After the core team has refactored five or six implementations of the new service and made any necessary changes to adapt it to specific circumstances, the rest of the refactoring should be turned over to the remaining members of the team with specific instructions on how to implement the new pattern. Because this is probably the team's first exposure to dependency injection and service location, developers might need help learning how to apply the patterns.

The important thing in this phase is to keep the entire team constantly updated about the new techniques and patterns that are introduced. Doing something one way today and a different way tomorrow with no warning that the change is being implemented can be a frustrating experience for the developers. This uncertainty can foster distrust of the new patterns and make it much more difficult to introduce the necessary changes.

Unit testing is probably introduced for the first time in this phase, which can cause a lot of confusion. If this is the first time your team has seen unit tests, plan sufficient time for team members to understand how to build these tests and what effect they have on the application. Developers new to unit tests typically require more attention by the architect to ensure that they create the necessary tests in the proper way. Mocks make this even harder because they are not an easy concept to grasp, and they are required from the start to test some classes properly.

Introducing unit tests also creates a new way for the build to break on code check-ins. This can be a major source of frustration as developers new to the process want to "just get their code in" but must first fix all the unit tests that have broken. A common argument revolves around who is "really" responsible for a unit test and ensuring that it runs properly. If a developer has made no changes in an area where unit tests were recently introduced, and some of those seemingly unrelated tests break, the developer is likely to resist the responsibility for making the necessary changes. The team lead needs to stress that regardless of the reason of a unit test failure, any check-ins need to pass all tests.

Management expectations also need to be managed when introducing unit tests. Though unit tests can dramatically increase code quality and velocity for subsequent system change, writing these tests take time. Development of new code is slower with unit tests than without, especially when first introducing the necessary framework around the tests. Also, adding test coverage to existing code can seem like wasted time to management because no additional features are produced from this effort.

When discussing these topics with management, a good measurement to use is how many defects are caught by the QA team for code that has unit test coverage versus code without coverage, and how much QA time is necessary to catch those defects. You should find that though development time increases, QA time should decrease. More importantly, development time increases only once to write the tests, while

QA time decreases for every subsequent product release. Also, the number of defects caught by QA should fall dramatically for code that has unit test coverage.

Refactoring to Use Advanced Services

By this phase, the whole development team should be involved in the reengineering process. The special reengineering team should be merged back with the normal team so that development tasks are no longer thought of as belonging to one team or the other.

This phase can be traumatic for the team because it introduces services that are even more abstract and difficult to grasp than in the previous phase. These services make the application appear more complicated than before, and there is resistance from those who don't see the long-term benefit. Care should be taken to teach the team the advantages of the new structures and ensure as much agreement as possible from the team.

The repository and data validations can be introduced first to get the team used to having significant services being used via dependency injection and the service locator. Region managers are a more difficult topic to introduce. It is often quite difficult to get the entire team to understand the idea of regions, much less accept it.

Reporting Progress to Stakeholders

Normally a reengineering project is selected instead of a rewrite because the application needs to continue being released with new features while simultaneously being updated to a better structure. This is a valid expectation, and it can be delivered using the approaches in this book, but customer and management expectations must be managed appropriately if the project is to be a success.

Start to finish, a reengineering project that includes no feature enhancements (that is, releases are stopped similar to a rewrite) should take less time and resources than a rewrite. However, a principle advantage of reengineering is the capability to continue releasing new features during the reengineering phase. Combining the reengineering effort with continued feature enhancement is likely to make the reengineering effort take more time end-to-end than a rewrite. This can be the source of much consternation by upper management. Quite often, just after the 50 percent completion point, you will begin to hear comments about how long the project is taking, how it is barely halfway done, and how if we had been rewritten from scratch, it would have be done by now.

This is a dangerous time in the life of the project because the architecture, which is invisible to management, is just being completed and the real enhancements are beginning to be introduced. Nearly all of the early work in a reengineering project lays the groundwork for improvements to be made later. This work is difficult to demonstrate to nontechnical people and has no effect on application performance until later when it is used. Therefore, to someone who is not involved in the actual coding, it appears as if a lot of time and money are going into the project with little in return.

To prepare for this resistance, define specific deliverables for the project with delivery dates. Frequent management updates on the progress of the project compared to the project plan should help keep complaints at bay.

Though continued feature delivery is enabled by reengineering, the pace of feature delivery slows. Customer expectations need to be managed so the normal pace of feature introduction is not expected. Often the decrease in the number of new features in each release can be managed by the marketing and sales departments in their communications with the customers. However, a wise project manager or architect invests the time and effort to keep in touch with the customer service department to see whether they are receiving any negative feedbackand whether any specific features have been furtively promised to customers. A passionate complaint by an important customer can derail a reengineering project regardless of how well it progresses.

Managing Communication and Training

Communication and training are important parts of any reengineering project. There are broad ranging code changes and new development practices introduced; if the team does not adopt to these new ways of building the software, the effort will fail.

The training frequency and depth can vary depending on the attitude of the team and whether they accept the new direction. For a team that is eager to adopt the new approaches, a weekly or bi-weekly meeting to review upcoming changes might be sufficient because the team members will put forth the effort to learn and adopt the new procedures. An unwilling team, however, might require more frequent meetings and personal attention for each developer to ensure he understands and adopts the new procedures. Also, frequent code reviews are required for both types of teams to ensure that improper use of the new patterns is caught and corrected early.

The architect should not underestimate the amount of time and effort required to make a reengineering project a success. Group training and one-on-one sessions are critical to managing a reengineering project.

Summary

A reengineering project is more complicated than a project to build a new system. If the foundation for the development process is not in place (source control, defect tracking, CI server, unit tests, and so on), time and effort must be spent on these efforts, which, though they improve the environment, add no new features to a product. Much of the work that is required is not visible to users, so to those who are unfamiliar with the process, it might seem as if there is a lack of progress. Extensive training and behavior modification might be necessary to train the team in the correct procedures, and management unfamiliar with the process can have unrealistic expectations.

All of these potential pitfalls can be avoided with the proper planning and expectation management.

8

Identifying Development Tools and the Build Process

Reengineering a legacy application is a difficult process. With the correct tools, however, much of the labor can be automated, making the task easier, faster, and more pleasant. This chapter discusses the tools and processes that can help make your reengineering project a success.

Using Source Control

Source control is a tool you must have in place for any software development project, whether it's a reengineering project or not. Source control is a way of saving the code for your application with version numbers so any version of any file can be retrieved. It is critical that you have a source control system in place before you begin editing code so that if you make a change that breaks anything, you can always revert back to the previous version. Source control is indispensable for a reengineering project because some refactoring efforts can go awry. Having a source control system in use enables you to experiment without fear of losing changes or introducing defects. This tool is important for a single developer, but even more so if you have a team working on the same codebase because it provides a single area where all code can be automatically merged together so you don't lose any work.

There are many source control systems on the market, and all the major ones do a good job of saving versions of your code. Some are better with large teams, others excel with distributed teams or open source, and others focus on speed and ease of use. Which you pick is completely up to you, but having one is critical. The three listed later in this chapter in the section on evaluating a hosting service have been used on real projects, so we can see the advantages and disadvantages of each. Each is an excellent choice, but one might be more appropriate than another depending on your situation.

Types of Source Control

There are two main types of source control systems available: centralized and distributed. In centralized systems, there is a central machine somewhere that is responsible for keeping the latest copy of the code, serving update requests, serving check-in requests, and keeping the history. The current version and the history for the project is stored on this server only, and everyone who wants to get a copy of the code or make changes to it must have appropriate permissions on that server.

Distributed Source Control (DSC) systems, on the other hand, are more free-form. In DSC systems, the code is distributed among all the developers on the project. Each developer has a full copy of the repository, including the history and the files. Changes are made to the developer's local copy of the code and then merged with a central point (if desired). There is no technical requirement to have a central server holding all the code and history, but this central server often exists to make the workflow easier.

A significant difference between the centralized and the distributed systems is where the code history lives. With a centralized scheme, there is one main server that holds all code and history. To look at the history for a file, a user must ask the server to display the history; it cannot be determined from the information on the user's local workstation. With a distributed system, participants in the project have a full copy of the repository including the history. If a user of a DSC system is offline and requests a full history of the application, it can be delivered immediately.

With distributed systems, in order to have a single authoritative source for the code, the development team agrees on a single source to be the main branch. This branch requires submitters to have appropriate permissions so only authorized people can submit changes. During development, changes are made and committed to each developer's local copy of the repository. When the developer is satisfied with his changes, he submits the incremental changes to the central repository at one time.

The process becomes clearer with an example. In the following descriptions, we assume the developer in question has the appropriate permissions to take the actions we describe. In both distributed and centralized systems, it is possible to lock down the code so only authorized people can access it.

A Process Example: Using a Distributed System

Assume you have just joined a development team using a distributed system. The team lead tells you the Uniform Resource Identifier (URI) for the main branch of the code and you pull a copy of it to your local machine.

When you are given a feature to work on, you decide it would be best to do it in five distinct steps. As you make changes to the code, you commit each of the steps to your local repository only. Nobody else on the team is able to see your changes. If you want others to do a code review for you, you can tell them where those changes are located on your local machine so they can pull a copy of your repository.

Because you make changes only to your local repository, checking in code with build errors does not affect the rest of the team. Also, unit tests are run at your own discretion (instead of on a centralized build server) so failing tests do not affect others. Note that you must periodically refresh your local repository with changes that others have submitted to the main branch. If you don't refresh, you will encounter merge conflicts when you try to submit your changes back to the main branch. Any conflicts that arise in your code after a refresh from the main branch is your responsibility to resolve.

> **NOTE**
>
> A merge conflict is when two developers have changed the same code file and the changes conflict with each other. All the source control systems mentioned later have a merge function that merges two edited files if the changes are compatible. For example, if one developer adds a method at the top of the file and another edits a method at the bottom, these changes can be merged. However, if these two developers change the same line of code, the merge utility does not know which version to pick and generates a merge conflict. The chances of having a merge conflict increase with the amount of time between check-ins, so the distributed systems can cause problems.

After a lot of changes and commits to your local repository, you decide that your feature is ready for others to use, so you merge your local repository with the main branch located at the URI agreed to by the team. If you don't have permission to merge with the main branch (as is typically the case with open source software), you email the administrator and send the URI of your local repository so the admin can review your changes and merge it into the main branch. After your changes are merged into the main branch, you refresh your local copy and begin work on the next feature. Note that in this workflow, the entire feature goes into the main branch at once, not individual pieces as they are developed.

A Second Process Example: Using a Distributed System

Another possible process exists for distributed systems that does not exist for centralized systems. Any developer can decide if he wants to start his own "main" branch and publish it. In this scenario, the developer gets a copy of the code from the centralized system to work on. This becomes the main branch. Before working on a new feature, he creates a new "MyFeature" branch off of his local Main branch so both are on the same local machine.

After completing work on the new feature, this developer merges his changes to his personal main branch, and then publishes that branch by emailing interested parties and telling them where his personal main branch is kept. This developer can also search for patches that others have published and selectively merge those patches into his main branch. This feature enables a single developer to work on multiple features at the same time without one feature interfering with another.

A Third Process Example: Using a Centralized System

Now let's look at the process flow for using a centralized system. When you first join the group, you are given the URI for the central repository. Using that, you pull a copy of the code to your local machine.

As previously, break your feature into five distinct steps. As you work on each step, you save the changes to your local machine. However, when each step is completed, you check the code back into the central server. This means that if another developer refreshes his code, he will get your changes. Therefore, you need to ensure that your code builds and passes all unit tests before checking into the source control system.

After checking in the code for the first step, continue working on your feature, checking in code after each step. After checking in the code for the final step, your feature is fully implemented and you can move on to the next feature.

During this development process, it is wise to continue refreshing your local copy of code from the main branch, just like when using the distributed system. This helps avoid merge conflicts and limits the amount of rework necessary if a conflict does occur.

Understanding the Pros and Cons of Centralized Systems and Distributed Systems

Both centralized and distributed systems work well and keep your code safe with the capability to retrieve previous versions of code. Each has its own advantages and disadvantages.

Consuming Shared Code from Others

Distributed systems enable much easier sharing of code updates than centralized systems. The user of a distributed system can merge specific patches from others into his version of the code, customizing the local version.

This process is possible with centralized systems but is more difficult. Customizing an application based on a centralized system requires much more manual labor because individual patches published by others must be applied to the local code by hand. After it is applied and submitted to the main branch, there is no connection back to the code that was imported. If the feature you imported into your code is updated, you must apply those updates by hand.

If you want to consume code from others and continually keep that code up to date, choose a distributed system. If you want to consume code from someone else but want to keep it static (after you've tested it and it works, you don't care about further updates), choose a centralized system.

Sharing Code with Others and Reviewing Changes

If you build code that you want to share with others, the main decision point is how much input do you want from those external developers. Trusting unknown developers to directly update your code can result in a lot of work backing out bad changes. In this case, it is prudent to implement a preliminary review structure to evaluate the quality of changes. This is much easier to do with a distributed system.

If you are going to be the main gatekeeper of the system and are not interested in submissions from others, either distributed or centralized systems work well.

If you are concerned about others taking the code and creating their own competing main branch, a centralized system cannot prevent this, but it does make it more difficult. The only way to completely guard against this is not to share the code in the first place.

Backing up the Code

Distributed systems encourage accumulation of changed code on the local system until a feature is completely ready for merging into the main branch. Centralized systems collect those changes in a central place throughout the development cycle.

If the local machines on your network are not backed up frequently and you are concerned with losing work due to hardware failure, use a centralized system where commits to the repository are stored on a server (which we assume has a more rigorous backup process). If this is not a concern for you, either distributed or centralized systems will work.

Managing Check-in Frequency

Frequently checking code in is a good practice regardless of which type of system you use. Each time you check in code, you save a reversion point so that if your next development effort goes awry for whatever reason, you do not have to try to manually reverse the changes. You can easily revert back to the last save point and try again. For example, when building a feature, we check the code each time we make a significant step that we know we want to keep. This results in about five or more check-ins per day.

Using a centralized system forces check-ins to be in a state where they build and pass unit tests. This is not a technical restriction; it's enforced by the team. If a check-in does not build and another developer refreshes his code, the second developer also has a broken build and must waste time trying to figure out why. With a distributed system, this is not the case because small check-ins can be made to local repositories, which do not affect the team.

A distributed system can give a slight time and code-safety advantage in not requiring check-ins to build or pass unit tests.

Managing Merge Conflicts

On the other side of the "check-in frequency" coin is the problem of merge conflicts. The more time that elapses between a refresh of the main branch and checking in new code, the greater the chances of a merge conflict. Merge conflicts can cost precious time and effort to resolve and so should be avoided when possible.

Developers who object to checked in code passing unit tests are also the ones who tend to go long periods without refreshing their code from the main branch. This results in significant merge conflicts that can be time-consuming.

If your team tends to have a lot of merge conflicts due to extensive time without refreshing code from the main branch, using a centralized system might help.

Managing Control

A common theme that runs through the previous topics is control. How much control do you want to have over your source code and your development team? Distributed systems provide a loosely controlled environment where individual development habits and discipline have more of an effect on the overall process. Centralized systems impose more control over the code and developers to impose the processes you want your team to follow. Both of these approaches are valid and have their advantages over the other.

A Final Word About Pros and Cons

So there are pros and cons to each type of source control. The type you choose depends a lot on team dynamics, the type of software you are building (open source or commercial), and the amount of control you would like to exercise over the code.

Evaluating a Hosting Service

All of the source control options in the following section are available either as an onsite installation or as a hosted service. The obvious tradeoff here is convenience versus security. If you are concerned someone mght try to steal your source code, or you don't trust the hosted services to back up its data properly, you can install your source control server inside your own firewall. This gives added protection against code theft or loss due to hardware failure (assuming your internal network administrators are doing a proper job of managing the server). If you do not have these concerns, there are many hosting services that are quite good and can have your source code repository up and running within minutes, often for free if you have a small project.

When deciding among the many possible hosting services, check to ensure the provider has sufficient bandwidth to support you, your team, and the rest of its customers. Insufficient bandwidth can make updates to your code slow and also increase the time it takes for an automated build server to build the code. Because automated build servers can be configured to pull all code before a build, having a responsive hosting service is important.

Also ask the hosting service how frequently it backs up the data on its servers. They should back up their code repositories at least daily, and preferably hourly. Some will offer to send you a backup of the repository with all history if you would like to have a copy onsite.

Using Apache Subversion (SVN)

Apache Subversion (or SVN) is a commonly found system that works well for small and large teams and excels at supporting distributed teams. It is easy to use and integrates well with Visual Studio. SVN is a centralized system and so must be hosted either internally to your company or at a hosted site. The code for Subversion is open source so it can easily be installed inside your own data center.

The Subversion server is command-line driven, but there is a graphical interface called TortoiseSVN that is so well integrated that it's virtually indistinguishable. If you choose to use SVN for your repository, TortoiseSVN is indispensable. It integrates into Windows Explorer, showing on screen what folders are managed by SVN. These indicators change when files within the folder have changed, letting you know that you have updates waiting to be committed.

Using TortoiseSVN, it's easy to update your local copy of the code and to submit changes. Simply right-click in the folder with the code, and you get the basic TortoiseSVN menu. It is possible to integrate SVN into the Visual Studio Solution Explorer with AnkhSVN, a freely downloadable utility.

Using Microsoft Team Foundation Server (TFS)

Microsoft Team Foundation Server (TFS) is a centralized source control system that Microsoft publishes, so it integrates deeply into Visual Studio. TFS and SVN take different approaches to maintaining the list of updated files. SVN makes no attempt to control how you edit files during a coding session. When it's time to check in your changes, SVN scans the folder and looks for files that are different. TFS, on the other hand, watches what you are doing throughout your editing session inside Visual Studio, and it keeps track of the files you edit. As you touch each file, TFS automatically marks files as "in use" on the server.

This approach enables anyone to see whether someone else is editing a file, which can help avoid merge problems. A manager can also see what files people are working with.

The real-time file tracking also enables the lock feature to be more proactive. SVN has a lock feature that enables a developer to lock a certain file, which prevents anyone else from checking that file in, but not from editing it. Locking a file can cause problems in SVN because a developer who needs to change a locked file is unaware of the locked status and can make changes to it but not be able to check it back in. TFS, on the other hand, prevents the second developer from editing the file in the first place.

A helpful feature in TFS is the shelf function. When editing code, you can put it on a shelf in TFS, which essentially checks it in to a temporary holding area. This ensures the code is safe on the server but does not merge it with the main branch. A developer can also share these shelve sets with others, which can be useful if one developer needs to hand off work on a feature to another developer. The first developer can put all code onto a shelf and share it with the second, who can complete it and check it in.

We don't discuss defect tracking until the next section, but an important feature of TFS is the built-in defect tracking. TFS has a database built in that can track defects internal QA or anyone else reports. These defects can then be assigned to developers to be fixed. When a fix is ready to be checked in, the code set can be linked directly to the defect. It has similar tracking of other tasks, such as feature development or documentation creation, that can be assigned to appropriate people. TFS also supports calculating code churn, which is a measurement of the quality of a code base calculated using the number of changes submitted. As a set of features nears release, the number of changes submitted to source control should decrease.

The advantages of TFS become more important with medium-sized teams (5–20) and become even more important with larger teams. In other words, as the solution grows, management of the project and team becomes more difficult, and TFS provides more team-management features than the other offerings.

Using Git

Git is a popular distributed system. Linus Torvalds created it when BitKeeper (which was hosting the Linux kernel) was changed to a pay service.

As with other distributed source control systems, it is well suited to exploratory development when you want to keep track of what you've done but don't want to submit it to the main branch yet. It allows check-ins to be done to your local machine and later merged into the main branch.

A feature that is particularly attractive with Git is the capability to email changes. If you are the administrator for an open source project and receive many suggestions for additions to your application, you probably want to review those submissions before merging them into the main branch. With Git, the developer contributing code to your project can generate an email via Git that has all appropriate changes encoded in the email. The administrator can import this email using Git and have all changes applied to a local repository. After review, these changes can be either rejected or merged into the main branch.

For contributors that are accustomed to using CVS source control clients, Git has an interface that enables it to integrate with those clients so the developers do not have to learn a new process.

Managing Features and Defects

A system to manage features and defects is also a critical tool for any development project. Regardless of how small or simple a project is, there will be defects, and tracking them is difficult without help. There are many on the market, both free and paid, and they range from adequate to extremely customizable. Having a defect tracking system is invaluable because you encounter many problems as you refactor an existing system, and you cannot address them as you find them. You must have a place where you can write down the issues you see and then come back later and fix them.

There are so many defect-tracking systems on the market that it is difficult to pick any to suggest here. However, there are certain questions to ask of the different vendors to ensure they meet the needs of your development process.

Managing Custom Workflow

The more advanced defect tracking systems allow a custom workflow that can be adapted to your team. For example, a small team might need no workflow at all; both QA and developers can set the status of a defect to whatever value they think appropriate. A larger shop might want to ensure that QA is the only department that can mark a defect Closed, so it would want to enforce this workflow. A large shop might want to force defects to be routed first to development, then QA, then documentation, and finally closed.

These and many other options are workflows that can be supported by some defect-tracking systems. When picking a system to use, be sure it can accommodate the workflow you have now and the one you might adopt in the future.

Managing Agile Development

Different development shops use different procedures for building their software. Some are agile, some are waterfall, and others are hybrids. They are all valid as long as they support the needs of the business. However, when it comes to defect tracking, they work differently.

If you are an agile shop, the defect-tracking system should also work as a product backlog. Combining these two tools makes managing the development process convenient and transparent. Only a single source is available for developers to go to when looking for more work. When picking a defect-tracking system, ensure that it can handle the backlog in the way your team likes to work.

Managing Reporting

If you intend to use your defect-tracking system as a source of progress reports, ensure that the reporting capabilities comply with your needs. Many of the defect-tracking systems are sparse on reports, assuming you use everything in an interactive manner. If the reporting is insufficient for your needs, you might be able to create your own reports if the database holding the information is available.

Using a Continuous Integration (CI) Build Server

A continuous integration (CI) server is a key piece of the development infrastructure because it enforces the rules that you apply to the team and the project. The purpose of a CI server is to build your application and run unit tests each time new code is checked in. The server can watch the source code repository, and when it senses a new check-in, it automatically pulls the new code and does a complete build of the system. If the build is unsuccessful, it sends an email to all team members telling what the build problem is and who checked in the code that broke the build.

If you also set up your CI server to run unit tests (which you should), it runs all unit tests immediately after the build completes successfully. If one of these tests fails, a similar email is sent to all team members. For the immediate builds, normally integration tests are not included because they tend to take a long time, but if you have a small project, the integration test can be included also. Normally nightly build also goes through the build unit test process, but it also runs the integration tests.

If you use TFS, the build server is integrated with your source control, so it is a simple matter to set up the CI server functionality. TFS can already sense when new code is checked in and automatically launches a build and unit tests. If using SVN or Git, you might have to set up your CI server to periodically poll these repositories to see whether any changes have been checked in. Either way, the build should be launched automatically and send an email to the entire team when something fails.

Using Visual Studio 2010 Developer Tools

Visual Studio 2010 is an open ecosystem that is easy for third-party companies to build extensions for. Deciding among the many possibilities is largely personal preference, but there are certain functions that any coding enhancement tool should be capable of accomplishing.

Refactoring Tools in Visual Studio

Reengineering an application is equal parts refactoring existing code and writing new code. Therefore, having good tools to help with the refactoring is important. Visual Studio comes with many useful tools right out of the box.

Variable and Method Renaming Tools

As you reengineer your system, you change the names of variables and methods to make them more legible and to describe their purposes better. Making these changes by hand can be a tedious and error-prone process. Visual Studio has variable and method renaming features built in that can make these chores much easier.

Visual Studio can also automatically reorder or remove parameters from method signatures, change return types, and change the order of the method parameters.

The Clone Location Tool

A new feature in Visual Studio 2012 is the Find Matching Clones in Solution option. By selecting a block of code, you can search the entire solution for similar blocks to merge the logic into a single method. This feature can help find patterns in legacy code.

Method Extraction Tools

The idea of an interface did not even exist in many legacy languages, but it plays a key role in modern architectures, so the capability to take an existing class and automatically create an interface from it is useful. This can save hours or days of development time over the life of the project.

Equally important is taking a large method and breaking it into smaller parts. This is called *method extraction* and is done frequently when adapting existing code to unit tests. A method extraction tool should take a highlighted set of code and move it to a method while replacing that code with the appropriate method call. The necessary parameters are added to the method signature to satisfy any data needs.

An associated refactoring feature that is available in third-party tools moves methods to parents or descendants. You often find code that is duplicated in many descendants of a particular class and would like to move the method to the parent class to make it more accessible. Conversely, if a base class contains a method that is appropriate for only one descendant, these methods can easily be moved down to the descendant with a few clicks.

Find All References Tools

The enhanced Find feature is one of the items used the most in daily routines. Visual Studio provides a Find References function that shows you all of the places where a particular symbol is used. This feature is invaluable because you constantly explore where and how things are used. It can tell how frequently a particular variable or method is used before embarking on an effort to change it in some way.

Code Snippet Tools

Code snippets are an excellent Visual Studio tool that lets the developer save frequently used pieces of code (snippets) and reapply them when necessary. These snippets are saved as a pattern so variable names and other parts of the code that change with each implementation can be easily updated. Visual Studio comes with many snippets already defined, or the developer can define his own.

One way a project lead can make the development process easier is to add project-specific snippets where all developers can access them. Because Visual Studio searches specific locations on startup looking for snippets, each developer can reference a network location for Visual Studio to search. Any snippets in this common folder are automatically added to the developer's snippet library. A project lean can add new snippets and easily distribute them to the entire team.

Third-Party Refactoring Tools

Though Visual Studio has many of the refactoring tools you need, there is still a place for some of the add-on tools that can take the basic refactoring features to another level. Several good commercial packages and some open-source versions are on the market.

Code Navigation Tools

Finding your way around the code can be a time-consuming task, especially with a particularly large solution. Navigation among all the files can be a critical tool in the developer's belt. Visual Studio comes standard with some navigation tools, and the third-party tools can extend these features.

Visual Studio comes standard with the F12 key, which enables the user to go to the declaration of a particular variable or method. However, if the code you are working with uses an interface instead of a concrete class, navigating to the interface is not useful. Add-on tools provide a way of navigating to the concrete class that implements the given interface method so you can see the code that is executed.

With large systems, it is also difficult to remember which project some classes reside in. Navigation tools can help in this situation by maintaining a list of all files in the solution regardless of which project they are contained in. You simply type the name of the file and it is opened. The class names can also be cached, so if you tend to keep more than one class inside a single file, you can navigate to the appropriate place easily.

Editing Tools

Rearranging code to make it more legible is a primary activity in a reengineering project. The enhanced editing tools can make this task much easier and faster. Some of the advanced features provided are as follows:

- **Move method up or down within the file**: By easily grouping methods together that have associated behavior, it is easier to maintain the code. Some tools can also automatically move a method into a particular code region.

- **Pattern completion**: Type in the first few characters of a key word, and it can be expanded out into any kind of template you would like. This functionality can improve productivity when building loops, events, or anything else that requires a standard set of code to be repeated with only small changes in the parameters.

Summary

Having the proper development tools and build process in place can make a significant difference in the quality and speed of the reengineering process. Source control, a continuous integration server, and defect management are significant pieces of the puzzle and need to be in place before any real reengineering work can begin. When the development process is supported by the proper tools, the team can build the application much more quickly with more quality and less risk of data loss.

9

Cleaning Up Legacy Solutions

This chapter discusses cleanup tasks that can be done to the legacy application without changing any business logic. By cleaning up the legacy application before starting the reengineering effort, you can make the entire project go quickly and smoothly. Simply moving classes and interfaces around in your solution, you can make the application more manageable and easier to enhance. The correct project structure can also help avoid the need for circular references.

> ### ■ NOTE
>
> For this cleanup process, we assume that the project runs under Visual Studio 2008 or greater, not Visual Studio 6 or any other development environment. If the project is still under Visual Studio 6, many of these techniques have to wait until it is ported to Visual Studio 2008 or greater.

Organizing the File System

The file structure underlying a solution is often ignored and left to grow and change in a haphazard manner. As long as the Visual Studio solution file has proper references to the files it needs, the underlying file structure is technically unimportant. However, occasionally you need to find files in that structure, so it's convenient to have it structured well. A predictable structure also makes it easier for new developers on the project to get oriented. The outcome of the reengineering project does not depend on the structure laid out here, but if you do not have a personal preference, this structure is easy to use and learn.

One folder that is indispensable to have in the root of your code folder is the Libraries folder. This folder should contain all the outside DLLs necessary for the application to build. By "outside DLLs," we mean anything that is not compiled during a build. After these DLLs are collected in one place, projects should refer to them in this folder.

For example, the DLLs for any tools we use, such as open source libraries, IoC container, and everything else, should go in this folder. If you have many DLLs in this folder, it might make sense to further organize it by creating subfolders, but ideally, all files are in a flat structure so they are easy to find and replace when a library is upgraded. System DLLs should remain in the GAC; do not try to move them to the Libraries folder.

By adding the Libraries folder to the root of your source code file structure, you can also check these DLLs into source control for safety. This has several advantages aside from having your files in a safe place:

- It enables the build server to pull all the code and build it without having the required DLLs installed on the server itself. This can sometimes mean saving the cost of an additional license on commercial libraries (obviously you must check the licensing requirements on your libraries to make sure this is true in your case).

- Having the DLLs in source control ensures that checking out a previous version of the code can also check out the proper DLLs that code was built with. Imagine releasing a new version of your application, and then subsequently upgrading the UI tools on your local desktop. If you ever need to go back and pull the old version of code out of source control, you want to ensure that the proper version of UI tools is checked out with the source code. If the DLLs are not in source control, you have to uninstall the current version of the UI tools, reinstall the old version, make the necessary fix, uninstall the old version, and finally reinstall the new version. This same strategy applies to any DLLs for necessary COM libraries.

- Using a Libraries folder also ensures you avoid problems where two different projects reference different versions of the same DLL. A common error that can cause much wasted debug time is for a single developer to update a library on its machine while the rest of the team does not. If the project has a reference to this updated library in the GAC, the solution can build on one developer's machine but not on another machine. Putting all the DLLs in a single place would force the one who upgraded his library to also check in the upgraded DLLs, thus ensuring all developers are using the same libraries.

Enforcing this structure can be difficult at times. If you have ReSharper installed on your system, it has a convenient feature that automatically adds necessary project references for you as you edit your code. However, this feature first checks the GAC for the DLL, and if it's found, ReSharper adds a reference to the DLL in the GAC (not in your Libraries folder). Also, if you use a designer to create your data entry screens and you add a new component that requires a reference to a new DLL, this reference is for the version in the GAC. This can cause problems on the build server as described previously.

My personal preference for the rest of the file structure is to keep it flat. Trying to group projects in subfolders on the disk makes it difficult to find files when you need them. When creating a new project in Visual Studio, the default folder name is the name of the project, which should uniquely identify the folder. This default is a good choice.

Structuring the Project

A large part of creating a code base that is easy to manage comes from the structure of the solution itself. As you reengineer it to remove the tight coupling and introduce the new architecture, project references become important. With an improperly organized solution, it is easy to get into a position where you need to add a circular reference, which Visual Studio does not allow. A circular reference is where Project A needs a reference to

Project B, and Project B also needs a reference to Project A. This can leave you with the unenviable problem of having to restructure the classes and projects in your solution.

The potential for circular references, and thus the importance of the structure of the solution, gets greater as the solution grows larger. For a small solution, ease of use should be the primary concern because refactoring the solution would not be difficult or time-consuming. However, for large enterprise applications, references to projects can be distributed throughout the solution in such a way that moving a class from one project to another can be a difficult and an error-prone process. Also, large solutions typically require large teams, and moving files and projects around in a solution can cause temporary confusion for the rest of the team. Because small solutions can eventually become big solutions, it is worth the effort to design your solution properly from the start.

Keep in mind that the following structure is not a silver bullet. Loading an assembly in .NET is a time-consuming process, so (assuming each project has its own namespace) having more projects than necessary can add startup time to your application. We can't make a recommendation for your specific circumstance, but we describe the structure for a generic large solution (over 100 projects) and let you use your judgment about which projects can be combined to minimize startup time.

Working with Project Categories

A major goal of a reengineering project is to keep the application functional during the process. This means that we cannot indiscriminately remove the code that does not meet our standards. As a result of this approach, there are two general categories of projects we deal with:

- **Old pattern projects**: These are the original projects from which you try to transition away. They are often unwisely designed and have references that bind them too tightly to the other projects in the solution. These projects are too difficult to try to merge with the new pattern projects, so they should be kept in a different area until they can be migrated later.

- **New pattern projects**: These are the projects you are creating or trying to move code into. They contain only the allowed references to other new pattern projects, and they contain only code that is properly broken out into different classes. There are two types of new pattern projects:
    - **Specific new pattern projects**: These classes should hold only code that is specific to that application (they cannot be used in another unrelated application).
    - **Shared new pattern projects**: These contain code that can be shared among all the different modules you intend to implement and even other applications. These projects can be either application-agnostic (generic projects that have no knowledge of the application domain they are being used for), or application-specific. In either case, they should be held separately from the specific projects to maintain the proper reference hierarchy.

These categories of projects can often be separated using a different naming convention. For example, if you work for a company called Acme Software, you can keep the current naming convention for the old pattern projects (or use Acme.MyProjectName.Legacy) and name the new pattern projects Acme.MyProjectName and the shared new pattern projects Acme.Shared.MyProjectName.

Understanding Project Types

There are quite a few types of projects that you create in the solution. They have different properties that make it important to break them out into separate types. Failing to keep these properties in mind can lead to project references that make your solution brittle, prone to circular references, and generally difficult to work with.

> ■ **NOTE**
>
> In this chapter, we occasionally reference dead-end projects. This term refers to projects that have references to external DLLs only, not to other projects in the same solution. Dead-end projects are important to identify because any other internal project can reference them without fear of circular references.

Application-Agnostic Projects

These are projects that do not have any knowledge of your specific application. They can be lifted out and dropped into another application easily with no code changes. Typical items in these kinds of projects are Object Managers (`ToolbarManager`, `RegionManager`, `ConnectionStringProvider`, `MessageAggregator`, and so on). These kinds of classes typically live in a single project called `SystemServices`, though there is no reason not to break these classes apart further if it suits you.

Projects in this category should have no references to any other project in your solution. Referencing outside libraries is acceptable as long as those libraries can be ported to other applications as necessary. Possible references are an IoC container or third-party logging system.

These projects should also have no UI or data access logic in them. Application-agnostic projects should be useful in WPF applications, WinForms applications, ASP MVC, and even console applications and services. Including unnecessary UI references can make it more difficult to multi-target your application.

Generic UI Projects

It is best to keep UI-related projects separate from the rest of your application. With the many different types of UI targets that are available now (HTML, Silverlight, WPF, WinForms, Metro, Console, and so on), and if you are strict with your implementation of MVC, MVP, or MVVM, the UI projects can be changed out or upgraded separately from the back-end business logic. If code containing UI logic is put in projects with business logic, it makes reusing the project more difficult.

This structure also opens the door to multi-targeting, where there are multiple types of frontend to the same business logic. Though theoretically possible, this goal is difficult to attain. If you want to have multiple frontends to the same business logic at the same time, it must be planned carefully.

Model-agnostic Projects

Model-agnostic projects are those that do have knowledge of the specific application they are in but do not have references to the data model. This is an important distinction because there are services that can possibly be reused elsewhere within the business, specifically in applications that share some functionality but do not share a business model.

In the real world, projects such as this are few and far between. It is rare that code specific to an application (not generic) can make a significant contribution to a system without any knowledge of the data model. However, we have run across this type of service, and it was convenient to have the code in a separate project in order to be reused by other solutions that were related.

Model-specific Projects

These projects have the code that is specific to your particular application. There is no restriction to the types of other projects these can reference because they are difficult or impossible to use in any other circumstance except the application they are in (or something in the same domain with the same data model). These types of projects compose the majority of your solution.

Reengineering Project Recommendations

There are two distinct patterns that have arisen regarding organization of projects in the solution, and they are divided along the lines of the architectural pattern in use. For MVVM projects, all files for a particular module are placed in a project together. This means module-specific services, constants, DTOs, views, view models, and everything else except foundational architecture. This structure keeps code in a single DLL and can be loaded when the module itself is needed. This can save slightly on application load time but moves that delay to the first time a module is used.

The other structure slices the solution in a different way and is most often implemented when using MVP or MVC. This solution structure groups services together into one project, views into another, controllers and presenters into another, and so on. This structure causes almost all DLLs to be loaded at application start, but using a feature for the first time causes no delay.

Both of these structures are valid, and your choice does not affect the reengineering effort. The first method (for MVVM architectures) is difficult to describe in a generic way. To give advice on this, we would have to know the features of the application you are building and how the modules are defined. Furthermore, the structure of legacy applications is typically more similar to the MVC project structure than the MVVM. Therefore, we analyze the second structure here.

The following sections describe the projects that are typically created in a solution regardless of the type of business problem at hand.

Constants

The easiest new pattern project to create and populate is the constants project. The constants project contains all constants and enums defined in the system in one convenient place. Sometimes a legacy system already has this project in place, and it can be used as is.

A critical factor of the constants project is that it remains a dead-end project. There should be no danger of creating a circular reference using the constants project because constants are used everywhere in the reengineered system.

Refactoring a legacy system to use the Constants project is quite easy in Visual Studio. Scanning for the const or enum keyword is a good way to start populating this project. Once found, ReSharper has two refactoring tools that help immensely in updating your solution. If a given enum is embedded in the same file as another class, the Move to Another File command cuts the enum code out of the file and creates a new file with the same name as the enum and then pastes in the code. The new file is added to the same project the original file is in. ReSharper then has a Move refactoring method that attempts to move the new file to the constants project. With these two refactoring methods together, it is quite easy to populate your Constants project.

Because this type of change involves no business logic, it is a good project to give to a junior developer or someone just learning how to code. If the move is done correctly, the solution builds. If it was not done correctly, the solution does not build.

Data Transfer Objects (DTO) Projects

This project contains classes that are only data transfer objects (DTOs). A DTO is a class that has little or no logic except for storage and retrieval of data. A common use of a DTO is when a particular method needs a lot of parameters and it becomes unwieldy to specify them all in the method signature. Instead, you can create a DTO that contains all the parameters and pass that to the method. Another instance is if there is data that makes sense only as a set and needs to be passed around the application. Then a DTO can easily accomplish this purpose. A caller must create the DTO, fill it with appropriate data, and then pass it to the proper method.

> **▪ NOTE**
>
> Though a DTO typically has no logic, there is one method we sometimes add for complicated DTOs: a Validate method. Because DTOs are often created separately from the method call they are used in, it is easy to forget to specify the information necessary for a particular operation. The Validate method checks data in the DTO to ensure it has sufficient data to perform the necessary operation. The code that receives the DTO as a parameter can then simply call the Verify method and throw an exception if insufficient data has been specified. This centralizes the validation logic so it does not have to be duplicated in all places where the DTO is used.

Another type of class we put into the DTO projects is EventArgs descendants. It is common to create descendants of the EventArgs class to specify data to send into events. If you examine the properties of an EventArg, it is similar to a DTO in that it has little logic and is mainly used to transfer data. EventArgs can have the same reference problems as DTOs, so they are solved with the same techniques.

We keep DTOs in a separate project because they are often used in many different classes throughout the system. Each class that uses DTOs must have a reference to the DTO project, so we must be diligent in the references we allow so we can avoid circular references. The DTO project should be a dead-end project.

In the real world, keeping a DTO project as a dead-end project is difficult. Often the DTO needs to carry Model objects or some other class type that is defined deeper in the application. To get around this problem, the DTOs we create are often generic. With this approach, the DTO can contain the appropriate type of information without having knowledge of what that information is (and therefore not needing a reference to the model).

Another option is to use a dynamic object. This type of DTO can carry any type of data without fear of requiring project references that can cause circular references (however, dynamics are only available in .NET 4).

Listing 9.1 shows an example of a generic DTO that can carry any kind of data model entity.

LISTING 9.1 An Example of Generic DTO

```
namespace CodeSamples.Ch09_LegacySolutionCleanup.Listing01
{
    /// <summary>
    /// This DTO can carry any type of data without
    /// requiring unnecessary project references.
    /// </summary>
    public class SelectedEntityDto<T>
    {
        public T Entity { get; set; }
    }
}
```

Interfaces

The Interfaces project is the lynchpin for the application. When using the ServiceLocator to resolve necessary services, the business logic needs to provide the name of an interface that represents the service it needs; therefore, nearly every project in the solution needs a reference to the Interfaces project. Views in MVC and MVP also expose their functionality via the Interfaces project.

The contents of this project should be obvious from the name Interfaces. Due to the importance of this project, much care should be taken to limit the references that are allowed. Ideally the Interfaces project is a dead-end project, but that is rarely possible. Remember that interfaces can be generic also, so the generic example used previously for DTOs can also be applied to interfaces.

If you still find it necessary to have business-specific references in the Interfaces project, it is best to create a shared Interfaces project that is maintained as a dead-end project and another Interfaces project that has references to business logic. Whenever possible, put new interfaces into the shared version to keep the chance of circular references low.

Services

The Services project is where the service classes live. In a well-designed system, there are many small services; each performs a specific duty, so the number of classes in the Services project can grow quite large. This is not a technical problem, merely an organizational one. With so many classes, it is often convenient to organize them using folders internal to the project. Note that each of these services should be associated with an interface that lives in the Interfaces project.

In a large system where the number of services can grow to an unmanageable number, it can sometimes be helpful to divide the services into several different types. Two appropriate types that are useful are Providers and Managers. When necessary, you can create Providers and Managers folders and move these types of services in there.

Providers are just services that provide access to some resource, usually locating and returning it but without changing it. For example, one frequent pain in the development process is the number of connection strings that are needed by the developers. Each developer on the team usually has his own copy of the database so when making data changes, it does not obstruct the work of other team members. These connection strings are difficult to manage because they are unique to each developer. To get around this problem, we use a ConnectionStringProvider, which has the logic to find the appropriate connection string depending on which developer runs the application. This service does not have the logic to make changes to data, just to choose which connection string to use and return it.

The second type of service that is frequently used is a Manager. The responsibility of a Manager service is to keep track of other objects that are needed for the proper operation of the system. An example of this is the RegionManager, which tracks all of the display regions that are available in an application. This service does not create or destroy regions; it just tracks those that are registered to it.

Another example of a manager is a CacheManager. Often in a complicated system, there is a need for multiple different caches of data entities. A CacheManager maintains these different data caches, creating, managing, and destroying them as appropriate during the lifetime of the application. The CacheManager does not use the caches or change any data in them; it just manages the caches.

There is one notable exception to the general statement that all services should be in a Services project: model or entity services. These are services that the model entities need for performing common business logic. These services cause a problem because the Services project invariably needs a reference to the Model project. If model entities need services and those services lived in the Services project, they would produce a circular reference. To get around this thorny problem, we sometimes must introduce an Entity Services Proxy project. This type of project can be complicated and obtuse, so it should be avoided if possible. However, in reengineering projects where you must adapt to the structure you are given, it is often difficult to avoid.

Domain Model Projects

The Domain Model project (or Data Model, or just Model) is the project that holds all the business entity classes. These are classes that typically each represent one table in the database (though this is not a hard rule). The Model project should be a dead-end project because many other projects refer to it. Depending on the type of data access technology you are using (Entity Framework, Linq to SQL, NHibernate, IdeaBlade, and so on), this project can contain different specific classes, but it always contains the classes that represent the data your project manipulates.

An important thing to note about the model is that it should not be tightly coupled to a specific database. In other words, a well-designed model can be used with Microsoft SQL Server just as easily as with Oracle or MySQL. The model project does, however, tightly couple to the ORM that is chosen. The model has different code and attributes depending on whether Microsoft Entity Framework is chosen, NHibernate, Linq to SQL, IdeaBlade, or any of the other ORM tools. If you would like to be able to swap one ORM for another, the data model project is the place to do that.

Repository Projects

The Repository project is where the data repository lives. The Repository pattern is covered in much more detail in Chapter 12, "Advanced Refactoring to Services," but in general, the repository is the service that interacts with the database on behalf of the rest of the system. All queries for data should come from this service.

As opposed to the Data Model project, the Repository project can be tightly coupled to a specific database instance. The queries needed to get a set of data from MS SQL Server can be different from those used to get data out of MS Access or even a flat file. These differences are implemented in the repository. The ORM being used should not be tightly coupled, however. Whether you use Entity Framework or NHibernate, the data model objects returned from the Repository project should be the same.

In the real world, sometimes this separation of repository and ORM can break down if the ORM has its own query language. The repository must use that language to query the data, and so it cannot be reused if the ORM changes. Most ORMs now support Linq, though, so the frequency of this problem is diminishing.

Controllers, View Models, and Presenters

If you use the MVC pattern, you will have a project called Controllers. This same project can go by the name ViewModels if you use the MVVM pattern, or Presenters if you use MVP. Whatever you call it, this project contains classes that control a large part of the business logic of the application.

Refactoring to the Solution Structure

This section discusses tips for changes that can be made to the solution to make it more flexible, but without changing business logic. We try to avoid changing business logic until that logic is covered by unit tests, so making a distinction between changes that do and do not affect logic is important. The changes discussed here can safely be made without test coverage.

It is convenient to make these changes in the order given, but not required. I recommend not making these changes in parallel with each other because they affect entire projects and often the solution itself. Having more than one person making these changes at the same time can result in a lot of rework during check-in. If possible, it is best to make these changes during off hours when the rest of the team is not actively working on the project.

> ## ■ NOTE
>
> A note to architects on large teams: It's better to over-communicate than under-communicate. The changes described in this section can dramatically change where things are located and how they are structured. References that were allowed before will become invalid. Developers who are unaware of the changes you are making can quickly become frustrated when an approach that was used yesterday no longer works today. During this process and until the project structure settles down, have frequent architectural meetings with the team to keep them abreast of the changes being made.

Remove Unnecessary Using Clauses

Using clauses are often ignored by developers because they apparently cause no harm. An unused Using clause does not cause the application to break, but a missing Using clause does, so many think it's better to leave them where they are "just in case." This is a mistake.

The references required in the project are determined by the Using clauses in the contained files. If a class has a Using clause, whether it's necessary or not, the project must have a reference to the appropriate DLL.

Therefore, especially when reengineering an application, it is important to remove unnecessary Using clauses so that only the necessary references are required.

Though Visual Studio makes it easy to identify unnecessary Using clauses in a file, unfortunately it is more difficult to identify unnecessary project references in a project. There is no indication that a reference is unnecessary and can be removed. The only way to identify unnecessary references is to remove one and try to build. When starting a new reengineering project, this tedious process is well advised because it can clear up potential problems. With unnecessary references, Visual Studio can report circular references that are unnecessary.

Separate Unit Tests and Integration Tests

If you are lucky enough to have existing unit tests in the application you are reengineering, then you must determine the quality of those tests. Many developers new to unit testing confuse unit tests with integration tests, resulting in "unit tests" that run for hours.

Unit tests do not interact with any outside services. In other words, they do not access the database in any way, nor do they access web services or anything else that is not in memory. This restriction makes unit tests fast, often running in milliseconds. An entire suite of unit tests should run in less than a minute or two. Because they are so fast, all unit tests should be run by the developer before any code check-in.

Integration tests, on the other hand, are allowed to interact with outside services. Due to this interaction, integration tests are typically slow. Repository tests are a typical example of an integration test, and a normal sized repository with full coverage can take over an hour to run. Therefore, these tests are typically run only at night.

Time should be taken to divide the unit tests and integration tests into separate projects so they can be run individually via the test runner. By dividing them into separate projects, they are easily recognizable and the unit tests are easy to run. If the unit tests are difficult or slow to run, developers eventually stop running them before check-ins, resulting in decreasing quality and increasing defect reports.

If separating the tests into different projects is too difficult, unit tests and integration tests can also be separated using test categories that are assigned using a attribute on the test. Using these attributes, the automated build can run either or both categories depending on the type of build.

Move Classes to Appropriate Projects

A good way of cleaning up an existing application and getting an idea of how difficult the project is going to be is to start by moving interfaces into the Interfaces project. As described previously, the Interfaces project should be a dead-end project so that it references no other projects in the solution. By maintaining the restriction on the project references, you can eliminate circular references.

This is a good project to start with because interfaces anywhere in the project are easy to identify. You can do a text search for the word "interface" to find all the declarations. Or, assuming you've maintained the standard naming convention of putting an "I" in front of interface names, using the ReSharper tools, you can press Ctrl+T to bring up a dialog box asking for the name of a Type to locate. Type "I" and all the interfaces in the solution are listed. You can then use ReSharper again to move this class in the interfaces project. This is done by first moving the class to the appropriate namespace. Using ReSharper to change the namespace also updates the other projects' Using clauses as necessary.

After changing the name space, simply cut and paste the file into the appropriate project or use the ReSharper Move command.

After cleaning up the interfaces, similar work can be done with DTOs, EventArgs, constants, and so on. Note that none of this work should require refactoring code; all that should be necessary is adding Using clauses and references to certain projects. If code needs to be refactored, the change made should be examined more closely before moving the class. Because only insignificant changes are necessary with this cleanup effort, it is a task that is easily undertaken by a junior member of the team.

Move Shortcuts to Libraries

Often in legacy Visual Basic applications (especially those that were ported from Visual Basic 6), you find shortcuts to files embedded in projects. These shortcuts can be created by adding an existing item to a project using the Add As Link option.

Though shortcuts have their place in modern code (most notably when you wish to compile a view in both WPF and Silverlight), in legacy applications, they were typically a clumsy way of reusing code. A better way of reusing this code is to create a library project that contains all the code to be reused and have other projects link to that library. Combining code into a library project is a good idea now because shortcuts are just disguised references and we need to take stock of the required references as early in the process as possible.

Shortcuts in projects can be difficult to find. If you know there are shortcuts to a particular file but cannot find them, you can make a change in the class that makes it fail to build. All projects that then fail a build are suspects for having a shortcut to the file. Other than using this technique, the only way of finding shortcuts is to look for them by hand.

Refactorings that Affect Logic

The changes described in the previous section should not affect business logic. They can safely be made without having unit tests in place because the only changes being made are to Using clauses. In this section, we discuss some changes that will affect business logic so they should only be made with appropriate unit tests in place.

There is a risk/reward decision that must be made at this point. While creating unit tests to validate existing logic, you may find a defect in the legacy code, and you must make a decision on whether to fix that defect. It is easy to get sidetracked when you discover a defect and try to fix it because this results in a full testing cycle and possible down-stream changes to fix other problems that surface as a result. However, finding defects and leaving them in the code is an unpleasant experience for any conscientious developer.

If you decide fixing a defect is not worth the repercussions in added QA time, create unit tests that validate the existing faulty logic to ensure that the changes we will make here do not break that logic. Make a note in the test describing the defect and how the test should be changed once you are to a point where logic changes can safely be made. It would be convenient to add a predictable string that can be found later to ease in the fix-up effort. Also, add a defect to your defect tracking system and set it to be dealt with at a later date.

If you decide to fix the defect, just be aware that this effort can affect your timeline.

Move Initialization Logic into the Constructor

This change is not necessary but saves time in debugging later and can reduce code bloat. You might find variable initialization code located in the declaration of a variable, as demonstrated in Listing 9.2.

LISTING 9.2 **Setting Up Logic Outside the Constructor**

```
using System;

namespace CodeSamples.Ch09_LegacySolutionCleanup.Listing02
{

  public class FormController
  {
    Uri myUri = new Uri("invalid string");

    public FormController()
    {
      //Controller logic goes here.
    }
  }

}
```

This is a problem because this code is run before the first line of the constructor. Therefore, if you place a breakpoint on the first line of the constructor, the application fails before arriving at the breakpoint. You can lose many hours because of this type of error if you put a breakpoint on the first line of a constructor. When it is not encountered, you might assume this class has nothing to do with the error.

Another problem with this type of coding is that it hides the variable initialization. If you have a class with an especially large number of properties (as View Models can have), then variables initialized in the declaration can easily become lost when they scroll off the screen.

A third reason to avoid initializing variables outside the constructor is to avoid code bloat and possible double-initialization of variables. When initializers are put outside of the constructor, behind the scenes the compiler copies this code into each constructor for execution, making your code bloated. Also, if you have a structure where one constructor calls another, this extra work done by the compiler can result in the same variable being initialized twice.

The solution here is simple; move the initialization code into the constructor, as demonstrated in Listing 9.3.

LISTING 9.3 Moving Initialization Code Inside the Constructor

```
using System;

namespace CodeSamples.Ch09_LegacySolutionCleanup.Listing03
{

  public class FormController
  {
    Uri myUri ;

    public FormController()
    {
      myUri = new Uri("invalid string');
      //Controller logic goes here.
    }
  }

}
```

With this structure, it is easy to find initialization code, and exceptions are thrown from the appropriate classes.

Replace Nested If Statements with Guards

In legacy code, you often see methods with many nested If statements checking various parameters before taking an action. To the developer writing the code at the time the logic probably made perfect sense, but to someone coming in after the fact and trying to decipher what the intent is, it is difficult to understand.

These nested If statement can be replaced by guard statements that return proper values. Replacing nested Ifs with guard statements makes the code much more legible without changing the logic. Adding the guard statements can also decrease the cyclomatic complexity of the method, which is a measure of how complicated your code is.

Listing 9.4 shows a complicated version of a method with many nested If statements.

LISTING 9.4 A Complex Nested IF Statement

```
namespace CodeSamples.Ch09_LegacySolutionCleanup.Listing04
{

  public class OrderEntryService
  {
    public OrderLineItem CreateInventoryOrderLineItem(
      InventoryItem pItem, Customer pCustomer,
      int pQuantity, float pPrice)
    {
      OrderLineItem result = null;
      if (pItem != null)
      {
        if (pCustomer != null)
        {
          if (pQuantity > 0)
          {
            if (!pItem.Discontinued)
            {
              if (pPrice > 0)
              {
                if (!pItem.Discontinued)
                {
                  result = new OrderLineItem(
                    pItem, pQuantity, pPrice);
                }
              }
              else
              {
                if (pCustomer.AllowFreeSamples)
                {
                  if (pItem.FreeSamplesAllowed)
                  {
                    result = new OrderLineItem(
                      pItem, pQuantity, pPrice);
                  }
                }
              }

            }
          }
        }
```

```
        }
      }
      return result;
    }

  }

  public class InventoryItem
  {
    public bool Discontinued { get; set; }
    public bool FreeSamplesAllowed { get; set; }
  }

  public class OrderLineItem
  {
    public OrderLineItem(InventoryItem item,
      int quanty, float price)
    {

    }
  }

  public class Customer
  {
    public bool AllowFreeSamples { get; set; }
  }
}
```

In this code, it is difficult to follow the logic flow because the condition tree is so deep. The only way to decipher this code is to use the brace-matching feature of Visual Studio by putting your cursor on an opening or closing brace and looking for its highlighted partner.

Now let's look at the equivalent code shown in Listing 9.5.

LISTING 9.5 A Simplified IF Statement with Guards

```
using System;

namespace CodeSamples.Ch09_LegacySolutionCleanup.Listing05
{

  public class FormController
  {
    public OrderLineItem CreateInventoryOrderLineItem(InventoryItem
➥pItem,
            Customer pCustomer, int pQuantity, float pPrice)
```

```csharp
    {
      if (pItem == null) throw new ArgumentException("Item is null");
      if (pCustomer == null) throw new ArgumentException("Customer is
➥null");
      if (pItem.Discontinued)
        throw new ArgumentException("Item Discontinued");
      if (pQuantity < 0) throw new ArgumentException("Invalid
➥Quantity");
      if (pQuantity == 0 && !FreeSampleAllowed(pCustomer, pItem))
        throw new ArgumentException("Free Samples Not Allowed on this
➥item");
      return new OrderLineItem(pItem, pQuantity, pPrice);
    }

    internal bool FreeSampleAllowed(Customer pCustomer, InventoryItem
pItem)
    {
      return pCustomer.AllowFreeSamples && pItem.FreeSamplesAllowed;
    }

  }

  public class InventoryItem
  {
    public bool Discontinued { get; set; }
    public bool FreeSamplesAllowed { get; set; }
  }

  public class OrderLineItem
  {
    public OrderLineItem(InventoryItem item,
      int quanty, float price)
    {

    }
  }

  public class Customer
  {
    public bool AllowFreeSamples { get; set; }
  }
}
```

This code is more easily understood by someone coming in fresh. The guard statements eliminate the possibility of invalid data entering the method so the remaining code can assume all parameters are valid. They also more easily present to the new developer the possible error conditions that have already been considered.

Some developers prefer putting the guard statements on a single line, as shown in the Listing 9.6.

LISTING 9.6 All Guard Statements in a Single Line

```csharp
using System;

namespace CodeSamples.Ch09_LegacySolutionCleanup.Listing06
{

  public class FormController
  {
    public OrderLineItem CreateInventoryOrderLineItem(InventoryItem
➥pItem,
            Customer pCustomer, int pQuantity, float pPrice)
    {
      if (pItem == null || pCustomer == null || pItem.Discontinued
        || (pQuantity <= 0
        && !FreeSampleAllowed(pCustomer, pItem)))
        throw  new ArgumentException("Invalid Arguments");
      return new OrderLineItem(pItem, pQuantity, pPrice);
    }

    internal bool FreeSampleAllowed(Customer pCustomer, InventoryItem
➥pItem)
    {
      return pCustomer.AllowFreeSamples && pItem.FreeSamplesAllowed;
    }

  }

  public class InventoryItem
  {
    public bool Discontinued { get; set; }
    public bool FreeSamplesAllowed { get; set; }
  }

  public class OrderLineItem
  {
    public OrderLineItem(InventoryItem item,
      int quanty, float price)
    {

    }
  }
```

```
public class Customer
{
    public bool AllowFreeSamples { get; set; }
}
}
```

Though these two examples of the refactored If statement achieve the same goal of guarding against bad input, the second example provides much less information about the reason the inputs have been rejected. By putting the conditions into the same If statement, it is not possible to provide detailed information about which of the conditions have been violated, leaving users to guess what input they need to correct.

This structure is also more difficult to debug because the Visual Studio debugger considers the entire If condition as a single statement, making it more difficult for a developer to determine the cause of the failure.

Before refactoring an If statement like this, it is best to create unit tests that accurately reflect the results of the If statement before refactoring. This ensures that the refactored method produces exactly the same results as the original version. It is easy to unintentionally make slight changes to the logic of the If statement during the refactoring without realizing it until a defect shows up.

Removing Access to Entity Class Constructors

When using the Repository pattern, it is a good idea to restrict creation of any entity objects to the repository. Only the repository should be able to "new-up" a new entity, and all other classes that need to create entities should call the repository to do so.

In day-to-day development, this practice is difficult to enforce. If the constructor for an entity class is public, developers often take the easy way and create what they need in the business logic, causing defects that are difficult to find.

The solution to this problem is to make the constructors of the entities internal and give access to these constructors only to the repository using the InternalsVisibleTo attribute. Doing this forces any business logic using the repository to create the entity because any attempt to "new-up" the entity does not build.

This refactoring is a good idea but often difficult to implement in a legacy system. The places where new entities are created tend to proliferate over time, and refactoring to limit where creation is possible can be a time-consuming and error-prone task. Trying to replace entity-creation code with a call to the repository implies that the ServiceLocator and repository are already in place. Also, creating unit tests to cover the code that must be refactored is typically not possible at this early stage, so refactoring can introduce defects.

Try to do this on several entities to see how difficult it is. If refactoring to implement this rule is too difficult, postpone this until the reengineering effort is further along. If you are able to do a few easy ones now and the rest later, it is at least a step in the right direction. It can also set an example for the team to use in any further development they may have to do.

Summary

Cleaning up the legacy solution is an important step when reengineering an existing system. The proper project structure plays an important role, especially in large systems, so the effort to structure things well before the reengineering process starts is worthwhile. A poorly organized project structure can force certain design decisions due to the project references that exist in the solution. By organizing the legacy project into the proper structure, many of those bad references can be broken, making the entire solution more loosely coupled.

10

Establishing the Foundation

Now that the legacy system is arranged well for our reengineering effort, it is time to start adding the foundation for all the work we will do. The work in this chapter has little effect for a while because we want to introduce our architecture and get it to build before we begin integrating it into our solution. The work in this section can be done while other team members continue adding features and maintaining the application in the same way they always have. If a release date occurs during this phase, it presents no problems releasing the application with this code partially implemented. Because we won't integrate it into the business logic until it is in place, you can release it with extra unused code in your application.

We start the process by introducing a Bootstrapper, a new shell, and the all-important ServiceLocator. When these are in place, we can create the first unit test project to test these two classes. This establishes the pattern used throughout the rest of the project and sets the stage for the next chapter where we will start to reengineer the solution to use services.

Adding New Projects

At this point, we create our first new projects: the Infrastructure project, Controllers, Views, and Interfaces. The Infrastructure project holds our ServiceLocator and other core services that we create along the way. We also enhance the existing shell project that holds the Bootstrapper and core program, while the Controllers and Views projects hold the respective items.

The Infrastructure, Interfaces, Controllers, and Views projects should be created as Class Library projects, whereas the existing shell should be either a Windows Forms Application or Windows Presentation Foundation (WPF) Application.

Using Prism, Unity, and Enterprise Library Versions

Before moving on, we need to specify the Prism version we are going to use and how you can get the same version. We use Prism 4.1.0.0, Unity 2.1.505.0, EntityFramework 4.2.0.0, and EnterpriseLibrary 5.0.414.0. Using the proper version of these libraries is important because the interface has changed slightly from its lower version numbers, and some functionality that we use was introduced.

Using these libraries is not as easy as it seems. First, you must download Unity at http://www.microsoft.com/download/en/details.aspx?id=17866.

Run the installation program, and it installs Unity on your machine (in the Program Files folder). You can ensure you have the correct version by finding the Microsoft.Practices.Unity.dll file in the Bin folder where Unity was installed and by viewing the properties (right-click Properties for mouse lovers; press Alt+Enter for the keyboard-oriented). Click the Details tab to see the version number. Figure 10.1 shows the dialog box you should see when viewing properties of the file.

Now download the Prism 4.1 package at http://www.microsoft.com/download/en/details.aspx?id=28950.

The Prism package comes as full source code that you must build yourself. However, the default Prism 4.1 uses Unity 2.0, not the 2.1 version that we want to use. Therefore, you must replace the Unity that comes with Prism with the newer one you downloaded. As shown in Figure 10.2, copy all four Unity DLLs in the Unity Bin folder into the Prism4.1\Lib\Desktop\Unity folder. This replaces Unity 2.0 with Unity 2.1.

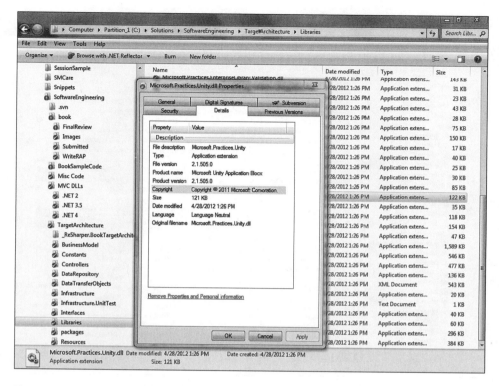

FIGURE 10.1: Required file version for Unity

Now open the Prism Desktop solution from Prism4.1\PrismLibrary\ PrismLibrary_Desktop.sln and rebuild. All projects should build successfully.

Download the Microsoft Enterprise Library 5.0 at http://www.microsoft .com/download/en/details.aspx?id=15104. You need the source code.

After extracting the Enterprise Library, it asks if you want to build the application blocks. Choose Yes and let the install build the libraries. If you look in the Bin folder where the Enterprise Library was installed, you should see the DLLs for EntLib.

Locate the Lib folder and copy the same Unity DLLs into this folder that you copied for the Prism build. Open the EnterpriseLibrary.2010.sln file in the Blocks folder and rebuild the solution. You now have an EnterpriseLibrary and Prism version that uses Unity 2.1. All DLLs we use in our project should come from the Bin folder of either the Unity, Prism, or EntLib versions we just built.

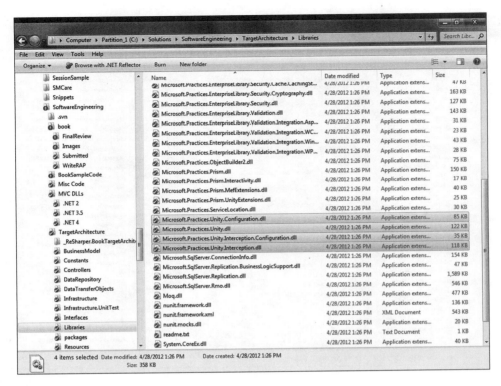

FIGURE 10.2: Unity files to copy

> **▪ NOTE**
>
> If you ever encounter build errors claiming you are missing a refer-
> ence to one of these DLLs when the reference is clearly there, check
> the path where the DLL is referenced. These libraries sometimes get
> registered in the GAC by other programs, and Visual Studio defaults
> to referencing them in that location. Also check the version number
> in the reference to make sure it is the proper one.

Adapting the Shell

The first thing you need to adapt is the shell the legacy application runs
under. The shell is the application window that contains the other windows and controls that make up the application. It is common for business
applications to have a shell that is designed similarly to Microsoft Outlook.

In other words, there is a menu and ribbon or toolbar at the top, a way to navigate around the application on the left, and a workspace on the right. Because it's not possible to know what your shell should look like, we assume that the Outlook design is how yours is designed. Figure 10.3 shows what our shell design looks like. If your shell does not look like the one shown here, don't worry. All the techniques described here still apply.

Your current legacy shell probably already has business logic in the code behind, which we leave in place. Over the course of this project, we refactor that code into the controller, but for now, because we introduce so much at once, it is best to leave the code behind alone.

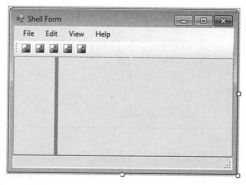

FIGURE 10.3: Target shell design

> **■ NOTE**
>
> In the following discussion, we use two terms (View and Form) to refer to windows that display on the screen. A *form* is a full window that can be displayed on its own in an application. A *view* is a collection of UI elements that must be displayed inside a form or another view. It's best to think of a view as a panel and all of its contents, whereas a form descends from System.Windows.Form.

Creating the IBaseView

In this step, we lay the foundation for the rest of the views by creating a base interface they inherit. In the Interfaces project, create the interface described in Listing 10.1.

LISTING **10.1: Providing the Foundation for the Views**

```
namespace CodeSamples.Ch10_EstablishFoundation.Listing01
{

    /// <summary>
    /// Basic components of every view
    /// </summary>
    public interface IBaseView
    {

        /// <summary>
        /// This activates the given view in the region,
        /// displaying the view.
        /// </summary>
        void SetActive();

        /// <summary>
        /// Makes this view invisible, but leaves it registered for
        /// future activation
        /// </summary>
        void SetInActivate();
    }
}
```

The IBaseView is an interface that views implement via inheritance through their specific interfaces (see the next section for an example). By declaring these methods in this base view, we can later treat all views similarly when working with the navigation system. The only two methods on the IBaseView interface are SetActive and SetInActive. These two methods are called when any view either gains focus or loses focus. We enhance this interface later.

Adapting the Current Shell

We adapt the current program shell by simply introducing a new interface to the current form. In the code listing that follows, we create a new interface IShellForm that descends from IBaseView. This form interface descends from a view interface because in the core window management code, we want to be able to treat our shell form the same as any other view.

Listing 10.2 displays the basic structure of the shell form and the accompanying interface.

LISTING 10.2: The Basic View and Interface Other Views Inherit

```
using System.Windows.Forms;
using CodeSamples.Ch10_EstablishFoundation.Listing01;

namespace CodeSamples.Ch10_EstablishFoundation.Listing02
{

  /// <summary>
  /// This interface should be created in the Interfaces project
  /// </summary>
  public interface IShellForm : IBaseView
  {
    //initially, this interface can be empty
  }

  public class ShellForm : Form, IShellForm
  {
    /// <summary>
    /// This activates the given view in the region,
    /// displaying the view.
    /// </summary>
    public void SetActive()
    {
      //do nothing for main shell
    }

    /// <summary>
    /// Makes this view invisible, but leaves it registered for
    /// future activation
    /// </summary>
    public void SetInActivate()
    {
      //do nothing for main shell
    }

    //the rest of the legacy codebehind code goes here
  }
}
```

By editing the current ShellForm, we introduce the IShellForm interface and implement the two required methods. For now, these methods can be empty.

For the first step, we simply introduce a marker interface that we can register with the ServiceLocator so we can resolve the shell when necessary. This interface expands to much more later, but for now it has everything we need.

Adding a Shell Controller

We want to connect a controller to the view to migrate business logic to it, so create the Listing 10.3 interface and class in the Controllers and Interfaces projects.

LISTING 10.3: **Creating the Shell Form Controller and Interface**

```csharp
using CodeSamples.Ch10_EstablishFoundation.Listing02;
using CodeSamples.Ch10_EstablishFoundation.Listing04;

namespace CodeSamples.Ch10_EstablishFoundation.Listing03
{

  /// <summary>
  /// This interface should be created in the Interfaced project
  /// </summary>
  public interface IShellFormController
  {
    IShellForm View { get; }
  }

  /// <summary>
  /// This class should be created in the Controllers project
  /// </summary>
  public class ShellFormController : IShellFormController
  {
    public IShellForm View { get; internal set; }
    public ShellFormController()
    {
      View = ServiceLocator.Resolve<IShellForm>();
    }
  }

}
```

The only functionality in the `ShellFormController` is code to resolve our `ShellForm` via the `ServiceLocator`. Eventually all of the code in the shell codebehind is moved into the controller to make it testable, but for this first step, we just introduce the controller architecture.

Creating the Service Locator

The `ServiceLocator` is the next class we add to our reengineered application. It is a core piece that is used throughout the application so we create it in the Infrastructure project where all other projects can reference it. As discussed earlier, the ServiceLocator is one of the few classes that we allow to be a static class.

Our ServiceLocator looks like Listing 10.4.

LISTING 10.4: Implementing the Service Locator

```
using System;
using Microsoft.Practices.Unity;

namespace CodeSamples.Ch10_EstablishFoundation.Listing03
{
  /// <summary>
  /// Provides locator services for client code that
  /// needs access to those services.
  /// </summary>
  public class ServiceLocator
  {
    /// <summary>
    /// Unity Container that can resolve required items.
    /// This is set in the Bootstrapper.
    /// </summary>
    /// <remarks>
    /// Make getter private so others don't try to use it
    /// to register stuff. Force them to resolve using
    /// the Resolve method.
    /// Getter is internal to give access to testing code.
    /// </remarks>
    public static IUnityContainer Container { internal get; set; }

    /// <summary>
    /// Create and return an instance of the class registered to T.
    /// </summary>
    public static T Resolve<T>()
    {
      return Container.Resolve<T>();
    }

    /// <summary>
    /// Create and return an instance of the class registered to T
    /// that was registered with the given name.
    /// </summary>
    public static T Resolve<T>(string pName)
    {
      return Container.Resolve<T>(pName);
    }
```

```csharp
    /// <summary>
    /// Create and return an instance of the class registered to T.
    /// </summary>
    public static object Resolve(Type T)
    {
      return Container.Resolve(T);
    }


    /// <summary>
    /// Register the given object with the proxy object T.
    /// </summary>
    public static void RegisterInstance<T>(T pObject)
    {
      Container.RegisterInstance<T>(pObject);
    }


    /// <summary>
    /// Register the given object with the proxy object T
    /// and label it with the given occurrence name.
    /// </summary>
    public static void RegisterInstance<T>(
      string pOccurranceName, T pObject)
    {
      Container.RegisterInstance<T>(pOccurranceName, pObject);
    }


    /// <summary>
    /// Register the given proxy type to create and return a class
    /// of the given type.
    /// </summary>
    public static void RegisterType<T, U>() where U : T
    {
      Container.RegisterType<T, U>();
    }


    /// <summary>
    /// Register the given proxy type to create and return a class
    /// of the given type. Name this instance so that this particular
    /// one can be accessed by callers.
    /// </summary>
    public static void RegisterType<T, U>(LifetimeManager
➥pLifetimeManager)
      where U : T
    {
      Container.RegisterType<T, U>(pLifetimeManager);
    }
  }
}
```

This is the same ServiceLocator discussed previously, so there should be no surprises here. Note that there is no code to register services or interfaces. That logic is placed in the Bootstrapper, which we create next.

Setting Up the BootStrapper Class

The Bootstrapper is the class that we use to start necessary processes in the application. It is the entry point for everything we are going to do, so it is obviously a key component. Depending on the framework you use, there are different types of Bootstrappers you can implement. For example, CaliburnMicro has one, Prism has a different one, and so on. All the Bootstrappers operate on the same basic principle, though, to initialize the application and show the program shell.

Because we base our application on Prism, we use the Prism Bootstrapper. Creating the Prism Bootstrapper is a bit different for Winforms and WPF, so we discuss the basics of the two separately and then continue the discussion for features that they share.

> **■ NOTE**
>
> In the Bootstrapper examples that follow, the bare minimum code that is needed to make the Bootstrapper work shows. In later chapters, we add many new service and interface registrations to these Bootstrappers. If you would like to see what the full Bootstrapper looks like, refer to the TargetArchitecture solution provided with the book.

Creating the Winforms BootStrapper

The Bootstrapper should be placed in the project that contains the application shell. This structure enables us to change the Bootstrapper depending on the shell we wish to use, which opens up the possibility of having dramatically different shells that use different domain models and repositories but share basic services with other applications.

Because we use Unity for our Dependency Injection, we make our Bootstrapper descend from the UnityBootstrapper that lives in the Microsoft.

Practices.Prism.UnityExtensions namespace. This provides us a lot of functionality, including creating the Unity container, as demonstrated in Listing 10.5.

LISTING 10.5: A Bootstrapper Implementation for a Winforms Application

```
using System.Windows;
using CodeSamples.Ch10_EstablishFoundation.Listing02;
using CodeSamples.Ch10_EstablishFoundation.Listing03;
using CodeSamples.Ch10_EstablishFoundation.Listing04;
using Microsoft.Practices.Prism.UnityExtensions;
using Microsoft.Practices.Unity;


namespace CodeSamples.Ch10_EstablishFoundation.Listing05
{
  /// <summary>
  /// This class will be created in the Shell project.
  /// </summary>
  public class BootstrapperWinforms : UnityBootstrapper
  {

    /// <summary>
    /// This is the entry point into our custom bootstrapper
    /// and is called by the base.
    /// </summary>
    protected override void ConfigureContainer()
    {
      base.ConfigureContainer();
      ServiceLocator.Container = Container;

      RegisterControlsAndControllers(Container);
      RegisterServices(Container);
    }

    /// <summary>
    /// Registers all services for the application.
    /// </summary>
    protected void RegisterServices(IUnityContainer container)
    {
      //Service registrations will go here.
    }

    /// <summary>
    /// Registers the views and controllers.
    /// </summary>
    protected void RegisterControlsAndControllers(IUnityContain
➥er container)
    {
```

```
      //Our shell should also be a singleton.
      container.RegisterType<IShellForm, ShellForm>(
        new ContainerControlledLifetimeManager());
      container.RegisterType<IShellFormController, ShellFormController>(
        new ContainerControlledLifetimeManager());
    }


    /// <summary>
    /// Returns the controller for the shell so Program.cs
    /// can run the app shell.  This is Winforms specific
    /// and should be replaced in the WPF version.
    /// </summary>
    public IShellFormController ShellController
    {
      get
      {
        var x = Container.Resolve<IShellFormController>();
        return x;
      }
    }


    /// <summary>
    /// This is a requirement by the UnityBootstrapper because
    /// it was built with WPF in mind.  For Winforms
    /// this makes no sense so we just return null.
    /// </summary>
    protected override DependencyObject CreateShell()
    {
      return null;
    }
  }


}
```

Our Bootstrapper gets control in the ConfigureContainer method, which is called by the UnityBoostrapper base class when it is created. The first action in the Bootstrapper is to initialize ServiceLocator with the Unity container created in the base UnityBootstrapper. We then initialize the container with services, views, and controllers. We break the service and controller registrations out into separate methods just for clarity.

As we register each class, we must decide whether we want that class to be a singleton or not. For most services, we want them to be singletons to save on memory and processing time for the garbage collector. We turn a normal service into a singleton simply by adding the ContainerControlledLifetimeManager in the registration call as can be seen in the `RegisterType` method call in the `RegisterControlsAndControllers` method. If you decide to make your service a singleton, however, remember that singletons must be stateless. There should be no variables saved inside the service that can affect the results of a method from one call to the next.

On the other hand, most controllers and views are not singletons because we want to have more than one created at the same time, so they are registered without this parameter. The one exception to this is the shell view and controller because we want only one active at a time. (If you are unfamiliar with the Singleton pattern or how to register a service with Unity as a singleton, see Chapter 4, "Understanding the Dependency Inversion Principle.")

With the basic `Bootstrapper`, we register only the shell form and controller, but eventually there will be many more registrations here. Each form has an interface associated with it that is registered with the container.

In the `ShellController` property, we resolve `ShellFormController` via the container so if this class is referenced anywhere else, the same controller is always returned. Notice that the controller is registered as a singleton. This enforces the rule that there be only one shell for the application. For other views, if more than one is allowed in the application at a time, the view and controller are registered as nonsingletons.

In the `CreateShell` method, we simply return null. The `Bootstrapper` was created with WPF in mind, and we adapt it to be used with Winforms. This base `Bootstrapper` has an abstract property called `CreateShell` that is used to create the WPF shell. In our case, we create the shell via the controller, so this is not necessary.

Updating the Winforms Program Class

Up to this point, we have not changed anything about the way the legacy system works, except to introduce some new (and far unused) classes. Now we update the `Program` class so we can start using our work with the `Bootstrapper`. Notice that no business logic has changed, however. When we are done making our changes to the `Program` file, the legacy application should function exactly as it did before, except with critical functions delegated to classes that are now fully testable.

Listing 10.6 shows the Main method of a Program class for an application. This is where the Bootstrapper should be created and initialized, so that it is available for use at the earliest point in the life of the application.

LISTING 10.6: The Main Program Class with Bootstrapper Initialization

```
using System;
using System.Windows.Forms;
using CodeSamples.Ch10_EstablishFoundation.Listing05;

namespace CodeSamples.Ch10_EstablishFoundation.Listing06
{
  /// <summary>
  /// This class already lives in the Shell project.
  /// </summary>
  static class Program
  {
    /// <summary>
    /// The main entry point for the application.
    /// </summary>
    [STAThread]
    static void Main()
    {
      BootStrapperWinforms bootStrapper = null;

      try
      {
        Application.EnableVisualStyles();
        Application.SetCompatibleTextRenderingDefault(false);

        bootStrapper = new BootStrapperWinforms();
        bootStrapper.Run();
      }

      catch (Exception ex)
      {
        MessageBox.Show("Error occurred during application startup. "
        + "Application will now exit. Error details:\r\n " + ex);
        return;
      }

      try
      {
        // The cast is necessary in order to treat the Shell
        // as an interface for the rest of the app.
        var shellController = bootStrapper.ShellController;
        var mainShellForm = shellController.View as Form;
        Application.Run(mainShellForm);
      }
```

```
      catch (Exception exc)
      {
        //This is where we handle exceptions that were
        //unhandled in the rest of the application.
      }
    }
  }
}
```

We begin modifying the Program class by adding calls to the BootStrapper. Because the BootStrapper is how we get everything initialized in our application, it is tightly coupled with the Program class in the Shell project. To initialize everything we need for our application, we create a Bootstrapper and call the Run method. This runs the ConfigureContainer method in the BootStrapperWinforms, initializing all of the registrations. If we encounter an error in the first Try..Catch block, it originated in the base architecture and so is probably unrecoverable. We show a message and exit. This can easily be enhanced later to log the error for future analysis.

In the second Try..Catch block, we resolve the controller for our shell via the Bootstrapper. The controller exposes its view via the View property as an IShellView. Winforms does not understand this interface, so we must cast the view as a form to use it as a parameter to the Application.Run method. Running with this view makes this window the main shell for the application.

In the Catch block for this section, we process any exceptions that were not handled anywhere else in the application. In other words, this is our "last resort" error-handling block that gets called when an exception has bubbled all the way up to the top. Eventually, we introduce an error logger service that is added to this catch block to log any unexpected errors.

Creating a WPF Application and Bootstrapper

In WPF, we initialize the application and run the shell slightly differently. The IBaseView and IShellView are the same, as is the ServiceLocator. The ShellViewController has been renamed to ShellViewModel and modified slightly, so let's examine that first.

Listing 10.7 shows the core code necessary for implementing the WPF version of the Shell Form ViewModel and interface.

LISTING 10.7: WPF Application Class

```
using CodeSamples.Ch10_EstablishFoundation.Listing02;
using CodeSamples.Ch10_EstablishFoundation.Listing04;

namespace CodeSamples.Ch10_EstablishFoundation.Listing07
{

  public interface IShellFormViewModel
  {
    IShellForm View { get; }
    void Activate();
  }

  public class ShellFormViewModel : IShellFormViewModel
  {
    public IShellForm View { get; internal set; }
    public ShellFormViewModel()
    {
      View = ServiceLocator.Resolve<IShellForm>();
    }

    public void Activate()
    {
      //Child views must be resolved here instead of in
      //the constructor
      //so view has time to register its regions.
    }
  }

}
```

The only difference between the View Model class and the Controller class is the additional Activate method that is added to the View Model class. We need to add this method to get around some startup problems regarding when the regions are declared in the shell and when they can be used. Any dependent views that the shell uses must be resolved and used in the Activate method rather than in the constructor. If used in the constructor, WPF has not yet had enough time to register the views with RegionManager, so they cannot be used. We talk more about the RegionManager in Chapter 12, "Advanced Refactoring to Services," but for now, in WPF, some item creation and use must be delayed slightly.

The main difference between the WPF and Winforms applications is in the Bootstrapper and the way the application is started up. First, let's examine the Bootstrapper that is shown in Listing 10.8.

LISTING 10.8: **The WPF Application Class**

```
using System.Windows;
using CodeSamples.Ch10_EstablishFoundation.Listing01;
using CodeSamples.Ch10_EstablishFoundation.Listing03;
using Microsoft.Practices.Prism.UnityExtensions;
using Microsoft.Practices.Unity;

namespace CodeSamples.Ch10_EstablishFoundation.Listing07
{
  public class BootstrapperWPF : UnityBootstrapper
  {
    private IShellFormViewModel _shellVM;

    protected override void ConfigureContainer()
    {
      base.ConfigureContainer();
      ServiceLocator.Container = Container;

      RegisterControlsAndControllers(Container);
      RegisterServices(Container);
    }


    /// <summary>
    /// Registers services for the application.
    /// </summary>
    protected void RegisterServices(IUnityContainer container)
    {
      //Service registration will go here, for example
      //container.RegisterType<ILogger, Logger>(
      //  new ContainerControlledLifetimeManager());
    }


    /// <summary>
    /// Registers the views and view models.
    /// </summary>
    protected void RegisterControlsAndControllers(IUnityContain
er container)
    {
      //Our shell should also be a singleton.
      container.RegisterType<IShellForm, ShellForm>(
        new ContainerControlledLifetimeManager());
      container.RegisterType<IShellFormViewModel, ShellFormViewModel>(
```

```
                new ContainerControlledLifetimeManager());
    }

    /// <summary>
    /// Creates the application shell. This is WPF specific and should
    /// be replaced in the Winforms version.
    /// </summary>
    /// <remarks>
    /// This runs before InitializeShell.
    /// </remarks>
    protected override DependencyObject CreateShell()
    {
        _shellVM = ServiceLocator.Resolve<IShellFormViewModel>();
        return _shellVM.View as DependencyObject;
    }

    /// <summary>
    /// Initializes the shell. This is WPF specific and should be
    /// replaced in the winforms version.
    /// </summary>
    /// <remarks>
    /// This runs after CreateShell.
    /// </remarks>
    protected override void InitializeShell()
    {
        base.InitializeShell();

        _shellVM.Activate();

        App.Current.MainWindow = (Window)Shell;
        App.Current.MainWindow.Show();
    }


    }


}
```

The initial part of the Bootstrapper has not changed from our Winforms implementation. The ConfigureContainer is still the method called during initialization and is still responsible for registering all interfaces and classes with the IoC container. The difference comes in how the view and view model are instantiated.

In the WPF Bootstrapper, instead of returning Null for the CreateShell method like we did in the Winforms Bootstrapper, we resolve and return the IShellFormViewModel. Notice that we create the view model, not the view.

Also, we cast this view model as a `DependencyObject` so the WPF infrastructure can use it.

The last change we made in the `Bootstrapper` is to override the `InitializeShell` method the base `UnityBootstrapper` provides. This method is called by the WPF architecture to initialize the application shell. We call the `Activate` method on the shell that we discussed earlier, letting the shell resolve any additional view models and register the views in the appropriate regions. We then take care of some windows housekeeping by setting the current application window to the shell and then showing the shell.

Finally, let's examine the App WPF class shown in Listing 10.9.

LISTING 10.9: The Main Application Class for a WPF Application

```
using System.Windows;
using CodeSamples.Ch10_EstablishFoundation.Listing08;

namespace CodeSamples.Ch10_EstablishFoundation.Listing09
{
  public partial class App : Application
  {
    protected override void OnStartup(StartupEventArgs e)
    {
      base.OnStartup(e);
      var bootstrapper = new BootstrapperWPF();
      bootstrapper.Run();
    }
  }
}
```

This must be one of the simplest classes we've encountered so far. This simply creates a new `Bootstrapper` and calls the `run` method.

Using Alternative Bootstrapper Configurations

In all of our examples so far, we registered the interfaces and concrete classes in code. There is another registration method that the IoC containers support: registering classes and interfaces via an XML file. These two approaches achieve the same goal, so either can be used in your project. Let's briefly examine the advantages and disadvantages of each registration method.

> ### ■ NOTE
>
> This discussion applies to both WFF and Winforms Bootstrappers.

Configuring the IoC container in code provides the build-time assertion that the specified class implements the given interface. The compiler gives a build error if the registered class does not implement the given interface. If registering classes via an XML file, this build time checking is not available, so the registration error is not found until the unit tests are run or the application is run. If there is an error in the code, it is best to discover it as soon as possible, so registering items in code is the best way to avoid this problem.

Something to note about the point made in the previous paragraph, if registering classes in an XML file, the mistaken registration might be the result of a simple typo in the class name. As the number of services, views, and other items registered in the IoC container grows, the difficulty of finding these typos grows also. Mistyping the name of a class or interface in code should be immediately noticeable due to the "red squiggly" that Visual Studio places under invalid class names.

Another argument for placing these registrations into code instead of XML files is the rename functionality available in Visual Studio. A change to a class or interface name can be propagated throughout the application using the built-in rename feature of Visual Studio. However, the class names in the XML files will not be changed using this feature, introducing a run-time defect when the registered class cannot be found.

It might be necessary to register different classes for the same interface depending on application conditions. For example, depending on whether a customer has bought a certain add-on module, you can register either a service that performs the extra tasks or a dummy service that implements the same interface but takes no action.

Listing 10.10 shows an example of an interface that is implemented by two different services. At runtime, we can check to see whether a customer has purchased the currency conversion feature and register the fully functional service if appropriate. If the customer has not purchased this feature, we register a dummy service that does nothing. With this approach, the rest of the code never needs to consider whether the customer has the proper license. It simply uses the currency converter that is registered.

LISTING 10.10: **Implementing a Dummy Service and a Real Service**

```csharp
using System;
using System.Collections.Generic;

//This example shows how we can have two different services
//that each implement the same interface, then at runtime
//decide which service is registered for use.
namespace CodeSamples.Ch10_EstablishFoundation.Listing10
{
  public enum Currency
  {
    Dollar,
    Euro,
    Yen
  }

  public interface ICurrencyConverter
  {
    decimal Convert(Currency destinationCurrency, decimal sourceAmt);
  }

  /// <summary>
  /// Very simple currency converter available only to
  /// those customers that purchase it.
  /// </summary>
  public class CurrencyConverter : ICurrencyConverter
  {
    private Dictionary<Currency, decimal> _conversionRates;

    public CurrencyConverter()
    {
      _conversionRates = new Dictionary<Currency, decimal>();
      //add code to fill the _conversionRates dictionary
    }

    public decimal Convert(Currency destinationCurrency, decimal
➥sourceAmt)
    {
      var conversionFactor = _conversionRates[destinationCurrency];
      return conversionFactor * sourceAmt;
    }
  }

  /// <summary>
```

```
    /// Dummy currency converter that is provided to customers
    /// that do not purchase the fully functional converter.
    /// </summary>
    public class CurrencyConverterDummy : ICurrencyConverter
    {
       public decimal Convert(Currency destinationCurrency, decimal
➥sourceAmt)
       {
         if (destinationCurrency != Currency.Dollar)
            throw new ArgumentException("Please purchase currency module");
         return sourceAmt;
       }
    }
}
```

In this example, our customer must purchase an extra currency converter module to convert the currency into a target currency. It is too cumbersome to put If statements throughout code to check to see whether a currency converter is registered or not, so instead, our business logic always assumes there is a currency converter available and uses it appropriately. We then register a dummy currency converter that does nothing so those customers who did not purchase this module gets no added functionality. Implementing this strategy using an XML file is difficult because we cannot add the necessary logic to check whether the currency module has been purchased.

While we discuss customers and how they use the system, let's examine the issue of the customer who "knows what's best" with your application. Registering services in an XML file can open the possibility of a customer deciding he would like to remove or replace a certain registration with a configuration he thinks is better. This experience requires extensive debugging time and eventually a site visit to determine that the configuration file to remove an "unnecessary" registration has been altered.

There is one advantage of registering items in an XML file, and that is the removal of the tight coupling necessary between the Shell project and supporting projects. If the Bootstrapper lives in the Shell project and the registrations are made in code, the shell must have hard references to the supporting classes. Using an XML registration strategy can remove these references, creating a more loosely coupled Shell project.

Which approach you use is your choice, though a hybrid is the preference. Register necessary services in code and then read the XML file (if it exists) to replace any of those registrations as necessary. This allows the configuration file to override any of the default services with a customized version and add new ones if necessary, while still guaranteeing that at least the default version of each class is available.

Summary

In this chapter, we discussed the critical step of introducing the foundation of our application. The items we discussed here outline the core of what we use throughout our project and determine many aspects of how our application works and grows. Now that we have this in place, we can move on to separating out the pieces of our application to make it more loosely coupled and easier to work with.

11

Basic Refactoring to Services

In this phase of the project, we begin to change existing code to use the infrastructure we have installed. To this point, we have made few changes in the logic of our legacy system. We've introduced the new architectural elements, but we haven't started using them anywhere except the startup process and the Shell. This chapter discusses the first changes necessary to start integrating the new architecture into the existing legacy system.

The refactorings suggested in this chapter should be taken in order because they are listed from the least impactful to the most. It is important to start with the service that has the smallest and most predictable impact because there are structural changes that must be made when introducing the first service. Project references must be added to access the ServiceLocator, the interfaces, and other projects. You also want to create the appropriate on-demand service resolution properties in the base classes so descendants do not have to declare these properties again. Implementing one of the more advanced services first requires not only adding this infrastructure to the legacy projects, but also possibly refactoring the business logic that surrounds the method calls being replaced. It is best to make as few changes as necessary in each step of the process, so we start with the services that require the fewest logic changes.

Using DialogService

The first service to add to the application is DialogService. The only respon-sibility of this service is to show a message to the user and potentially get a reply and return it to the caller. The service is unaware of the content of the message or the significance of the reply. It simply takes a message as a parameter, creates a dialog of the appropriate type depending on some parameters sent in by the caller, displays the message, and returns the reply. There is no internal state kept, and the service can be called by any component at any time without concern for other things that might happen within the system.

The DialogService is a good early service to add because it is focused and easy to create. It is also a critical piece of the unit testing strategy for any application. Refactoring to use a DialogService is typically an easy chore, and the locations where the service should be called are easy to find.

The DialogService is meant to be a replacement for the built in .NET MessageBox method. You use the DialogService anytime you want to interact with the user either by displaying a message or getting input. This is a simple refactoring and should present no problems with your legacy code.

The first step is to write DialogService. This is a simple service initially but can easily be expanded to meet additional needs. Add the class in Listing 11.1 to your Services project and add the interface to the Interfaces project.

LISTING 11.1: A Sample DialogService

```
using System.Windows.Forms;

namespace CodeSamples.Ch11_RefactorToBasicServices.Listing01
{
  /// <summary>
  /// The dialog service will show a message to the user
  /// and accept an appropriate response as requested
  /// by the caller.
  /// </summary>
  public class DialogService : IDialogService
  {
    /// <summary>
    /// Show the given message to the user in a dialog
    /// with just an OK button.
    /// </summary>
```

```csharp
    public void Show(string pUserMessage)
    {
      MessageBox.Show(pUserMessage);
    }


    /// <summary>
    /// Show a message to the user with the specified
    /// window caption and buttons.
    /// </summary>
    public DialogResult Show(string pUserMessage, string pCaption,
      MessageBoxButtons pMessageBoxButtons)
    {
      return MessageBox.Show(pUserMessage, pCaption, pMessageBoxButtons);
    }
  }

  public interface IDialogService
  {
    void Show(string pUserMessage);
    DialogResult Show(string pUserMessage, string pCaption,
      MessageBoxButtons pMessageBoxButtons);
  }
}
```

As shown in the listing, the DialogService is simple. It accepts a string from the caller and displays that string in a dialog box where the user is required to press the OK button. There is another signature that provides a little more control, but the intent is the same.

Now that we have our dialog service, we can refactor our legacy code to use it. Listing 11.2 shows an example of the legacy code before implementing DialogService.

LISTING 11.2: The Legacy Method Before Refactoring to DialogService

```csharp
using System;
using System.Windows.Forms;

namespace CodeSamples.Ch11_RefactorToBasicServices.Listing02
{
  public class BusinessLogicClass
  {
    /// <summary>
    /// Example of a method that can be refactored to use
    /// the dialog service.
    /// </summary>
```

```
      public bool ValidateDateRange(DateTime pStartDate, DateTime
➥pEndDate)
    {
      if (pEndDate < pStartDate)
      {
        MessageBox.Show("End Date must be after Start Date");
        return false;
      }
      return true;
    }
  }
}
```

To refactor this code, we first must register the new DialogService with the ServiceLocator via the BootStrapper. After that is done, we simply resolve a reference to the singleton IDialogService using the ServiceLocator. Using this reference, we call the Show method, and we are done. Listing 11.3 shows the reengineered code using the DialogService.

LISTING 11.3: The Legacy Method After Refactoring to DialogService

```
using System;
using CodeSamples.Ch10_EstablishFoundation.Listing04;
using CodeSamples.Ch11_RefactorToBasicServices.Listing01;

namespace CodeSamples.Ch11_RefactorToBasicServices.Listing03
{
  public class BusinessLogicClass
  {
    /// <summary>
    /// Example of a method that can be refactored to use
    /// the dialog service.
    /// </summary>
    public bool ValidateDateRange(DateTime pStartDate, DateTime
➥pEndDate)
    {
      if (pEndDate < pStartDate)
      {
        var dialogSvc = ServiceLocator.Resolve<IDialogService>();
        dialogSvc.Show("End Date must be after Start Date");
        return false;
      }
      return true;
    }
  }
}
```

In this code, we removed the call to MessageBox, replacing it with a call to the DialogService. Because our ServiceLocator was put into place in the previous chapter, it is easy to use it here to resolve the services we need.

A slightly different alternative to the code in Listing 11.3 is to use an on-demand service property. The logic is exactly the same; however, the dialog service resolution code is relegated to a property that caches the pointer to the service. This usage is convenient because you can use the property at will without being concerned whether it has been initialized yet. It also makes the code slightly faster because you don't have to resolve the reference on the second use. Whether you use this convenience feature or not does not affect the processes we recommend here, so implement what makes the most sense to you. Listing 11.4 shows the method from the legacy system after we refactor it to use DialogService. An on-demand service property is used at the top to resolve the reference to our service.

LISTING 11.4: The Legacy Method After Refactoring to DialogService with the OnDemand Property

```
using System;
using CodeSamples.Ch10_EstablishFoundation.Listing04;
using CodeSamples.Ch11_RefactorToBasicServices.Listing01;

namespace CodeSamples.Ch11_RefactorToBasicServices.Listing04
{
  public class BusinessLogicClass
  {
    private IDialogService DialogSvc
    {
      get
      {
        return _dialogSvc ?? (
          _dialogSvc = ServiceLocator.Resolve<IDialogService>());
      }
    }
    private IDialogService _dialogSvc;


    /// <summary>
    /// Example of a method that can be refactored to use
    /// the dialog service.
    /// </summary>
    public bool ValidateDateRange(DateTime pStartDate, DateTime
➥pEndDate)
    {
```

```
    if (pEndDate < pStartDate)
    {
      DialogSvc.Show("End Date must be after Start Date");
       return false;
    }
    return true;
  }
 }
}
```

As you can see, this change has no impact on the logic of the application. The message is shown just as it was before, and the logic continues along the same line as before. The only difference is that we hand off the responsibility for showing the message to our service. On the project level, though, many changes might have to be made to achieve this one line of code. A reference to the Infrastructure project is required to gain access to ServiceLocator. We must also reference the Interfaces project to get the IDialogService interface. These two projects are purposely maintained so that they do not reference any other projects in the system, reducing the chances of getting a circular reference. However, adding the first few new project references in a legacy system can often be a frustrating experience as the shortcomings of the legacy architecture are exposed. This is why we do the simple service first.

> **■ NOTE**
>
> The DialogService is a good example of a service that should be registered as a Singleton. This class can be used from anywhere, and it holds no state. Registering it as a singleton saves on resources and speeds up your application. Here is an example of registering a service as a singleton with the ContainerControlledLifetimeManager parameter:
>
> ```
> container.RegisterType<IDialogService, DialogService>(
>   new ContainerControlledLifetimeManager());
> ```

Unit Testing

With so little impact on the code, you wonder why the DialogService is necessary when MessageBox has served the same need reliably. We use the DialogService instead of MessageBox to make our code testable.

Imagine you have some code that checks for a certain error condition and then shows the user a message when that condition is found. When you create a unit test for this code, a successful test displays a message on screen, which requires someone to press the OK button. Showing a message on screen during a unit test dramatically reduces the effectiveness of that test because an automated build server stops execution of your test suite until someone presses the button. We can surround the call to MessageBox with conditional compilation directives (#if statements), but with this approach, we would never be completely sure that the code that runs in production has been fully tested. We also cannot test that the message is actually displayed.

This is where the DialogService comes in. By creating a service that is resolved via a service locator and using that service to display any messages, you are able to have live code display the appropriate error message while unit tests still run correctly. You might find that legacy code overcomes this problem by using condition compilation. If so, this code should be removed and replaced with the service resolution.

With our reengineered application, we can address the testing problem using a mock of the DialogService. By registering a mock of the DialogService with your container instead of the real service, there is no need for special code or compiler directives indicating whether you are running in Debug mode. Our mock is resolved by the live code instead of the real DialogService, and our mock DialogService registers only the fact that it has shown the message on screen in live code.

Referring to the legacy code example in Listing 11.4, your original unit tests would look something like Listing 11.5 (that is, these are tests for the legacy code before our refactoring).

LISTING 11.5: The Legacy Method After Refactoring to DialogService with the OnDemand Property

```
using System;
using System.Windows.Forms;
using Microsoft.VisualStudio.TestTools.UnitTesting;

namespace CodeSamples.Ch11_RefactorToEasicServices.Listing05
{
  public class BusinessLogicClass
  {
```

```csharp
    /// <summary>
    /// Example of a method that can be refactored to use
    /// the dialog service.
    /// </summary>
    public bool ValidateDateRange(DateTime pStartDate, DateTime
➥pEndDate)
    {
      if (pEndDate < pStartDate)
      {
        MessageBox.Show("End Date must be after Start Date");
        return false;
      }
      return true;
    }
}

[TestClass]
public class MockingExampleTestClass
{
  static BusinessLogicClass _bizLogic;

  [ClassInitialize]
  public static void ClassInitialize(TestContext context)
  {
    _bizLogic = new BusinessLogicClass();
  }

  [TestMethod]
  public void ValidateDateRange_ValidDates_NoMessage()
  {
    var startDt = new DateTime(2000, 1, 1);
    var endDt = new DateTime(2000, 1, 2);
    var result = _bizLogic.ValidateDateRange(startDt, endDt);

    //We can only assume no message was shown if the method
    //call returns to us.
    Assert.IsTrue(result);
  }

  [TestMethod]
  public void ValidateDateRange_SameDates_NoMessage()
  {
    var startDt = new DateTime(2000, 1, 2);
    var result = _bizLogic.ValidateDateRange(startDt, startDt);

    //We can only assume no message was shown if the method
    //call returns to us.
    Assert.IsTrue(result);
  }
```

```
    [TestMethod]
    public void ValidateDateRange_InvalidDates_ShowsMessage()
    {
        var startDt = new DateTime(2000, 1, 2);
        var endDt = new DateTime(2000, 1, 1);
        //This will show a dialog box on screen.
        var result = _bizLogic.ValidateDateRange(startDt, endDt);
        Assert.IsFalse(result);
    }
  }
}
```

If you step through the last test for invalid dates, you will see that the test shows a dialog on the screen, and you must press the OK button to continue. There is no automated way to push that button, so if you want the entire test suite to run on an automated server, you must remove that test. Use of the MessageBox in this example makes the method impossible to test.

Now refer to the reengineered version of the same method in Listing 11.4. If you run the same tests on this code, they still show the message on the screen. What we need to do is introduce a Mock DialogService, which does not show the message. We do this by creating the mock and registering it with our dependency injection container, which replaces the current registration.

The unit test is changed to look like Listing 11.6.

LISTING 11.6: Unit Tests Adapted to Use Mock Dialog Service

```
using System;
using System.Windows.Forms;
using CodeSamples.Ch10_EstablishFoundation.Listing04;
using CodeSamples.Ch11_RefactorToBasicServices.Listing01;
using Microsoft.Practices.Unity;
using Microsoft.VisualStudio.TestTools.UnitTesting;
using Moq;

namespace CodeSamples.Ch11_RefactorToBasicServices.Listing06
{
    public class BusinessLogicClass
    {
        private IDialogService DialogSvc
        {
            get
            {
                return _dialogSvc ?? (
```

```csharp
            _dialogSvc = ServiceLocator.Resolve<IDialogService>());
      }
    }
    private IDialogService _dialogSvc;


    /// <summary>
    /// Example of a method that can be refactored to use
    /// the dialog service.
    /// </summary>
    public bool ValidateDateRange(DateTime pStartDate, DateTime
pEndDate)
    {
      if (pEndDate < pStartDate)
      {
        DialogSvc.Show("End Date must be after Start Date");
        return false;
      }
      return true;
    }
  }

  [TestClass]
  public class MockingExampleTestClass
  {
    private BusinessLogicClass _bizLogic;
    private Mock<IDialogService> _mockDialogSvc;

    [ClassInitialize]
    public static void ClassInitialize(TestContext context)
    {
      var bootStrapper = new BootStrapper();
      bootStrapper.Run();
    }

    [TestInitialize]
    public void TestInitialize()
    {
      //Create a mock DialogService
      //that will do nothing when called.
      _mockDialogSvc = new Mock<IDialogService>();

      //Replace the real DialogService with our mock.
      ServiceLocator.Container = new UnityContainer();
      ServiceLocator.RegisterInstance<IDialogService>(
        _mockDialogSvc.Object);

      _bizLogic = new BusinessLogicClass();
    }
```

```csharp
        [TestMethod]
        public void ValidateDateRange_ValidDates_NoMessage()
        {
          var startDt = new DateTime(2000, 1, 1);
          var endDt = new DateTime(2000, 1, 2);
          _bizLogic.ValidateDateRange(startDt, endDt);

          //Ensure that the message was NOT shown to the user.
          _mockDialogSvc.Verify(mds =>
            mds.Show(It.IsAny<string>()), Times.Never());
        }

        [TestMethod]
        public void ValidateDateRange_SameDates_NoMessage()
        {
          var startDt = new DateTime(2000, 1, 2);
          _bizLogic.ValidateDateRange(startDt, startDt);

          //Ensure that the message was NOT shown to the user.
          _mockDialogSvc.Verify(mds =>
            mds.Show(It.IsAny<string>()), Times.Never());
        }

        [TestMethod]
        public void ValidateDateRange_InvalidDates_ShowsMessage()
        {
          var startDt = new DateTime(2000, 1, 2);
          var endDt = new DateTime(2000, 1, 1);
          _bizLogic.ValidateDateRange(startDt, endDt);

          //Ensure that the message was NOT shown to the user.
          _mockDialogSvc.Verify(mds =>
            mds.Show(It.IsAny<string>()), Times.Once());
        }
    }


    /// <summary>
    /// The reader should remove this BootStrapper and replace with the
➥normal one
    /// used to set up the application.
    /// </summary>
    public class BootStrapper
    {
      public void Run(){}
    }

}
```

This unit test looks much more complicated, but that is deceptive. Let's look at it one piece at a time.

The first addition is to the `ClassInitialize` method to create and run a `BootStrapper`. This is now necessary to set up the `ServiceLocator` properly and register all of the services in our system. Something to note here is that by running the `BootStrapper`, the test mimicks as closely as possible the setup of the production system. If the business logic used any other services during its processing, they would already be registered by running the `BootStrapper`. This also means that any time new services are introduced into the application, we do not have to visit each test and add appropriate service registrations; they are automatically included in the `BootStrapper`.

Because the `BootStrapper` registers all live services as if the application is running for real instead of under test, we must replace some of those services in the dependency injection container so that they do not interfere with the test. The `DialogService` is one of the services that must be replaced so that it does not show messages on the screen that a user needs to respond to. To do this, we create a mock of the `IDialogService` and register that with our dependency injection container as you can see in the `Setup` method.

> ■ **NOTE**
>
> Note that re-registering a service with Unity replaces the previous registration. If you use a different dependency injection container, you should verify that it behaves in a similar fashion or update the code so that the real `DialogService` is replaced by the mock.

Now we are ready to revisit each test and add the necessary assert logic. Because we use MOQ, we can verify that a particular method was called on our service with the Verify call, which is the last line in each of the previous tests. This ensures that the Show method was never called for correct date ranges, or exactly one time if the dates are incorrect.

If you examine the code closely, you might notice that it seems to be a waste of resources to create the mock in the `TestInitialize` method instead of the `ClassInitialize`. Creating the mock once for all tests in the

`ClassInitialize` seems like it should satisfy the needs of each test. This is true; however, it introduces a subtle defect that is difficult to find. MOQ does not have a method for resetting the call counter for each method, so each call to `Times.Never()` tests to see whether that method had been called since the mock was created. Depending on the order that your tests run, these asserts might succeed or fail depending on whether another test changes the number of times the method is called. By creating the Mock in the `TestInitialize` instead of the `ClassInitialize` method, a new mock is created for each test and we do not fall victim to this problem.

Refactoring for DialogService

There are two reasons we picked `DialogService` as the first one to implement. First, there is no logic change introduced by this refactoring. As long as your legacy application is displaying an informational message, you can replace that call with the service without other changes. If your legacy application has some business logic wrapped around the message display, you can move that same logic into `DialogService` by adding an additional method. The main point is that there should be little or no impact on the business logic by introducing `DialogService`.

The second reason for introducing this service first is because the places where we need to refactor are easily identified. Often by simply searching the code for `MessageBox.Show`, you will find the majority of places where the `DialogService` needs to be implemented. In some systems, there will already be a utility class that implements the same idea as the `DialogService` by providing a single method callers can use to show a message. If so, these methods are also easily identified and located in the legacy code.

If you do encounter a utility class that provides the same services as the `DialogService`, it might be tempting to register this existing class with your dependency injection container and use it in place. As long as that utility class follows the rules of services, the conversion in place should save some time. However, these utility classes often have broad-ranging responsibilities and do not lend themselves well to our definition of a service.

Other factors that can keep an existing class from being converted to a service are static properties. Static properties cannot be mocked by Moq, and so there is little point in creating a service for classes that contain these.

It is also unlikely that the existing class will be located in the proper project. Keeping our project structure clean is critical, especially for large projects, so leaving a class in the wrong place can cause reference problems later. If you decide to convert a class in place instead of replacing with a new `DialogService`, keep this in mind.

Though this refactoring is not technically challenging, it is often time-consuming. A good way to get a time estimate for this task is to do a text search for `MessageBox.Show` (or the appropriate utility method) and allocate about 10 minutes per occurrence. This might seem excessive for what appears to be a simple search and replace, but because this is the first service that we use throughout the system, you will probably have to add project references to use the Interfaces and Infrastructure projects. You will also need to allocate time for testing the changes, though for such a small refactoring, that testing should not be significant.

> ■■ **NOTE**
>
> Refactoring efforts that are technically simple but time-consuming are excellent tasks for junior developers or new developers who are getting accustomed to the code.

Adding Unit Tests

Refactoring to add the calls to the `DialogService` can decouple some of the legacy methods enough so that unit tests can be created for them. Now is a good opportunity to begin creating the unit testing classes and adding tests for the updated methods where you have added the `DialogService` calls. Doing this now can result in many new test projects and test classes, and creating this infrastructure can be time-consuming. If you pursue this option (we highly recommend you do), be sure to increase your time estimates.

While refactoring to use this service, you will run across `MessageBox.Show` calls that use different signatures. For now, it is easiest to just add the different signatures to your `DialogService` and leave the basic logic of the legacy code in place. It is tempting to simultaneously refactor the code to use an existing DialogService method signature; however, this is often a losing battle. You may end up doing the same refactoring many times throughout the project, spending precious time and getting little benefit.

Refactoring for DialogService is often a two-phase task. First refactor by copying the signatures into your service just as they are in the legacy code. This will most likely create many different signatures that are nearly identical. When this is completely done and the code is checked in, use your refactoring tools to count the number of usages for each of the signatures in your dialog service. If some of the signatures have only a few references, you can simplify the service by refactoring those signatures out.

Using LogWriterService

Along with DialogService, LogWriterService is one of the first services to introduce. This is the service that takes care of writing to any log files you wish to maintain. You can add logic to decide what the logging situation is (in debug or live code) and write to a flat file, database table, or anywhere you choose. This basic component is often used just before a call to the DialogService to log the fact that something went wrong and you are about to notify the user about it. This service is critical for debugging issues that happen only in the field.

Using a LogWriterService instead of writing directly to a log file can centralize the code that writes to the log making additions to the log writer easier and also allows substituting a "do-nothing" log writer for testing. By replacing the LogWriterService in tests with a mock of ILogWriterService, which just throws away the attempts to write to the log, there is no impact on the local drive as a result of unit tests.

Implementing LogWriterService is similar to the pattern for implementing the DialogService; however, even in legacy systems. you find a separate class that writes to the log. If that class functions well and there is no need to change it (that is, it has a single responsibility and is not tightly coupled to other classes), you can extract an interface for it, register it with your Dependency Injection container, and use it like it is (after moving it to the correct project). These legacy log writer classes are sometimes static or have static variables. By registering them with Unity as singletons, there is no need to make them static, so these modifiers should be removed.

If there is no log writer class yet, you can use the one in Listing 11.7, which takes advantage of certain .NET functions to make the log more meaningful by adding a stack frame to each log message. It's a simple logger that writes to a text file, but it can be enhanced any way you choose.

LISTING 11.7: A Sample Error Logger

```
using System;
using System.Diagnostics;
using System.IO;
using System.Windows.Forms;
using Microsoft.Practices.Prism.Logging;

namespace CodeSamples.Ch11_RefactorToBasicServices.Listing07
{
  /// <summary>
  /// Logger implementation.
  /// This class should go in the Services project.
  /// </summary>
  public class Logger : ILogger
  {
    private string _logFilePath;

    /// <summary>
    /// Constructor - initializes the location of the log file to the
    /// same folder where the application is running.
    /// </summary>
    public Logger()
    {
      _logFilePath = Path.GetDirectoryName(Application.ExecutablePath)
        + "\\MyLogFile.log";
    }

    /// <summary>
    /// Log a message to the log file.
    /// </summary>
    public void Log(string format, params object[] arg)
    {
      Log(String.Format(format, arg));
    }

    /// <summary>
    /// Log a message to the log file.
    /// </summary>
    public void Log(string pMessage)
```

```csharp
    {
      writeLogInfo(pMessage, Category.Info, Priority.None);
    }

    /// <summary>
    /// Log an exception to the log file.
    /// </summary>
    public void Log(Exception pException)
    {
      if (pException == null) return;
      writeLogInfo(pException.ToString(), Category.Exception, Priority.
➡High);
    }

    /// <summary>
    /// Log a message to the log file.
    /// </summary>
    public void Log(string pMessage, Category pCategory, Priority
➡pPriority)
    {
      writeLogInfo(pMessage, pCategory, pPriority);
    }

    /// <summary>
    /// Writes the log message to the log file.
    /// </summary>
    internal void writeLogInfo(string pMessage, Category pCategory,
      Priority pPriority)
    {
      if (string.IsNullOrEmpty(pMessage))
        pMessage = "Empty message received in LogWriterService";

      //For 10,000 test calls, adding the stack frame
      //added 0.5 seconds to exe time so getting stack
      //frame each time adds negligible performance hit.
      var callingStackFrame = new StackFrame(1);  //1 for our caller

      string msg = String.Format("{0} - {1} - {2}",
        pMessage, pCategory, pPriority);
      using (var file = new StreamWriter(_logFilePath))
      {
        file.WriteLine(callingStackFrame + Environment.NewLine + msg);
        file.Close();
      }
    }
  }

  /// <summary>
  /// This interface should go in the Interfaces project.
```

```
/// </summary>
public interface ILogger
{
  void Log(string msg);
  void Log(Exception exc);
  void Log(string format, params object[] arg);
  void Log(string pMessage, Category pCategory, Priority pPriority);
}
}
```

Refactoring for LogWriterService

Reengineering to use the LogWriterService is similar to the refactoring we used for the DialogService. If there is an existing log writer, we do a text search for the appropriate method name and replace it just like we did for the Dialog Service. With the log writer, however, it is also possible for code to write directly to a log file. These occasions are more difficult to find and may require that you search for the filename as a text string.

In the example that follows, you see two possible versions of legacy software writing to a log. One uses a dedicated log writer service, and the other writes directly to the file. Both of these can be refactored to use the log writer service with either the on-demand property or point-of-use resolution. You can see both versions of each refactored method in Listing 11.8.

LISTING 11.8: A Legacy LogWriterService Example

```
namespace CodeSamples.Ch11_RefactorToBasicServices.Listing08
{
  public class LegacyCodeSample
  {

    /// <summary>
    /// Legacy method of writing to a log file using
    /// a dedicated log writer class.
    /// </summary>
    public void LegacyLogWriterCallUsingLogWriterClass()
    {
      LegacyLogWriter.Log("log this message");
    }

    /// <summary>
    /// Legacy method of writing to a log by accessing the
```

```
    /// file directly.
    /// </summary>
    public void LegacyLogWriterCallWritingDirectlyToFile()
    {
      using (var file = new System.IO.StreamWriter("c:\\test.txt"))
      {
        file.WriteLine("log this message");
        file.Close();
      }
    }
  }

  public static class LegacyLogWriter
  {
    private static string _logFileName = "c:\\test.txt";
    public static void Log(string msg)
    {
      using (var file = new System.IO.StreamWriter(_logFileName))
      {
        file.WriteLine(msg);
        file.Close();
      }
    }
  }
}
```

Listing 11.9 shows this same legacy code refactored to use the log writer service via the ServiceLocator. In this example, we refactored the legacy log writer into a service in order to keep the current functionality.

LISTING 11.9: Legacy Log WriterService Refactored for ServiceLocator

```
using CodeSamples.Ch10_EstablishFoundation.Listing04;

namespace CodeSamples.Ch11_RefactorToBasicServices.Listing09
{
  public class LegacyCodeSample
  {
    /// <summary>
    /// Legacy method of writing to a log file using
    /// a dedicated log writer class.
    /// </summary>
    public void LegacyLogWriterCallUsingLogWriterClass()
    {
      ServiceLocator.Resolve<ILegacyLogWriter>().Log("log this
  message");
    }
```

```
      /// <summary>
      /// Legacy method of writing to a log by accessing the
      /// file directly.
      /// </summary>
      public void LegacyLogWriterCallWritingDirectlyToFile()
      {
         ServiceLocator.Resolve<ILegacyLogWriter>().Log("log this
 ↳message");
      }
   }

   public interface ILegacyLogWriter
   {
      void Log(string msg);
   }

   public class LegacyLogWriter : ILegacyLogWriter
   {
      private string _logFileName = "c:\\test.txt";
      public void Log(string msg)
      {
         using (var file = new System.IO.StreamWriter(_logFileName))
         {
            file.WriteLine(msg);
            file.Close();
         }
      }
   }

}
```

Note that if you use an existing logger by converting it to a service, it is easy to accidentally continue using the concrete class instead of converting to the service. A trick you can use to detect any method calls that you might have missed during refactoring is to change the name of the logging method slightly in the interface and the class. The project does not build until you have converted all of the method calls to the new name. After the application is building again, you can use your refactoring tools to rename the method as the original name in just a few keystrokes.

For example, if the legacy method name is LogMessage, change it to LogMessageNew (without allowing Visual Studio to propagate that change) and create an interface. This breaks any calls to the old logging method and forces you to update these calls to service calls. After the solution is building again, use the refactoring tools to change the method name in the interface back to LogMessage, and this time, allow Visual Studio to propagate that change throughout the application.

> ### ▪ NOTE
>
> Sometimes what not to test is just as important as what you should test. For example, when we write a test for the logger itself, we test to make sure the messages are actually written to the disk. This is contained in an integration test. When testing code that uses the logger, however, test only to ensure that the logger was called. Do not try to test for a message that was written to the disk. As long as you can prove that the logger received the Log method call, you can rest assured that the message was logged as appropriate.

Tracking Session Information

As much as we resist having global session information available, it is sometimes unavoidable. There are some values that we need to have access to throughout the application. This is especially true when reengineering an existing application because older designs used global variables extensively. We cannot change this design all at once, so for the short term we need to move our global variables somewhere that is more compatible with our service-oriented architecture (SOA). This is where the SessionInformationService comes in. This service can obey the rules we've set forth for our architecture and at the same time provide access to the variables by all parts of the code. It also centralizes the global variables in a single place, making the eventual removal of the SessionInformationService easier.

When legacy systems use these global variables, they are often marked static. When moving to the session information service, this annotation can and should be removed. Static variables and methods cause many problems with modern applications and should be avoided (the only exception to this is the ServiceLocator, which must be a static class).

Please keep in mind that we do not advocate the validity of a global information store. During the reengineering effort, creating such a service is usually necessary to decouple some components while the reengineering effort is underway. If you architect a reengineered application correctly, this class grows large through the first half of the reengineering effort as you move the legacy global variables into the service, and then shrink down again as your structure improves and the global variables are no longer needed. Ideally, this class is deleted after the reengineering effort is complete and all global variables have been moved to other places.

Refactoring for Session Information

Fortunately, it is relatively easy to implement a Session Information service. We call ours `ApplicationSession`. This class is a service that typically provides little functionality; it is just a holding place for global data to be accessed by different components. It often just has a series of properties of various types and no logic inside.

Implementing this service couldn't be easier. Just create a class with the proper parameters, attach an appropriate interface, and register it with your Dependency Injection container as a singleton. It can then be resolved anywhere necessary and the values updated when appropriate.

> **▪ NOTE**
>
> One potential problem with the session information service is how your application handles login and logout logic. If your application shuts down when a user logs out, this service should work well. If you allow one user to log out and another to log in without the application closing, you have to refresh your session information service with a new copy. Our `ApplicationSession` looks like Listing 11.10.

LISTING 11.10: An ApplicationSession Service

```
using System;
using CodeSamples.Ch10_EstablishFoundation.Listing04;

namespace CodeSamples.Ch11_RefactorToBasicServices.Listing10
{
  public class BusinessLogic
  {
    public void SampleCallToApplicationSession()
```

```
    {
      var svc = ServiceLocator.Resolve<IApplicationSession>();
      var usrName = svc.UserName;
    }
  }


  /// <summary>
  /// This class that contains application session
  /// information, which may
  /// be used throughout the application.
  /// </summary>
  public class ApplicationSession : IApplicationSession
  {
    /// <summary>
    /// Holds the username for the currently logged in user.
    /// </summary>
    public string UserName { get; internal set; }

    /// <summary>
    /// Holds the ID for the customer currently logged in.
    /// </summary>
    public Guid CurrentCustomerId { get; internal set; }

    public ApplicationSession()
    {
      //This is where data would be populated, possibly
      //from the database or other permanent store.
      UserName = "CurrentUser";
      CurrentCustomerId = Guid.NewGuid();
    }
  }

  public interface IApplicationSession
  {
    string UserName { get; }
    Guid CurrentCustomerId { get; }
  }

}
```

This is just a sample; your implementation will be much different and probably hold much more information. Change this class at will to meet your needs.

The easiest way to implement this service is to first find a global variable in your code that you need to remove. Copy the variable into a property of the service and also add it to the interface. Now delete the original legacy variable and try to build. You should be able to repair any build errors by simply replacing the legacy reference with a call to our new service.

Accessing Resources the SOA Way

Resources for an application have always been difficult to work with. Managing the images and text required for a nice UI is time-consuming and unrewarding work. Additionally, if you have many images in the application, they can slow down the build and make things generally unwieldy. To add to the problem, the .NET ResourceManager can be difficult to use in a decoupled fashion. Reengineering the resources for a legacy application can be particularly difficult because when the legacy applications were initially designed, there were rarely any accepted ways of accessing assets. Therefore, there are many different ways that such functionality is implemented.

This is a problem that SOA can help with. Once the ServiceLocator is installed in your application, resolving a resource image or text or anything else can be as simple as getting a service reference and asking for the item.

The resource provider is a service that accepts requests for strings, icons, pictures, and other application resources that are needed. It retrieves these resources out of its local store and returns them to the caller without the caller being concerned about where they came from. This is in contrast to the built-in ResourceManager, which must be told by the caller where to find the resources.

Take a look at the code for the ResourceProvider in Listing 11.11. This is a simple wrapper around the built-in ResourceManager, but it enhances the ResourceManager in several ways.

LISTING 11.11: The Code for Resource Provider

```
using System;
using System.Drawing;
using System.Reflection;
using System.Resources;
using CodeSamples.Ch10_EstablishFoundation.Listing04;
```

```
namespace CodeSamples.Ch11_RefactorToBasicServices.Listing11
{
  public class ResourceProvider : IResourceProvider
  {
    internal Assembly _currAssembly;

    /// <summary>
    /// Value to return if the requested string is not found.
    /// </summary>
    public string MissingStringValue { get; set; }

    /// <summary>
    /// Value to return if the requested Icon is not found.
    /// </summary>
    public Icon MissingIconValue { get; set; }

    /// <summary>
    /// Value to return if the requested Image is not found.
    /// </summary>
    public Image MissingImageValue { get; set; }

    internal ResourceManager ResourceMgr
    {
      get
      {
        return _resourceMgr ??
          (_resourceMgr = new ResourceManager(
          "Resources.Resource1", _currAssembly));
      }
    }
    internal ResourceManager _resourceMgr;

    public ResourceProvider()
    {
      _currAssembly = Assembly.GetExecutingAssembly();
    }

    /// <summary>
    /// Returns a resource identified by the given name.  If the
➥resource
    /// is not found, it will make an attempt to return something
➥useful.
    /// </summary>
    public T GetResource<T>(string pName) where T : class
    {
      var obj = ResourceMgr.GetObject(pName) as T;
      if (obj != null) return obj;

      return HandleObjectNotFoundError<T>(pName);
```

```csharp
    }

    private T HandleObjectNotFoundError<T>(string pName) where T : class
    {
      if (typeof(T) == typeof(string))
      {
        if (MissingStringValue == null)
          throw new ArgumentOutOfRangeException(
            "String resource not found " + pName);
        return MissingStringValue as T;
      }

      if (typeof(T) == typeof(Icon))
      {
        if (MissingIconValue == null)
          throw new ArgumentOutOfRangeException(
            "Icon resource not found " + pName);
        return MissingIconValue as T;
      }

      if (typeof(T) == typeof(Image))
      {
        if (MissingImageValue == null)
          throw new ArgumentOutOfRangeException(
            "Image resource not found " + pName);
        return MissingImageValue as T;
      }

      throw new ArgumentException("Unsupported object type " +
➥typeof(T));
    }
  }


  public interface IResourceProvider
  {
    T GetResource<T>(string pName) where T : class;
    string MissingStringValue { get; set; }
    Icon MissingIconValue { get; set; }
    Image MissingImageValue { get; set; }
  }

  public class ResourceProviderExample
  {
    public ResourceProviderExample()
    {
      var svc = ServiceLocator.Resolve<IResourceProvider>();
      svc.MissingStringValue = "missing string value";
    }
```

```
    public string GetStringResourceExample()
    {
      var svc = ServiceLocator.Resolve<IResourceProvider>();
      return svc.GetResource<string>("String resource name");
    }
  }
}
```

Let's start looking at this code with the three properties at the top. These three properties contain the values that the service should return if the requested resource does not exist. Adding these properties allows the calling code to assume that something valid is always returned. This is useful in applications that require images to enhance their appearance, but you do not want the application to throw an exception if the image does not exist for some reason. You can simply add a value for the MissingImageValue property, and that will be returned to the caller if the requested image does not exist.

Next let's look at the on-demand property ResourceMgr. This opens the current assembly and creates a ResourceManager to do the actual work of retrieving the resources. For simplicity, we assume that all resources are contained in the current project, but this can easily be changed if necessary.

> **■ NOTE**
>
> Those building applications that must handle multiple languages will notice this implementation of the ResourceProvider does not handle the case properly. Enhancing for multiple languages is not difficult, however, and is left as an exercise for the reader.

The GetResource method is where all the magic happens. It makes a call to the embedded resource to get the resource that has been requested. We then cast the returned object as the appropriate type and return it. We have made this method generic to save the caller the trouble of trying to cast the object to the proper type.

If the object returned is a null, we handle the error by examining the type of object requested to see whether we should return a default value. If no default value is specified, we throw an exception.

In the last class shown in Listing 11.11, we see an example of how to use our new resource provider. If we want to specify the value to return when a resource is missing, we simply resolve the provider as is done in the constructor. Resolving a resource is a simple method call specifying the type of resource we want and the name. This resource provider can now be mocked to return any value (even the "missing" value) and your calling code tested appropriately to ensure it can handle the various values properly.

Refactoring for ResourceProvider

The concept behind the `ResourceProvider` is the same as for any other service. It provides a service to the rest of the application by granting access to standard strings and images, and it is unaffected by the state of the application, so regardless of when a caller asks for a particular resource, the same one is always returned. However, the details here are different. This service typically goes in a project by itself while the interface for the `ResourceProvider` still lives in the Interfaces project like the other interfaces.

This service is put into a project by itself for several reasons. Projects with a lot of images can take a long time to build. However, in a mature system, they rarely change, so spending the time to build them can be unnecessary. When a standard build is requested, Visual Studio is smart enough to build only projects that have changed, but there are times when a full rebuild is required. This is particularly true in large systems or on projects with a lot of team members where the rapid pace of change can cause Visual Studio to get out of sync. By separating the Resources project on its own, in large projects, you can create a solution that contains only this one project and only when necessary. The main solution does not contain the source code for this project, just a link to the DLL. This introduces the extra overhead of remembering to load a different solution when working with resources, but this price is often worth the improved build times and responsiveness of the IDE.

A separate project can also be advantageous when you need to significantly customize your application for separate clients. You can create two projects called `ResourcesClient1` and `ResourcesClient2` where they share

ResourceProvider code. Simply replacing the necessary images and text in the proper resource project and then sending the proper DLL when distributing the application can make this multi-customer-targeting much easier.

To implement the ResourceProvider, scan your legacy code for a string that identifies a resource, such as ".ico," ".bmp," and so on. You should find code that tries to read the specified resource from a disk file and probably other code that handles the case where the resource does not exist. All of that code can be replaced by the simple call to the ResourceProvider.

We added some error-handling features to the provider to minimize the impact of a missing resource. The caller can set a value to use as a default in case a resource is missing. With this approach, if a resource is missing, at least the application continues to function, though it may have an "under construction" image instead of the proper one.

Using a Message Aggregator

One of the main points of all the work we are doing here is to make the classes in our application more loosely integrated. To achieve this, we want to limit the hard references any class has to another class. However, this goal does not reduce the need for different classes to communicate. This is where a message aggregator (also known as an EventAggregator) comes in.

A message aggregator provides a publish and subscribe mechanism that enables two classes to communicate without having references to each other. One of the classes acts as a publisher while one or more other classes act as the subscriber. The two classes agree on a message type to be used to communicate, and then the message aggregator receives this message type from the publisher and delivers to the subscriber(s) without either class knowing anything about the other.

This description makes the message aggregator sound like a regular event, and indeed it is. Messages can be used in place of events if desired, but the indirection provided by messaging can be a hindrance in the wrong situation. As a general rule, if a class already has a direct reference to another class, then use events for communication. If there is no direct reference, use messaging.

Refactoring for MessageAggregator

Because we are basing our work on Prism, there is an `EventAggregator` provided for us with all the functionality we need, as demonstrated in Listing 11.12. Our message aggregator subclasses the `EventAggregator` but adds no additional functionality. We do this just in case we need to add functionality to it later. By adding our own class into the hierarchy, we make it easier to control the way the aggregator grows and changes to meet our needs.

Using a message aggregator is not nearly as easy as creating one. Listing 11.12 shows you how to create and use a `MessageAggregator`.

LISTING 11.12: **A MessageAggregator Example**

```
using System;
using CodeSamples.Ch10_EstablishFoundation.Listing04;
using Microsoft.Practices.Prism.Events;

namespace CodeSamples.Ch11_RefactorToBasicServices.Listing12
{

  public interface IMessageAggregator : IEventAggregator
  {
  }

  /// <summary>
  /// Provides messaging services for the application.
  /// </summary>
  public class MessageAggregator : EventAggregator, IMessageAggregator
  {
    // This is an extension point for the Prism EventAggregator.  It
➥allows
    // us to enhance the EventAggregator later if necessary without
➥having
    // to change any calling code.
  }

  /// <summary>
  /// DTO class that carries the payload for a status message.
  /// </summary>
  public class StatusMessageDto
  {
    public StatusMessageDto(string pMsg)
    {
      Message = pMsg;
    }
```

```csharp
      //Put any kind of relevant information here that is necessary.
      public string Message { get; set; }
    }



    /// <summary>
    /// Container class that organizes all the messages for the system.
    /// </summary>
    public class MessageEvents
    {
      /// <summary>
      /// This message is used when the caller wants to set app status.
      /// </summary>
      public class StatusMessage : CompositePresentationEvent
➥<StatusMessageDto>
      {
      }
    }


    public class MessageAggregatorExample
    {
      /// <summary>
      /// This publishes a message to all subscribers.
      /// </summary>
      public void PublishMessage()
      {
        var msgAgg = ServiceLocator.Resolve<IMessageAggregator>();
        var msg = msgAgg.GetEvent<MessageEvents.StatusMessage>();
        var dto = new StatusMessageDto("Hello World");
        msg.Publish(dto);
      }


      /// <summary>
      /// This listens for publications having the given message type.
      /// </summary>
      public void SimpleSubscription()
      {
        var msgAgg = ServiceLocator.Resolve<IMessageAggregator>();
        var msg = msgAgg.GetEvent<MessageEvents.StatusMessage>();
        var subscriptionToken = msg.Subscribe(SetApplicationStatus);
      }


      /// <summary>
      /// This listens for publications having the given message type
      /// and filters to only those starting with the word "Hello".
      /// </summary>
      public void FilteredSubscription()
      {
        var msgAgg = ServiceLocator.Resolve<IMessageAggregator>();
```

```
    var msg = msgAgg.GetEvent<MessageEvents.StatusMessage>();
    msg.Subscribe(

        //Method to call with payload.
        SetApplicationStatus,

        //Thread to use for the subscription.
        ThreadOption.PublisherThread,

        //Strong reference flag.
        false,

        //Filter for the message.
        pParam => pParam.Message.StartsWith("Hello"));
    }

    /// <summary>
    /// Process the message as appropriate.
    /// </summary>
    public void SetApplicationStatus(StatusMessageDto pStatusMessage)
    {
        Console.WriteLine(pStatusMessage.Message);
    }


    }
}
```

Listing 11.12 shows the infrastructure necessary for any module anywhere in the application to write a message to the status bar on the main shell. This is a common need for applications and has always been something overly difficult to do. Let's start at the top and work our way down.

The first classes we see are the `MessageAggregator` and its interface, which adds nothing to the base `EventAggregator` Prism provides.

The next class is `StatusMessageDto`, which is simply a data transfer object that is meant to carry any information necessary to make the message meaningful. This class can contain literally anything, so enhance it as necessary. In the example, we need only the string that should be written to the status bar on the shell.

The next class is the `MessageEvents` class, with a subclass called `StatusMessage`. Use this structure because it groups messages into a single place that is easy to find. By the time your system is reengineered to use the message aggregator, you will have many messages to reflect the plethora of topics the modules need to discuss. Placing all these messages under MessageEvents allows developers to easily see the list of messages available to choose from and pick the appropriate one. There is no technical reason to use this container class structure, however, so if it does not appeal to you, everything will still function properly.

> ### ◾ NOTE
>
> It is easy for the number of messages in a system to get out of control. On a large team, developers tend to create new messages for their own purposes instead of reusing existing messages, resulting in duplication and confusion. The architect should keep an eye on the messages that are created to ensure they represent truly unique messages and information.

We declare the StatusMessage class to be a subclass of the Composite PresentationEvent<>. This is required by the EventAggregator to send the message properly. We make the message specify the StatusMessageDto so it contains the proper information for the message.

Now that we have the message type, we can get to the real coding effort of creating the publish and subscribe logic. The first method in the example shows how to publish a message with the MessageAggregator. We resolve a reference to the service just like normal, and then we use that reference to get a reference to the specific message we want to send. This reference is what we use to publish our message to all subscribers. If you publish the same message multiple times, you can use the same message object in all Publish calls.

So now we have published our message to all subscribers, but note that we do not know whether there are any subscribers out there listening. This Publish method gives no feedback to the publisher. This is by design. Publishers should not know and not care if there are any subscribers. They publish the necessary information and continue processing.

Now let's look at how to subscribe to a message. The SimpleSubscription method shows how to subscribe to a message using the MessageAggregator. Note that this has to be done only once, and the subscription continues until the subscriber goes out of scope and the garbage collector cleans up the memory. The Subscribe method returns a subscription token that can be used to unsubscribe from the message later if necessary.

The subscription process is similar to the publication process, where we get a reference to the aggregator via the ServiceLocator and then get the message we are interested in. Using the message, we subscribe to have all messages sent to a method of we choose (SetApplicationStatus in this example). Note that the parameter passed to SetApplicationStatus is the DTO that we created, not the message object itself.

The FilteredSubscription method shows another signature for the subscription that is worth noting because it allows more flexibility. This example is more complicated, but you probably need to use it more often than the simple version. The first parameter is just the method to call when a message is received. The second enables you to choose what thread to handle the subscription on. The options are as follows:

- PublisherThread receives the event on the publishers' thread. This is the default setting.
- BackgroundThread asynchronously receives the event on a .NET Framework thread-pool thread.
- UIThread receives the event on the user interface thread.

The third parameter is the strong reference flag, which indicates whether the aggregator should hold a weak or strong reference to the subscription. By default, the aggregator holds a weak reference to the subscription, which means if the module the subscription lives in ever goes out of scope and is garbage collected, the subscription is removed. Depending on how you structure the modules in your application, this can cause many headaches as it appears that the subscription sometimes works and sometimes doesn't. Specifically, it works in debug because Visual Studio itself keeps a reference to the module, keeping it in memory. However, when running outside the debugger, it appears the subscription does not work.

Setting this flag to true forces the message aggregator to hold a strong reference to the message handler. However, this can lead to memory leaks because the module where the message handler lives can never be garbage collected, so be cautious when using this flag.

The last parameter is a filter that is applied at the aggregator before your handler method is called. This filter should be used instead of having a filter in the message handler because adding the filter to the subscription causes it to run in the aggregator, not in the message handler. This can help speed up message handling because the aggregator does not have to send the message to the handler, which can potentially be across threads. Marshaling messages across threads is an expensive process that should be avoided when possible.

Converting Static Classes

After introducing the aforementioned services, there is another step that is necessary in this phase of the project. We need to convert any static classes into services so they can be properly used and tested.

When working with legacy systems, you will probably come across many classes and methods that are marked as static. Before Dependency Injection, static classes were an acceptable and easy way of creating singletons for an application. Static classes and methods, however, present difficult problems in modern architecture.

The main problem that concerns using static classes with a Dependency Injection container is that you cannot put an interface on a static class. In fact, it is not possible to register a static class with a DI container. Therefore, any calls to the static class are tightly coupled. Fortunately, static classes are just a syntactic way of creating a singleton, which we know how to do with our DI container.

> **▪ NOTE**
>
> A notable exception to the statement that we must refactor all static classes is a class containing an extension method. These classes should remain static.

Refactoring Static Classes

Review the sample in Listing 11.13 of a static class before and after refactoring into a service.

LISTING 11.13: Refactoring a Static Class

```
using CodeSamples.Ch10_EstablishFoundation.Listing04;

namespace CodeSamples.Ch11_RefactorToBasicServices.Listing13
{
  /// <summary>
  /// Static class before conversion to service.
  /// </summary>
  public static class StaticServiceClass
  {
    private static int _variable;

    public static void StaticMethodCall()
    {
      _variable++;
    }
  }

  /// <summary>
  /// Static class after conversion to service.
  /// </summary>
  public class NonStaticServiceClass : INonStaticServiceClass
  {
    private int _variable;

    public void NonStaticMethodCall()
    {
      _variable++;
    }
  }

  public interface INonStaticServiceClass
  {
    void NonStaticMethodCall();
  }

  public class ClassThatCallsStaticMethod
  {
    public void MethodCallingStaticClass()
    {
      //This is the old way of calling the method.
      StaticServiceClass.StaticMethodCall();
```

```
        //Replace the line above with this equivalent non-static call.
        var svc = ServiceLocator.Resolve<INonStaticServiceClass>();
        svc.NonStaticMethodCall();
    }
  }
}
```

Refactoring a static into a singleton begins with removing the Static keyword from the class, variables, and all methods. We then add an interface that exposes the public methods.

Note that logic still works because the _variable is a class global variable and we now work with an instance of the class instead of a static.

After registering this new service and interface with your DI container as a singleton, when you build the application, you find errors in all the places that the service is used as a static. Replace these static calls with ServiceLocator calls, as demonstrated the last method call in Listing 11.13.

Making this simple replacement throughout the system completes the conversion of a static class to a nonstatic singleton.

Summary

In this chapter, we looked at how to start refactoring your application toward an SOA. We removed or replaced many of the common coding concepts that make an application tightly coupled, enabling our application to be much more easily updated and tested. By changing the way we interact with the user, log errors, and track global information, we have begun breaking apart the pieces of our application to make it more flexible.

In the next chapter, we tackle some of the more difficult problems in reengineering a legacy system.

◗12◖
Advanced Refactoring to Services

When reengineering from a legacy system to the new architecture, some parts of the process take more time and planning. This chapter reviews these parts. Each of these tasks takes a significant effort to complete, sometimes spanning several days or even weeks depending on the size of the application.

Most of the refactoring can safely be done while the system is still being released. In other words, if one of these changes is introduced when the time comes to release the application, it does not have to hold up the release. The changes do not have a detrimental effect. When a task is so complicated or involved that it must be done all at once, we point this out.

The first thing we discuss is the repository pattern.

Using a Repository Pattern

The repository pattern provides a data access layer that can shield your business logic from the necessity of understanding the data layer. It is basically a service that executes the data interaction necessary for the whole application. Using a repository pattern, data access can be localized so that any details of the table structure, stored procedures, or anything else is hidden from code that needs to use it. This is an important service to implement because it can change a large percentage of tests from integration tests to unit tests.

We know that encapsulating functionality in a service is a key part of our testing and mocking strategy. By encapsulating all data access calls in a repository, we create a service that takes care of all database access for us by retrieving and saving all data. Once we have this functionality in a single service, it can be mocked in unit tests to fool the system under test into thinking it received any kind of data set we want to test.

Let's start our examples with a listing of a typical way for legacy software to access data (see Listing 12.1). Many legacy applications use ADO for their data access, so we assume that is where you are starting.

LISTING 12.1: Accessing Data with Legacy Software

```
using ADODB;

namespace CodeSamples.Ch12_RefactorToAdvancedServices.Listing01
{
  public class SecurityService
  {
    public bool ValidateUserPassword(int userId, string password)
    {
      var conn = new Connection();
      conn.ConnectionString = "connection string";
      conn.Open();

      var qryString = "select * from User where id = " + userId;

      var rs = new Recordset();
      rs.CursorLocation = CursorLocationEnum.adUseClient;
      rs.CursorType = CursorTypeEnum.adOpenForwardOnly;
      rs.LockType = LockTypeEnum.adLockOptimistic;
      rs.Open(conn, qryString);
      rs.ActiveConnection = null;

      //if locked out, fail
      if (rs.Fields["isLockedOut"].Value == "1") return false;

      //if password matches, succeed
      var validPW = (password == rs.Fields["password"].Value) ;

      //if last login was successful, no update needed
      var numBadLogins = int.Parse(rs.Fields["numBadLogins"].Value);
      var isLockedOut = int.Parse(rs.Fields["isLockedOut"].Value);
      if (validPW && numBadLogins == 0 && isLockedOut != 1) return true;
```

```
      //lock out user after 3 tries
      var updString = "update User set ";
      if (validPW)
      {
        updString += " numBadLogins = 0, isLockedOut = 0";
      }
      else
      {
        updString += " numBadLogins = numBadLogins + 1";
        if (numBadLogins >= 3)
          updString += " , isLockedOut = 1";
      }
      updString += " where id = " + userId;

      var cmd = new Command();
      cmd.CommandType = CommandTypeEnum.adCmdText;
      cmd.CommandText = updString;
      cmd.ActiveConnection = conn;
      object recordsAffected;
      cmd.Execute(out recordsAffected, null);

      return validPW;
    }

  }
}
```

In this example, we have a SecurityService that needs to validate a user password. Part of our business logic is that we lock the user out after three bad attempts at entering the password, so the code must retrieve the number of bad attempts and check it. Contained in this method is also the business logic to maintain the isLockedOut flag, the number of bad attempts, and so on.

With our business logic intermingled with the database access logic, there is no way to test this code without having a live database with the appropriate test data already set up. We have to use an integration test with three distinct user types set up in the database:

1. A valid user (not locked out, zero bad attempts)
2. A locked out user
3. A user with two bad attempts but not locked out

Maintaining this data is time-consuming, and it can easily get changed, breaking the tests. Notice that part of the testing should ensure that the num-BadLogins field and isLockedOut field are updated in the database, so even our integration test would change the data so that a second run would fail. Therefore, part of our tests would need to put all of our test data back again. This testing structure is so complicated and fragile, it will quickly be abandoned by the development team as unusable.

In the repository pattern, we move all the data access code into a service that can be resolved with the ServiceLocator. Listing 12.2 shows an example of using the repository to make data access calls. In this example, we moved the database access code out of the ValidateUserPassword method so that there are no queries or other specifics about what data is retrieved. All of the table and database details are encapsulated in the repository. The only database related code left in the ValidateUserPassword method is used to get access to the individual columns of the recordset.

LISTING 12.2: Legacy Code Refactored to Use a Repository

```
using ADODB;
using CodeSamples.Ch10_EstablishFoundation.Listing04;

namespace CodeSamples.Ch12_RefactorToAdvancedServices.Listing02
{
  public class SecurityService
  {
    public bool ValidateUserPassword(int userId, string password)
    {
      var repo = ServiceLocator.Resolve<IRepository>();
      var rs = repo.GetUserData(userId);

      //if locked out, fail
      if (rs.Fields["isLockedOut"].Value == "1") return false;

      //if password matches, succeed
      var validPW = (password == rs.Fields["password"].Value);

      //if last login was successful, no update needed
      var numBadLogins = int.Parse(rs.Fields["numBadLogins"].Value);
      var isLockedOut = int.Parse(rs.Fields["isLockedOut"].Value);
      if (validPW && numBadLogins == 0 && isLockedOut != 1) return true;

      //lock out user after 3 tries
      if (validPW)
      {
```

```
            rs.Fields["numBadLogins"].Value = 0;
            rs.Fields["isLockedOut"].Value = 0;
        }
        else
        {
            rs.Fields["numBadLogins"].Value = numBadLogins + 1;
            if (numBadLogins >= 3)
                rs.Fields["isLockedOut"].Value = 1;
        }
        repo.SaveUserData(rs);

        return false;
    }

}

public interface IRepository
{
    Recordset GetUserData(int userId);
    void SaveUserData(Recordset userData);
}

public class Repository : IRepository
{
    public Recordset GetUserData(int userId)
    {
        var conn = new Connection();
        conn.ConnectionString = "connection string";
        conn.Open();

        var qryString = "select * from User where id = " + userId;

        var rs = new Recordset();
        rs.CursorLocation = CursorLocationEnum.adUseClient;
        rs.CursorType = CursorTypeEnum.adOpenForwardOnly;
        rs.LockType = LockTypeEnum.adLockOptimistic;
        rs.Open(conn, qryString);
        rs.ActiveConnection = null;
        return rs;
    }

    public void SaveUserData(Recordset userData)
    {
        var updString = "update User set ";
        updString += " numBadLogins = " + userData.Fields[1].Value;
        updString += " ,isLockedOut = " + userData.Fields[2].Value;
        updString += " where id = " + userData.Fields[3].Value;

        var conn = new Connection();
```

```
      conn.ConnectionString = "connection string";
      conn.Open();

      var cmd = new Command();
      cmd.CommandType = CommandTypeEnum.adCmdText;
      cmd.CommandText = updString;
      cmd.ActiveConnection = conn;
      object recordsAffected;
      cmd.Execute(out recordsAffected, null);
    }
  }
}
```

Using the repository, the legacy code asks for the data it needs, and the repository (not the class itself), constructs the query and executes it against the database. The repository then returns the appropriate data, and the SecurityService operates on that data. This strategy separates the database access logic from the business logic, fixing the tight coupling between the database and our SecurityService. It also has little effect on the logic flow of the application, so it is easy to implement.

With a repository in place, it is much easier to test the business logic. By mocking the repository, we can arrange to return any dataset to the business logic, as shown in Listing 12.3.

LISTING 12.3: Tests for Legacy Code Refactored to Use a Repository

```
using ADODB;
using CodeSamples.Ch10_EstablishFoundation.Listing04;
using Microsoft.Practices.Unity;
using Microsoft.VisualStudio.TestTools.UnitTesting;
using Moq;

namespace CodeSamples.Ch11_RefactorToBasicServices.Listing05
{
  public class SecurityService
  {
    public bool ValidateUserPassword(int userId, string password)
    {
      var repo = ServiceLocator.Resolve<IRepository>();
      var rs = repo.GetUserData(userId);

      //if locked out, fail
      if (rs.Fields["isLockedOut"].Value == 1) return false;

      //if password matches, succeed
```

```
      var validPW = (password == rs.Fields["password"].Value);

      //if last login was successful, no update needed
      int numBadLogins = rs.Fields["rumBadLogins"].Value;
      int isLockedOut = rs.Fields["isLockedOut"].Value;
      if (validPW && numBadLogins == 0 && isLockedOut != 1) return true;

      //lock out user after 3 tries
      if (validPW)
      {
        rs.Fields["numBadLogins"].Value = 0;
        rs.Fields["isLockedOut"].Value = 0;
      }
      else
      {
        rs.Fields["numBadLogins"].Value = numBadLogins + 1;
        if (numBadLogins >= 3)
          rs.Fields["isLockedOut"].Value = 1;
      }
      repo.SaveUserData(rs);

      return false;
    }

}

public interface IRepository
{
  Recordset GetUserData(int userId);
  void SaveUserData(Recordset userData);
}

[TestClass]
public class SecurityServiceTestClass
{
  private SecurityService _svc;
  private Mock<IRepository> _mockRepo;

  [TestInitialize]
  public void TestInitialize()
  {
    _mockRepo = new Mock<IRepository>();
    ServiceLocator.Container = new UnityContainer();
    ServiceLocator.RegisterInstance<IRepository>(
      _mockRepo.Object);

    _svc = new SecurityService();
  }
```

```
[TestMethod]
public void ValidateUserPassword_WhenValidPassword_ReturnsTrue()
{
  //Arrange
  var rs = CreateNewUserRecordset();
  AddDataToUserRecordset(rs, 1, "password", 0, 0);
  _mockRepo.Setup(mr => mr.GetUserData(It.IsAny<int>()))
    .Returns(rs);

  //Act
  var result = _svc.ValidateUserPassword(1, "password");

  //assert
  Assert.IsTrue(result);
}

[TestMethod]
public void ValidateUserPassword_WhenBadPassword_ReturnsFalse()
{
  //Arrange
  var rs = CreateNewUserRecordset();
  AddDataToUserRecordset(rs, 1, "password", 0, 0);
  _mockRepo.Setup(mr => mr.GetUserData(It.IsAny<int>()))
    .Returns(rs);

  //Act
  var result = _svc.ValidateUserPassword(1, "badpassword");

  //assert
  Assert.IsFalse(result);
}

private void AddDataToUserRecordset(Recordset rs, int id,
  string password, int numBadLogins, int isLockedOut)
{
  rs.AddNew( );
  rs.Fields["id"].Value = id;
  rs.Fields["password"].Value = password;
  rs.Fields["numBadLogins"].Value = numBadLogins;
  rs.Fields["isLockedOut"].Value = isLockedOut;
}
private Recordset CreateNewUserRecordset()
{
  var rs = new Recordset();
  rs.CursorType = CursorTypeEnum.adOpenDynamic;
  rs.Fields.Append("id", DataTypeEnum.adInteger);
  rs.Fields.Append("password", DataTypeEnum.adVarChar, 250);
  rs.Fields.Append("numBadLogins", DataTypeEnum.adInteger);
  rs.Fields.Append("isLockedOut", DataTypeEnum.adInteger);
```

```
        rs.Open();
        return rs;
    }

  }
}
```

In the test class, you can see that we created a mock of the Repository service and registered that with our ServiceLocator. This enables us to change the results that the SecurityService receives, allowing us to create any database results we want.

In the first test method, we validate that we get a True value returned when we pass in a valid password. In the test, we create a valid recordset on the fly that contains the data we wish, including the password we want to verify. We set up the mock repository to return the dataset we've created when the SecurityService requests data. We can now verify that this method properly compares the incoming password with the one in the database.

If you look closely at the ValidateUserPassword method in the SecurityService you will notice that this test has exposed the first defect. Though the code compiled successfully with this line in Listing 12.2, as noted in the following, this is actually an error:

```
if (rs.Fields["isLockedOut"].Value == "1") return false;
```

The isLockedOut data field is defined as an integer, and we try to compare it to a string, which throws an exception at runtime. If you look at the same line in Listing 12.3, you will notice we have changed it to this:

```
if (rs.Fields["isLockedOut"].Value == 1) return false;
```

Continuing with the example, the second test method verifies we returned a false if a bad password was submitted to the SecurityService.

Creating a Repository with a Domain Model

The example we just saw is for a legacy system with no domain model. The process for creating a repository for an application that has a domain model is similar. Let's assume the legacy system is using some sort of Object

Relational Modeling tool (ORM), such as Entity Framework, NHibernate, or IdeaBlade. These tools provide a way of using Linq to query the database, and then return domain model entities that represent a row in the database. They each behave in roughly the same way, requiring that a data context be used for accessing the database. For our code examples, we assume Entity Framework. Listing 12.4 shows the domain model for the legacy system.

LISTING 12.4: An Example of an Application Domain Model

```csharp
using System;
using System.Data.Entity;

namespace CodeSamples.Ch12_RefactorToAdvancedServices.Listing04
{
  public class ReengineeringEntities : DbContext
  {
    public ReengineeringEntities()
      : base("MyConnectionString")
    {
    }

    public DbSet<Address> Addresses { get; set; }
    public DbSet<Person> People { get; set; }
  }

  public class Address : BaseEntity
  {
    public int Id { get; set; }
    public string Address1 { get; set; }
    public string Address2 { get; set; }
    public string City { get; set; }
    public string State { get; set; }
    public string Zip { get; set; }
  }

  public class Person : BaseEntity
  {
    public int Id { get; set; }
    public string FirstName { get; set; }
    public string LastName { get; set; }
    public DateTime BirthDate { get; set; }
    public string Email { get; set; }
    public int Age
    {
      get
```

```
      {
        DateTime now = DateTime.Today;
        int age = now.Year - BirthDate.Year;
        if (BirthDate > now.AddYears(-age)) age--;
        return age;
      }
    }
    public Address HomeAddress { get; set; }
    public DateTime DateJoined { get; set; }
    public bool MembershipCancelled { get; set; }
  }

  public abstract class BaseEntity
  {
    public DateTime CreatedDate { get; set; }
    public DateTime UpdatedDate { get; set; }
  }
}
```

This is a typical declaration of the database contexts used to query a database in Entity Framework. We declare a class that descends from DbContext (this comes from the EntityFramework DLL), and we list the entities included in our model. Note that we assume you use EF Code First, which means you create the entity classes by hand and then include them in the DbContext. We do this for clarity only, not because this method is superior to the other ways of generating a model in EF. The important thing is that the model exists.

Let's assume we have a task to email coupons to those who have just joined our website. In our legacy system, this context is used in the fashion demonstrated in Listing 12.5.

LISTING 12.5: Legacy Code to Send Coupons to New Users

```
using System;
using System.Linq;
using CodeSamples.Ch12_RefactorToAdvancedServices.Listing04;

namespace CodeSamples.Ch12_RefactorToAdvancedServices.Listing05
{

  public class CouponDistributor
  {
    private ReengineeringEntities _context;
```

```csharp
  public CouponDistributor()
  {
    _context = new ReengineeringEntities();
  }

  public void SendCouponToNewUsers(string pFirstName)
  {
    var people = (from p in _context.People
                  where p.DateJoined == DateTime.Today
                        && p.MembershipCancelled == false
                  select p);
    foreach (var person in people)
    {
      EmailCoupon(person);
    }
  }

  public void EmailCoupon(Person pPerson)
  {
    //code to send coupon goes here
  }
  }
}
```

There are several things to note here. Our database context is created within the class that uses it. The query to get all newly joined members is constructed in the method where the data is needed, and then the resulting dataset is acted upon. This is a poor design because we cannot test the SendCouponToNewUsers method without connecting to a real database with test data.

To reengineer this class, you first create the repository service and add the appropriate code to make a connection to the database. Listing 12.6 presents an example of the repository that uses Entity Framework to access the database.

LISTING 12.6: Creating a Repository Using a Domain Model

```csharp
using System;
using System.Linq;
using CodeSamples.Ch12_RefactorToAdvancedServices.Listing04;

namespace CodeSamples.Ch12_RefactorToAdvancedServices.Listing06
{
  public class Repository : IRepository
  {
```

```
  private ReengineeringEntities _context;

  public Repository()
  {
    _context = new ReengineeringEntities();
  }

  public IQueryable<Person> GetRecentlyJoinedUsers()
  {
    var people = (from p in _context.People
                  where p.DateJoined == DateTime.Today
                    && p.MembershipCancelled == false
                  select p);
    return people;
  }
}

public interface IRepository
{
  IQueryable<Person> GetRecentlyJoinedUsers();
}
}
```

In the repository, we create a method that retrieves the recently joined users. Doing this in the repository instead of in the business logic hides the logic of the query inside the repository so the individual business logic is not required to know how to query it. This is a real advantage because it would be easy for the calling code to forget to check the MembershipCancelled flag and issue coupons to members who signed up today but immediately cancelled their memberships.

You might notice that we do not use the ServiceLocator to create our database context. This is because we do not want the context used directly by any other part of the system. By putting an interface in front of the context and adding it to the ServiceLocator, we enable the rest of the application to bypass the repository and use the context directly.

We can now refactor the original code to use this repository for its data access, as demonstrated in Listing 12.7.

LISTING 12.7: A Reengineered Coupon Distributor Using a Repository

```
using CodeSamples.Ch10_EstablishFoundation.Listing04;
using CodeSamples.Ch12_RefactorToAdvancedServices.Listing04;
using CodeSamples.Ch12_RefactorToAdvancedServices.Listing06;
```

```
namespace CodeSamples.Ch12_RefactorToAdvancedServices.Listing07
{

  public class CouponDistributor
  {

    public void SendCouponToNewUsers(string pFirstName)
    {
      var repo = ServiceLocator.Resolve<IRepository>();
      var people = repo.GetRecentlyJoinedUsers();
      foreach (var person in people)
      {
        EmailCoupon(person);
      }
    }

    public void EmailCoupon(Person pPerson)
    {
      //code to send coupon goes here
    }
  }

}
```

Notice that the data context is now gone; we don't need it because we can use the repository for our data needs.

With this final change, we are done converting this class to use a repository. You can see that we changed the business logic very little. We still get the same set of classes to manipulate, and we execute the same commands against those entities. The only thing that has changed is where these queries are executed. This change, however, has opened many new possibilities for unit testing the application because we can now mock the repository to return any dataset we want to exercise our method.

Reengineering Methods to a Repository

For each individual method that we reengineer to use a repository, the process is simple and easy to test manually. Converting an entire application to use a repository is normally a large effort that can take days or weeks. The good news is that if a release date comes up during the reengineering effort, the product can be released with the repository only halfway in place. If done correctly, reengineering to a repository does not change the business logic at all.

As the conversion is being done, some methods become candidates for unit tests as the repository is extracted. It is a good idea to introduce those unit tests immediately to take advantage of the additional quality assurance they offer as soon as possible. This adds to the already long timeline for converting to a repository, but it is worth it.

Another approach to reengineering to a repository is not to refactor the entire application to use a repository all at once, but to wait and refactor as necessary when classes need other work done. Technically, this approach is just as effective as a concerted conversion effort, but in practice, doing this means the repository conversion is often neglected due to time pressure for the feature or defect change request. For example, if someone is fixing a defect on a class that is not converted to use your repository, it is common to put off the conversion because the defect is too important to be held up by the repository conversion.

Converting Existing Code to Use a Domain Model

For those who are working with a legacy system without a domain model, the next step is to introduce the domain model along with your choice of ORM tool. Using a domain model and ORM has many advantages, but this endeavor should be planned carefully. Trying to reengineer to a domain model is a difficult and time-consuming task when migrating a legacy system to modern technology. It affects a large portion of the application, requiring extensive refactoring of the business logic to use the new entities.

Following is a brief description of the process, assuming you have already migrated to the repository pattern as previously described. Having a repository that uses ADO makes the process of converting to a domain model easier.

1. Create the model project and entity classes for the ORM either by generating from the database or by writing by hand.

   Opting to "roll your own" ORM is not a sensible decision with the number of high-quality ORM products on the market (some free).

There is a lot of tedious work moving data around to implement an ORM, and the maintenance of this code is time-consuming and error-prone.

2. Choose a single repository method to convert to the new domain model and change the return type of the method to return the proper domain entity. Also change the logic inside the repository method to properly query the database.

3. Fix the build breaks resulting from changing the return type to a domain entity. This involves editing a lot of code to set values in your entity instead of in the Recordset. This is the part that will take the majority of the time and produce the most defects.

4. Ensure that any time the ADO data is saved, the repository Save method is also called. This is a key point and often causes problems during this type of conversion. Forgetting to save the changed data via the repository at the same time as data is saved via ADO can result in erroneous data in the database and a lot of debugging time. There are several potential problems with this step, which are outlined later.

5. Test thoroughly!

6. Choose another method to convert and continue.

There are many problems that can occur during this process, and they are not easily handled. For example, in ADO the queries are able to return multiple data sets in a single ADO query. This is not possible with any ORM. If the legacy code relies on this feature of ADO, then appropriate measures must be taken to fix the code to issue multiple queries instead.

Another problem that can arise is in saving. ORMs usually contain a cache of changed data that is saved all in one step. Unless you create different caches, all changes that are made to data are saved at once. Using ADO, the changes are saved one table at a time, thus opening the possibility of business logic that can decide not to save particular data. If the logic exists in the legacy application to save some data and not others, it must be removed to be compatible with an ORM.

Another problem with saving part of the data via ADO and part via ORM has to do with data relationships and foreign keys in the database. Suppose there is a master-detail relationship between tables A and B, and another similar relationship between B and C. Converting any repository methods that create rows in table B can cause foreign key conflicts if the proper master row is not yet available.

If the legacy code uses any ADO events, those must also be removed because these events typically have no equivalent in the ORM. Any events on the DataTable, DataRow, or DataColumn types probably have to be removed and the appropriate logic put somewhere else in the system.

In summary, even though ORMs and domain models bring many advantages to your application, converting from ADO to a domain model is a significant amount of work. Making a generic recommendation in this book on whether that effort is worthwhile is not possible. You will have to weigh your own situation to determine whether there is sufficient value. All processes described in this book still work with an ADO-based repository.

Adding Data Validations to the Domain Model

Data validation is a way of ensuring that the data that gets stored into the database is valid before the code attempts to issue the query to store it. The compiler ensures that data in properties and methods is the correct type, but data validations are needed to ensure those values follow business rules. For example, a data validation ensures that the start date of a contract is before the end date.

For this discussion, we assume you have a domain model and repository in your application already. If you use ADO and have decided not to convert to a domain model, then validating ADO data tables needs to be done in custom methods for each data row. This is a manual process and specific to your implementation, so we do not review that approach here.

Validation is such a common problem that Microsoft has released a standard approach to doing it called the Microsoft Validation Block. This is an excellent way of adding validation to your domain model in a standard way. First let's look at a data entity and how the validations are implemented, as demonstrated in Listing 12.8.

LISTING 12.8: A Sample Domain Model with Validation Logic

```csharp
using System;
using Microsoft.Practices.EnterpriseLibrary.Validation;
using Microsoft.Practices.EnterpriseLibrary.Validation.Validators;

namespace CodeSamples.Ch12_RefactorToAdvancedServices.Listing08
{
  [HasSelfValidation]
  public class Person : BaseEntity
  {
    public int Id { get; set; }
    public string FirstName { get; set; }
    public string LastName { get; set; }
    public DateTime BirthDate { get; set; }
    public string Email { get; set; }
    public int Age
    {
      get
      {
        DateTime now = DateTime.Today;
        int age = now.Year - BirthDate.Year;
        if (BirthDate > now.AddYears(-age)) age--;
        return age;
      }
    }
    public DateTime DateJoined { get; set; }
    public bool MembershipCancelled { get; set; }

    [SelfValidation]
    public void Validation_LastName_IsNotNull(
      ValidationResults results)
    {
      if (string.IsNullOrEmpty(LastName))
        results.AddResult(CreateValidationResult(
          "Lastname cannot be null."));
    }

    private ValidationResult CreateValidationResult(string errMsg)
    {
      var v = new ValidationResult(errMsg, this,
        Id.ToString(), "Person", null);
      return v;
    }
  }

  public abstract class BaseEntity
  {
```

```
      public DateTime CreatedDate { get; set; }
      public DateTime UpdatedDate { get; set; }
  }
}
```

The first thing to notice here is the attribute on the name of the entity class. The [HasSelfValidation] is a flag indicating that the Validation Service (which we discuss in a moment) should check the entity for bad data.

Moving to the bottom of the class, you see another attribute called SelfValidation. The method name is not important because we won't call it, so it is convenient to begin with the word Validation and then describe what is being validated. The body of the method can contain any code necessary to ensure that the entity is valid. If invalid data is detected, simply add a new ValidationResult to the ValidationResults object that is passed in by the validation framework, and you are done. It's that simple. We added a helper method called CreateValidationResult simply to ensure that all validation results have similar properties.

To turn on validations in your application, we turn to the repository SaveChanges method, as demonstrated in Listing 12.9.

LISTING 12.9: An Example of How to Use a Validation Service in a Repository

```
using System;
using System.Collections;
using System.Collections.Generic;
using System.Data;
using System.Linq;
using CodeSamples.Ch10_EstablishFoundation.Listing04;
using CodeSamples.Ch12_RefactorToAdvancedServices.Listing04;
using Microsoft.Practices.EnterpriseLibrary.Validation;

namespace CodeSamples.Ch12_RefactorToAdvancedServices.Listing09
{
  public class Repository : IRepository
  {
    private ReengineeringEntities _context;
    private IValidationService ValidationSvc
    {
      get
      {
        return _validationSvc ??
```

```
            (_validationSvc = ServiceLocator.
➡Resolve<IValidationService>());
        }
    }
    private IValidationService _validationSvc;

    public Repository()
    {
        _context = new ReengineeringEntities();
    }

    /// <summary>
    /// Verifies all edited items, then saves
    /// all pending changes to the database
    /// </summary>
    public ValidationResults SaveChanges()
    {
        try
        {
            //Validate data and exit if invalid
            var results = Validate();
            if (!results.IsValid) return results;

            //Save changes to DB
            _context.SaveChanges();

            return results;
        }
        catch (Exception e)
        {
            //add logic to handle data save errors
            throw;
        }
    }

    /// <summary>
    /// Validates all changed entities in this Repository
    /// </summary>
    public ValidationResults Validate()
    {
        var entities = GetUpdatedItems();
        return ValidationSvc.Validate(entities);
    }

    /// <summary>
    /// Returns a list of all updated entities
    /// </summary>
    internal List<BaseEntity> GetUpdatedItems()
    {
        var allEntities = _context.ChangeTracker.Entries()
```

```
              .Where(e => e.State == EntityState.Added
                 || e.State == EntityState.Modified)
              .Select(e => e.Entity)
              .OfType<BaseEntity>().ToList();
           return allEntities;
        }


    }

    public class ValidationService : IValidationService
    {
       public ValidationResults Validate(ICollection objectsToValidate)
       {
          var validationResults = new ValidationResults();
          foreach (var obj in objectsToValidate)
          {
             var validator = ValidationFactory.CreateValidator(obj.
➥GetType());
             validationResults.AddAllResults(validator.Validate(obj));
          }
          return validationResults;
       }
    }

    public interface IRepository
    {
       ValidationResults SaveChanges();
       ValidationResults Validate();
    }

    public interface IValidationService
    {
       ValidationResults Validate(ICollection objectsToValidate);
    }



}
```

When the SaveChanges method is called (usually from a controller or view model), the first thing it does is validate updated entities by calling the ValidationService with a list of entities that are about to be saved to the database. We can see that we get a list of all changed entities (we ignore deleted entities because they do not need validation), and we call the ValidationService to validate each one. We then return the ValidationResults to the caller to decide how to inform the user that something is wrong in his data.

Our validation service is quite simple. It loops through all elements in the list of incoming edits and gets the list of validations from the `ValidationFactory` (provided by Microsoft in `Microsoft.Practices.EnterpriseLibrary.Validation`). Calling `validator.Validate` returns a list of all failed validations or an empty list if the entity has correct data. After cycling through all entities, we return the full list of validation errors to the caller.

That's all there is to validation using a domain model. Enhance your entities to have appropriate self-validation methods, and it should not be possible to get bad data into the database.

Reengineering Domain Models to Use Validations

Reengineering an existing domain model to use validations is easy. Simply add the `ValidationService` and update the `SaveChanges` method of the repository. These two changes have no effect on your application until the validations themselves are added to the entities.

After the `ValidationService` is in place, add appropriate logic to indicate to the user when a validation has failed. This is the most difficult, time-consuming, and error-prone part of introducing validations; however, you must give the user feedback to let him know the save did not happen and what he needs to do to fix the situation.

Finally, begin introducing the attributes and validation methods necessary to validate the methods. This can be done gradually or at once because it should not prohibit releasing the product when necessary.

Care should be taken to test what happens when existing errors in the data are exposed. For example, because data validations have not been done before, there might be bad data in the database that is flagged now that validations are enabled. The user must be able to fix this situation, or he might have to abandon his changes to get out of the application.

Using a Generic Object Manager

Quite often, you have a list of things that need to be tracked and made available to the rest of the application. For example, if you have more than one repository at a time (one for each view that is open), you might need to keep track of them to ensure they are shut down properly on application exit.

Tracking objects is something that a Dependency Injection container does well, but some containers (such as Unity) do not allow unregistering a type or instance. This can cause objects to hang around for the life of the application, causing unnecessary memory usage. As an alternative to using a DI container to manage limited lifetime objects, we can use a generic object manager that achieves the same purpose but is more flexible where we need it.

Our object manager supports two types of references: weak and strong. A strong reference to an object is what one normally thinks of when considering object references. It prevents the garbage collector from releasing the memory allocated to the object, so if all references to the object are removed except the one in the object manager, the object still remains in memory. A weak reference is one that enables the garbage collector to release the object's memory so if the object manager is the only thing that has a reference to the object (that is, nothing else in our application needs it anymore), it is released. Note that the object manager doesn't "need" any of the objects it manages. It simply keeps track of them for us. If one is removed due to garbage collection, it should not affect the object manager.

Let's begin the discussion by looking at the component parts that the object manager uses. We need to dereference the object a little by defining a small class that holds only a reference to the object we want to track, plus a little bit of additional information. This is a perfect application for a Data Transfer Object, or DTO.

Depending on whether you want a weak or strong reference to the objects, you need to create either a WeakReferenceDto or a StrongReferenceDto. Making this decision is a simple matter of analyzing the expected lifetime of the object. An example of an object manager that uses a strong reference is an object cache. If a particular object is expensive to create but is needed often and only for a short period, that object should be kept in a cache so that the system can reuse objects that are created. In this instance, an object that is not needed by any business logic code currently should not be garbage collected because we might have to provide a new one again. This is a perfect use of a strong reference object manager.

Listing 12.10 shows the code for both the weak reference and strong reference objects. For our object manager to treat them identically, we also introduce an interface for them.

LISTING 12.10: A Weak Reference DTO and a Strong Reference DTO

```csharp
using System;

namespace CodeSamples.Ch12_RefactorToAdvancedServices.Listing10
{
  public interface IObjectManagerReference<T> where T : class
  {
    T Object { get; }
    bool IsAlive { get; }
    string Name { get; }
  }

  public class StrongReferenceDto<T>
    : IObjectManagerReference<T> where T : class
  {
    public virtual T Object { get; internal set; }
    public virtual bool IsAlive { get { return true; } }
    public string Name { get; internal set; }
    public StrongReferenceDto(T pObject, string pName)
    {
      if (pObject == null) throw new ArgumentNullException("pObject");
      Object = pObject;
      Name = pName;
    }
  }

  public class WeakReferenceDto<T> :
    IObjectManagerReference<T> where T : class
  {
    private WeakReference _reference;

    public string Name { get; internal set; }
    public T Object
    {
      get { return _reference.Target as T; }
      internal set { _reference = new WeakReference(value); }
    }

    public bool IsAlive
    {
      get { return _reference.IsAlive; }
    }
```

```
    public WeakReferenceDto(T pObject, string pName)
    {
      if (pObject == null) throw new ArgumentNullException("pObject");
      Object = pObject;
      Name = pName;
    }
  }
}
```

This interface exposes three properties, the first of which is the object we are tracking. Because this is a generic interface, we can maintain type safety in our DTO and use the property easily.

The `IsAlive` property is a flag indicating whether the object referred to is still alive. For weak references, this returns false if the garbage collector has disposed of the object we reference without us knowing about it, or true if the object is still available for use. For strong references, this always returns true.

Finally, the `name` property is a unique name for the object. You use this name as the key for a dictionary, so it must be unique among all the objects managed.

In the `StrongReferenceDto` class, we implement the items in the interface in a straightforward way. We can also add a constructor that accepts all possible parameters so that we can easily create our DTO.

The `WeakReferenceDto` also implements the interface but adds different logic for the properties. A `WeakReference` is a special class that enables the garbage collector to dispose of the item referred to. Therefore, when assigning the object to the `Object` property, we must create a `WeakReference` to that object. Likewise, when referring to the `Object` property, we must return the `Target` of the weak reference, not the weak reference itself.

A `WeakReference` also contains a property called `IsAlive` that we must return when requested.

With our component objects in place, we can turn our attention to the object manager itself. See Listing 12.11.

LISTING 12.11: Implementation of a Generic Object Manager

```
using System;
using System.Collections.Generic;
using System.Linq;
using CodeSamples.Ch12_RefactorToAdvancedServices.Listing10;
```

```csharp
namespace CodeSamples.Ch12_RefactorToAdvancedServices.Listing11
{
  public interface IObjectManager<T> where T : class
  {
    T Register(T newObject, string objectName);
    T Get(string pObjectName, bool pIncludeInactive = true);
    T Register(IObjectManagerReference<T> pObjectReference);
    bool Remove(string pObjectName);
  }

  /// <summary>
  /// Manages all the objects registered with it
  /// while optionally allowing them to be garbage
  /// collected when appropriate.
  /// </summary>
  /// <remarks>
  /// There is a small memory leak here in that the Dto
  /// used to keep track of the weak reference items
  /// is not cleaned up when the item itself is.
  /// This could be extended to add a Cleanup method that will release
  /// unused DTOs but that is left as an exercise for you.
  /// </remarks>
  public class ObjectManager<T> : IObjectManager<T> where T : class
  {
    /// <summary>
    /// Indicator whether caller wants to use
    /// strong or weak references
    /// </summary>
    internal bool _useStrongReference;

    /// <summary>
    /// Items being managed
    /// </summary>
    internal Dictionary<string, IObjectManagerReference<T>> _items;

    /// <summary>
    /// Constructor
    /// </summary>
    public ObjectManager(bool pStrongReference = true)
    {
      _useStrongReference = pStrongReference;
      _items = new Dictionary<string, IObjectManagerReference<T>>();
    }

    /// <summary>
    /// Registers a new item with the manager
    /// and returns the registered item (to enable
    /// fluent interfaces)
    /// </summary>
```

```csharp
      public T Register(T pNewObject, string pObjectName)
      {
        if (_useStrongReference)
          return Register(new StrongReferenceDto<T>(pNewObject,
➥pObjectName));
          return Register(new WeakReferenceDto<T>(pNewObject, pObjectName));
      }


      /// <summary>
      /// Registers a new item with the manager
      /// and returns the registered item (to enable
      /// fluent interfaces)
      /// </summary>
      public T Register(IObjectManagerReference<T> pObjectReference)
      {
        if (pObjectReference.Object == null)
          throw new ArgumentNullException("pNewObject");
        if (string.IsNullOrEmpty(pObjectReference.Name))
          throw new ArgumentNullException("pObjectName");

        if (_items.ContainsKey(pObjectReference.Name))
          throw new ArgumentException(pObjectReference.Name
            + " key already exists.");

        _items.Add(pObjectReference.Name, pObjectReference);
        return pObjectReference.Object;
      }


      /// <summary>
      /// Returns the named item to the caller
      /// </summary>
      public T Get(string pObjectName, bool pIncludeInactive = true)
      {
        if (pIncludeInactive)
          return (from x in _items
                  where (x.Key.Equals(pObjectName))
                  select x.Value.Object).FirstOrDefault();

        return (from x in _items
                where (x.Value.IsAlive && x.Key.Equals(pObjectName))
                select x.Value.Object).FirstOrDefault();
      }

      /// <summary>
      /// Removes the first occurrence of the object from the manager
      /// </summary>
      /// <returns>
      /// True if item is successfully removed; otherwise, false.
      /// </returns>
```

```
    public bool Remove(string pObjectName)
    {
      //must be a valid name
      if (string.IsNullOrEmpty(pObjectName))
        throw new ArgumentNullException("pObjectName");

      //if we can't find the name, object is not in the list
      if (!_items.ContainsKey(pObjectName)) return true;

      return _items.Remove(pObjectName);
    }
  }
}
```

Let's start with the constructor, which takes a single optional parameter that determines what the default registration type is for the manager, either weak or strong. This sets a flag in the manager for which type of DTO to create when a new object is registered. This is only a default, however, because the manager provides a way for the caller to decide on an object-by-object basis whether the references are weak or strong. We look at this later in this chapter.

To register an object with the object manager, we use the `Register` method, which has two different signatures. The first accepts the object itself and the name to register it with. This signature uses the default reference type that was specified in the constructor to determine whether a weak or strong reference should be created.

The second signature accepts an `IObjectManagerReference<T>` from the caller, allowing the caller to decide whether each object should have a weak or strong reference. This method is the one that does the actual work of validating the incoming reference and adding the reference to the internal dictionary. To enable a fluent interface, we return the object that was passed in.

After we register an object, we can later retrieve it again with the `Get` method. The logic in this method should be clear. It simply uses the dictionary to look up the object name and returns the object registered by that name. The flag for including inactive items is applicable only when the manager uses weak references. When using strong references, the reference is always active, so the method returns the same result set. If the `includeInactive` flag is set to true for weak references and the object has been garbage collected, a `null` is returned to the caller.

As discussed before, the advantage of an object manager over a DI container is the capability to remove objects from management. The `Remove` method accepts the object name and removes that object from the dictionary. For strong references, this enables the garbage collector to reclaim the memory, and for weak references it can be used to clean up the list of old references that are no longer needed.

Simplifying Complex Code with a Command Dispatcher Service

Another useful service for reengineering is the command dispatcher, which has its roots in the Strategy software pattern. This is a service that can help to transform large `IF..Then..Else` blocks into something easier to work with.

A word of warning with this service: It is difficult for junior developers to understand how it works. When it is in place, adding additional features is easy, but the architect should spend time to ensure that team members understand the service, what it is used for, and how it works.

The basic idea is to have a set of classes called Commands, each of which is self-contained and able to perform a specific function. These commands are registered with the command dispatcher service along with a specific condition that the command is capable of handling. During run-time, the business logic submits the parameters describing a certain condition that is possibly unpredictable at design time, and the dispatcher determines which one or more of the commands to execute.

An example of this might be interpreting command-line arguments for your application. Command-line arguments are supported in many legacy applications and offer a way of performing various duties without the overhead of running the entire UI for the application.

Typically, command lines are composed of commands and optional data elements for those commands. The commands are usually delimited by a slash or dash to indicate their keyword status. A good example of this is the DIR command you use in any command shell. Using the command line to ask for help is a convenient way to find all the command-line arguments that are supported. Just type dir /? and press Enter, as shown in Figure 12.1.

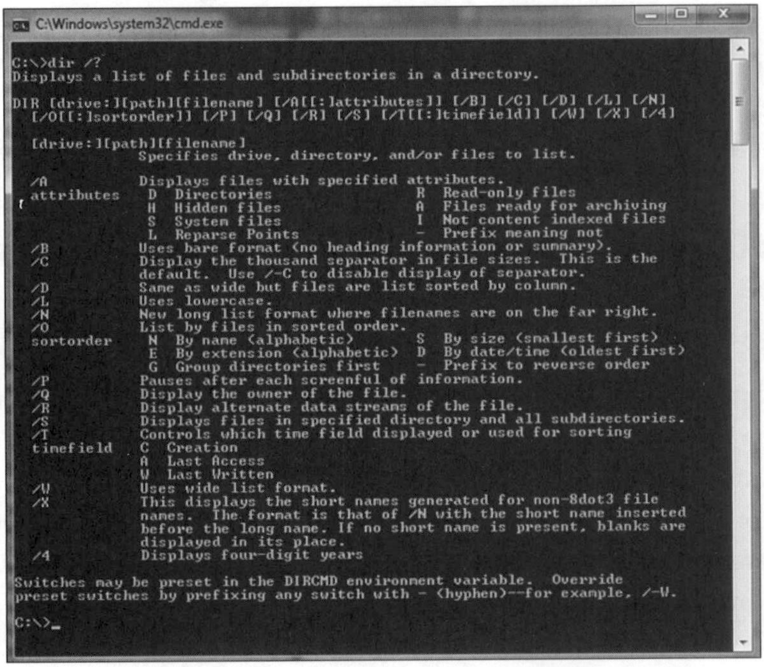

FIGURE 12.1: Results of a DIR command showing command-line help

For our command dispatcher, we can equate each of the parameters listed here to a command. We do not know at design time which of these options the user is going to pick, so we must be prepared to process any of them in any order, including the options parameters that follow some of them.

To implement our own command-line interpreter, the code must parse the command line looking for these slashes or dashes, split the command line into the individual pieces, and process each piece in order. The process gets complicated when you introduce optional parameters for these keywords or when there is a specific order to the commands. Using standard tools to implement this logic results in a large If..Then..Else structure where you need to test each keyword and process accordingly. If we support only a few keywords, this structure can be sufficient, but as the number of keywords expands, so does the complexity; therefore, a more powerful solution is needed. Replacing the If..Then..Else structure with a command dispatcher can make a much more understandable and easy-to-manage parser.

First, we look at the design of the commands, and then we examine the dispatcher service. Listing 12.12 shows how our commands are structured.

LISTING 12.12: An Example Command for the Command Dispatcher

```csharp
using System;

namespace CodeSamples.Ch12_RefactorToAdvancedServices.Listing12
{
  /// <summary>
  /// Base class for a command that is executed via the
  ➥CommandDispatcher.
  /// </summary>
  public abstract class BaseDispatchedCommand<T> : IDispatchedCommand<T>
  {
    public BaseDispatchedCommand(T pCommandKey)
    {
      CommandKey = pCommandKey;
    }

    /// <summary>
    /// Determines whether this command can be executed. Assume
    /// it is always available.
    /// </summary>
    public virtual bool CanExecute(object parameter)
    {
      return true;
    }

    /// <summary>
    /// Executes this command with the given parameter.
    /// </summary>
    public abstract void Execute(object parameter);

    /// <summary>
    /// Notifies subscribers that the status of CanExecute has changed.
    /// </summary>
    public event EventHandler CanExecuteChanged;

    /// <summary>
    /// Key used to lookup this command.
    /// </summary>
    public T CommandKey { get; internal set; }
```

```
    /// <summary>
    /// Number of times this command has been executed.
    /// </summary>
    public int ExecuteCount { get; set; }

}

internal class Cmd1Command : BaseDispatchedCommand<string>
{
  //Give the base the string used to invoke this command.
  public Cmd1Command() : base("/cmd1") { }
  public override void Execute(object parameter)
  {
    //Do something important.
  }
}

public interface IDispatchedCommand<T>
{
  T CommandKey { get; }
  bool CanExecute(Object parameter);
  void Execute(Object parameter);
  event EventHandler CanExecuteChanged;
  int ExecuteCount { get; set; }
}

}
```

The previous code has a `BaseDispatchedCommand` that provides most of the functionality needed for the command dispatcher. The generic argument `TCommandKeyType` is the type of key that is used to locate the proper command. For example, in our command-line interpreter, this is a string because the incoming command-line parameters are strings.

The constructor for the base type accepts the key to be used to identify the command. If you look at the `Cmd1Command` type that inherits from `BaseDispatchedCommand`, you can see that the constructor passes in the command-line parameter that this particular command handles. If the user ever enters the command-line parameter `/cmd1`, this command is chosen, and the `Execute` method is run.

The next parameter in the base command class is the `CanExecute` parameter. By default, we assume that all commands are enabled so the base class always returns true. However, the subclass can insert its own logic to decide whether that particular command is available or not.

Following the `CanExecute`, we have the abstract `Execute` method with an `Object` parameter. This is overridden in the `child` command, and any logic needed to process the `/cmd1` command is entered here. The parameter sent is provided by the dispatcher; we look at this in a moment.

The following properties are for convenience and enable callers to view the key for this command (notice the setter is internal so the key cannot be changed) and to see how many times this command has been executed.

Now let's examine the code for the dispatcher shown in Listing 12.13.

LISTING 12.13: Implementation of the Command Dispatcher Service

```
using System;
using System.Collections.Generic;

namespace CodeSamples.Ch12_RefactorToAdvancedServices.Listing13
{
  public interface ICommandDispatcherService<T>
  {
    void ExecuteCommand(T pCommandLine, object pParameter);
    void AddCommand(IDispatchedCommand<T> pCommand);
    IDispatchedCommand<T> KeyNotFoundCommand { get; set; }
    void ClearCommands();
  }

  public class CommandDispatcherService<T> : ICommandDispatcherService<T>
  {
    /// <summary>
    /// List of commands that can be executed.
    /// </summary>
    internal Dictionary<T, IDispatchedCommand<T>> _executableCommands;

    /// <summary>
    /// The command to execute if a given key is not found. If this is
null,
    /// an ArgumentException will be thrown.
    /// </summary>
    public IDispatchedCommand<T> KeyNotFoundCommand { get; set; }

    public CommandDispatcherService()
    {
      _executableCommands = new Dictionary<T, IDispatchedCommand<T>>();
    }

    /// <summary>
    /// Adds a given command to the list of available commands
    /// </summary>
```

```
      public void AddCommand(IDispatchedCommand<T> pCommand)
      {
        if (pCommand == null) throw new ArgumentNullException("Command");
        _executableCommands.Add(pCommand.CommandKey, pCommand);
      }

      /// <summary>
      /// Executes the command associated with the given key.
      /// </summary>
      public void ExecuteCommand(T pCommandKey, object pParameter)
      {
        if (pCommandKey == null) throw new ArgumentNullException
➥("CommandKey");

        var command = GetCommand(pCommandKey);
        command.Execute(pParameter);
        command.ExecuteCount++;
      }

      private IDispatchedCommand<T> GetCommand(T pCommandKey)
      {
        if (_executableCommands.ContainsKey(pCommandKey))
          return _executableCommands[pCommandKey];
        if (KeyNotFoundCommand != null) return KeyNotFoundCommand;
        throw new ArgumentOutOfRangeException(pCommandKey.ToString());
      }

      /// <summary>
      /// Clears out all commands from list.
      /// </summary>
      public void ClearCommands()
      {
        _executableCommands.Clear();
      }
    }

    public interface IDispatchedCommand<T>
    {
      T CommandKey { get; }
      bool CanExecute(Object parameter);
      void Execute(Object parameter);
      event EventHandler CanExecuteChanged;
      int ExecuteCount { get; set; }
    }
}
```

If you look at the ICommandDispatcherService interface, notice the few items listed. We see the property KeyNotFoundCommand, which enables the caller to specify a specific command to execute if a key is submitted to the dispatcher but not found in the dictionary. Often this is used to handle unexpected keys that do not have their own associated command. The unexpected key is typically logged, then ignored.

In addition to the `KeyNotFoundCommand` property, we see only three methods: one to allow adding commands to the dispatcher, one for executing a given command key, and one for clearing the list. This provides a simple user interface for calling code and hides the complexity of the logic inside the service.

When using a dispatcher service, we first instantiate the service, add commands to it, and then call `ExecuteCommand` with the incoming parameters. To add the commands to the dispatcher, the `AddCommand` method accepts an `IDispatchedCommand` and adds it to the internal dictionary of commands. Notice that the `dictionary` throws an exception if the command key already exists, so we do not have to add logic to ensure the uniqueness of the keys.

After the commands are entered into the dispatcher, the calling code can call the `ExecuteCommand` method with the incoming key and any type of command parameter that is desired. The dispatcher looks up the key in the internal `dictionary` to find the appropriate command, executes that command, and then increments the counter on the command.

Let's look at a specific implementation of the command dispatcher to get a better idea of how it is used. Listing 12.14 shows a command-line interpreter that handles a few command-line parameters. The set of commands is easily expanded to process any additional command-line parameters necessary.

LISTING 12.14: Implementation of the Command-Line Interpreter

```
using System;
using System.Collections.Generic;
using CodeSamples.Ch10_EstablishFoundation.Listing04;
using CodeSamples.Ch12_RefactorToAdvancedServices.Listing12;

namespace CodeSamples.Ch12_RefactorToAdvancedServices.Listing14
{
    /// <summary>
    /// This class will take a command line, parse it into
    /// the component parts, and then process each command.
    /// </summary>
```

```csharp
public class CommandLineInterpreter
{
  /// <summary>
  /// CommandDispatcher we will use for executing the commands
  /// </summary>
  internal ICommandDispatcherService<string> _dispatcher;

  /// <summary>
  /// Constructor will populate the list of commands.
  /// </summary>
  public CommandLineInterpreter()
  {
    _dispatcher = ServiceLocator
      .Resolve<ICommandDispatcherService<string>>();
    _dispatcher.KeyNotFoundCommand = new MissingKeyCommand();
    _dispatcher.AddCommand(new Cmd1Command());
    //add more commands here
  }

  /// <summary>
  /// This method executes a single command.
  /// </summary>
  /// <param name="pCommandLine">The command to be executed</param>
  public void Execute(string pCommandLine)
  {
    if (string.IsNullOrEmpty(pCommandLine)) return;
    pCommandLine = pCommandLine.Trim();
    var commandQueue = ParseCommandLineIntoCommands(pCommandLine);
    while (commandQueue.Count > 0)
    {
      var cmd = commandQueue.Dequeue();
      _dispatcher.ExecuteCommand(cmd, commandQueue);
    }
  }

  /// <summary>
  /// Parses into separate commands by splitting on spaces.  If
➥support
  /// for quoted strings and embedded spaces is necessary,
  /// this logic must be added.
  /// </summary>
  internal Queue<string> ParseCommandLineIntoCommands(string
➥pCommandLine)
  {
    var commands = pCommandLine.Split(' ');
    var result = new Queue<string>();
    foreach (var cmd in commands)
      result.Enqueue(cmd);
```

```
        return result;
    }

    /// <summary>
    /// Command to do something important.
    /// </summary>
    internal class Cmd1Command : BaseDispatchedCommand<string>
    {
        //Give the base the string used to invoke this command.
        public Cmd1Command() : base("/cmd1") { }
        public override void Execute(object parameter)
        {
            //Do something important.
        }
    }


    /// <summary>
    /// Command that is executed if the incoming command from the
    /// command line is not found.  This command can do nothing,
    /// log an error, or anything else that is appropriate.
    /// </summary>
    internal class MissingKeyCommand : BaseDispatchedCommand<string>
    {
        public MissingKeyCommand() : base(Guid.NewGuid().ToString()) { }
        public override void Execute(object parameter)
        {
            //Do error handling here.
        }
    }
}

public interface ICommandDispatcherService<T>
{
    void ExecuteCommand(T pCommandLine, object pParameter);
    void AddCommand(IDispatchedCommand<T> pCommand);
    IDispatchedCommand<T> KeyNotFoundCommand { get; set; }
    void ClearCommands();
}


}
```

The first thing to note is that the CommandLineInterpreter wraps the dispatcher; it does not descend from the dispatcher. This is done to hide the dispatcher method calls that are not appropriate for a command-line interpreter. There should be no need for an outside caller to manipulate the command dispatcher, but if your scenario requires this, it is trivial to add appropriate methods to the command-line interpreter that merely pass the request on to the underlying dispatcher.

> **■ NOTE**
>
> In our example, the commands are internal to the `CommandLineInter-preter`, but this is not necessary. With the Command Dispatcher Pattern, the number of classes in your system can grow significantly, and making the commands internal is one way of taming the beast. Some quality measurement tools do not list internal classes separately; they are counted as part of the containing class. Making the command classes internal decreases the noise generated by these tools. In the end, whether they are internal or external does not affect the way they work, so pick whichever makes the most sense to you.

In the constructor of the `CommandLineInterpreter`, we initialize the dispatcher with the commands that we are prepared to handle for the system. We also set the default command that we want executed if the given command-line parameter is unknown. This `MissingKeyCommand` is quite powerful, allowing you to log information, throw an exception, do nothing, or take any other action that makes sense. Processing continues after the unknown command is executed.

When the `Execute` method is called on the `CommandLineInterpreter`, it accepts a parameter for the command-line text. This text is parsed using the spaces between the words into a queue of incoming tokens. At this point, we do not know if these tokens are commands or parameters, though we do assume that the first item in the queue is a command. We also make the simplifying assumption that there are no strings with embedded spaces. Adding support for this is relatively simple.

We use a queue to contain the incoming commands instead of just a `List<string>` to ensure that the original order is maintained and also to allow any command to change the order if appropriate. For example, imagine a conditional command `/if` that examines a variable and executes the following logic only if that value is true. The command that processed the /if can evaluate the given variable and if false, pull commands off of the queue until it encounters the /endif command. Processing can then continue as normal.

The queue also enables us to add support for parameters to the command-line arguments. Assume we need a parameter for a certain command, such as sorting output by a certain field. The command line looks similar to /o, and the subsequent command executed by the dispatcher is SortColumnName. In the command execution code for this command, we can simply take the next item off the queue to get the SortColumnName parameter, and then processing continues as normal.

After the queue is created, the interpreter processes the queue by simply looping through all queued commands and calling the dispatcher with each one.

Refactoring for CommandLineInterpreter

To reengineer the existing system to use the new CommandLineInterpreter, we must know what commands we will support. We then create a new descendant of BaseDispatchedCommand for each of these commands and add the appropriate logic to the Execute method. Creating the command as separate classes is a perfect opportunity to add the appropriate unit tests for each command.

After we have the supported command-line commands created, we simply place a call to the CommandLineInterpreter.Execute with the string from the command line. Some languages provide the command line as an array of strings; our interpreter is easily updated to accept this as another option for the Execute method parameter.

Because a command line is typically interpreted only when the application is first run, it is not difficult to locate the place where the new interpreter should go. Just be sure that the BootStrapper runs before we interpret the command line so that the service can be registered. Also, the commands might use some services which are assumed to be registered.

Summary

In this chapter, we analyzed the more advanced services that are typically found in a legacy application and how to convert them to a service-oriented architecture (SOA). We tackled the difficult tasks of converting an existing repository and of reengineering to begin using a repository. These changes are difficult to make and can have far reaching consequences, but they make your application much easier to use and enhance. We also examined some new structures that are useful in managing the myriad of objects that are required in a modern system.

In the next chapter, we take the final step to reengineer to an MVC/MVP/MVVM pattern.

▌13▪

Refactoring to a Controller

The last step in the reengineering journey is to refactor the forms in our application that have business logic buried inside them to either a controller or view pair or a ViewModel and View pair. The process is similar, so we are going to assume you are refactoring to use the Model-View-Controller architecture and call everything a controller.

▪ NOTE

We assume MVC instead of MVVM to avoid the binding process that goes along with MVVM- and WPF -based applications. The binding engine in WPF-based applications is powerful and hides a lot of the plumbing that is necessary to connect a view and view model. In day-to-day development, this is advantageous, but when trying to demonstrate how to refactor for a controller or view model, we need to see how this code works. Therefore, we'd rather show how to build the plumbing when necessary and let those with a WPF-based application ignore these pieces of code, rather than show the MVVM approach and make the MVC proponents figure out how to do it on their own.

Strictly speaking, the code that follows is the Model-View-Presenter (MVP) pattern, not MVC. However, MVP is simply MVC where the view has no knowledge of the model, which makes MVP a special type of MVC. We use the term MVC in this chapter because the techniques described here apply to either MVC or MVP patterns.

By this time, we have created many services that encapsulate much of the architectural and business logic we need for our system. However, we still have business logic tied up in the individual forms and views that we need to pull out so it can be tested. As long as this logic is buried in the form files, we can never be absolutely sure that our application is fully tested.

Using the Legacy Approach to Form Creation

The first step in getting the business logic out of the forms and views is introducing a view model or controller. We got a hint of things to come in Chapter 10, "Establishing the Foundation," when we adapted our shell to be created by a controller. Now we make similar changes for the rest of the forms by moving the business logic into the controller where it can be tested.

Legacy applications often implement their UI by creating the form and showing it in the shell. We introduce our controllers so that the existing infrastructure of creating the forms changes as little as possible.

Let's start with a sample of how many legacy applications create their data entry forms. We assume we have a main shell that has a handler for a toolbar button that shows a new data entry form. Listing 13.1 shows how the code can look.

LISTING 13.1: **An Example of the Form Creation Logic Typical of Legacy Applications**

```
using System;
using System.Windows.Forms;
using CodeSamples.Ch10_EstablishFoundation.Listing04;

namespace CodeSamples.Ch13_RefactorToViewModel.Listing01
{
  public class ShellForm : Form
  {
    private Button _showViewBtn;

    public ShellForm()
    {
      _showViewBtn = new Button();
      Controls.Add(_showViewBtn);
```

```csharp
      _showViewBtn.Click += ShowViewRequested;
    }

    private void ShowViewRequested(object sender, System.EventArgs e)
    {
      var frm = new DataEntryView();
      frm.LoadUserData(1);
      frm.Show();
    }
  }

public class DataEntryView : Form
{
  private TextBox _userName;
  private User _user;
  private Button _saveBtn;

  public DataEntryView()
  {
    _saveBtn = new Button();
    Controls.Add(_saveBtn);
    _userName = new TextBox();
    Controls.Add(_userName);

    _saveBtn.Click += _saveBtn_Click;
  }

  void _saveBtn_Click(object sender, EventArgs e)
  {
    if (string.IsNullOrEmpty(_userName.Text))
    {
      var dlgSvc = ServiceLocator.Resolve<IDialogService>();
      dlgSvc.Show("You cannot leave name blank");
      return;
    }

    _user.Name = _userName.Text;
    var repository = ServiceLocator.Resolve<IRepository>();
    repository.SaveUser(_user);
  }

  public void LoadUserData(int userId)
  {
    var repository = ServiceLocator.Resolve<IRepository>();
    _user = repository.GetUser(userId);
    _userName.Text = _user.Name;
  }
}
```

```csharp
public class User
{
  public int Id { get; set; }
  public string Username { get; set; }
  public string Name { get; set; }
}

public interface IRepository
{
  User GetUser(int id);
  void SaveUser(User u);
}

public interface IDialogService
{
  void Show(string msg);
}

public class DialogService : IDialogService
{
  public void Show(string msg)
  {
    MessageBox.Show(msg);
  }
}

public class Repository : IRepository
{
  public User GetUser(int id)
  {
    //This code should retrieve the user from the database.
    var u = new User();
    u.Id = id;
    u.Name = "Joe User";
    u.Username = "JoeUser";
    return u;
  }

  public void SaveUser(User u)
  {
    //Code for saving the user to the DB goes here.
  }
}
}
```

This is a boiled-down version of nearly any data entry form. We have a ShellForm with a button that shows the DataEntryForm on the screen. That DataEntryForm is given some data to display to the user for editing. The user edits that data as appropriate and presses a Save button to indicate the edits are complete; the data is stored back to the database. This basic workflow is shown in the different classes and methods, using a repository for data storage.

Notice that in the SaveBtn_Click method, we have some business logic that ensures the user name cannot be blank. When we convert to a controller, this business logic must be maintained.

Our goal in this section is to get as much functionality as possible out of the DataEntryForm and into a controller without losing any of the functionality. Our first step is to introduce the controller.

Preparing the View

The first step is to prepare the view to be resolved by the ServiceLocator. In Listing 13.2, we create the IDataEntryForm interface and make the DataEntryForm class implement that interface. We also update the ShowFormRequested method to create the view using the ServiceLocator and the interface.

LISTING 13.2: The Legacy Form Refactored to Add the IDataEntryForm Interface

```
        .
        .
        .
    private void ShowViewRequested(object sender, System.EventArgs e)
    {
      var frm = ServiceLocator.Resolve<IDataEntryView>();
      frm.LoadUserData(1);
      frm.Show();
    }
  }

  public interface IDataEntryView
  {
    void LoadUserData(int userId);
    void Show();
  }

  public class DataEntryView : Form, IDataEntryView
  {
    private TextBox _userName;
```

```
private User _user;
private Button _saveBtn;
```

.
.
.

To do this, we simply add an interface and make the view implement that interface. This enables us to add a registration for the interface and form into the BootStrapper so the form can be resolved by the ServiceLocator. In Listing 13.2, you can also see that the Shell form now resolves the DataEntryForm via the ServiceLocator instead of using the New keyword.

Introducing the Controller

The next step is to introduce a controller for the view. To do this we create our controller class and add enough logic for it to resolve the DataEntryForm and display it. Listing 13.3 shows the changes we make to implement this. Notice that ShowFormRequested method has changed again; this time it changes to resolve the controller via the ServiceLocator instead of resolving the view.

LISTING 13.3: **Introducing a Controller**

.
.
.

```
private void ShowViewRequested(object sender, System.EventArgs e)
{
  var controller= ServiceLocator.Resolve<IDataEntryFormController>()
;
  controller.LoadUserData(1);
  controller.Show();
}
```

.
.
.

```
public interface IDataEntryViewController
{
  void LoadUserData(int userId);
  void Show();
}

public class DataEntryViewController : IDataEntryViewController
{
  public IDataEntryView View { get; internal set; }

  public DataEntryViewController(int userId)
  {
    View = ServiceLocator.Resolve<IDataEntryView>();
  }

  public void LoadUserData(int userId)
  {
    View.LoadUserData(userId);
  }

  public void Show()
  {
    View.Show();
  }
}
```

.
.
.

This is a critical step in the process of refactoring for a controller or view model. The logic that follows the call to the `ServiceLocator` in the `ShowFormRequested` method is exactly the same due to the few pass-through methods we put on the controller, so the impact on the legacy code is minimal. However, we made the important switch from the old paradigm where the shell passed logic flow to the form, to a new paradigm of the shell passing logic flow to the controller. This is the turning point in reengineering the forms to use a controller or view model instead of having the business logic buried in the form.

> ■ **NOTE**
>
> One note of caution: This refactoring to resolve the controller instead of the form needs to be made throughout the application all at once. If there are any instances where the form is resolved instead of the controller, it introduces a defect that slowly gets worse as the business logic is migrated out of the form and into the controller.

Enhancing the Controller

Now that we have introduced the critical idea of the controller, we can begin the process of migrating the business logic out of the form and into the controller. At no time during this logic migration should the form be unavailable for use. We should be able to use this form like normal at any time, but the business logic will become more and more testable as it migrates into the controller.

Our logic now only passes in the ID of the current user to the form, and the form uses the repository to retrieve the data and then store it again. A better structure would be for the controller to retrieve the user and give it to the form for display. With this logic, the controller is in full control of the data that is displayed, as well as any data validation that needs to be done along the way.

In Listing 13.4, we move the business logic into the controller.

LISTING 13.4: Migrated Code from Form to Form Controller

```
        .
        .
        .

public class DataEntryView : Form, IDataEntryView
{
  private TextBox _userName;
  private User _user;
  private Button _saveBtn;

  protected virtual void OnSaveRequested(object sender, EventArgs e)
  {
    var handler = SaveRequested;
```

```
      if (handler != null) handler(this, e);
  }
  public event EventHandler<EventArgs> SaveRequested;

  public DataEntryView()
  {
    _saveBtn = new Button();
    Controls.Add(_saveBtn);
    _userName = new TextBox();
    Controls.Add(_userName);

    _saveBtn.Click += OnSaveRequested;
  }


  public void LoadUserData(User currentUser)
  {
    _user = currentUser;
    //Bind the user data to the necessary controls.
  }
}

public class DataEntryViewController : IDataEntryViewController
{
  public IDataEntryView View { get; internal set; }
  private User _currentUser;

  public DataEntryViewController()
  {
    View = ServiceLocator.Resolve<IDataEntryView>();
    this.View.SaveRequested += View_SaveRequested;
  }

  void View_SaveRequested(object sender, EventArgs e)
  {
    if (string.IsNullOrEmpty(_currentUser.Name))
    {
      var dlgSvc = ServiceLocator.Resolve<IDialogService>();
      dlgSvc.Show("You cannot leave name blank");
      return;
    }

    var repository = ServiceLocator.Resolve<IRepository>();
    repository.SaveUser(_currentUser);
  }

  public void LoadUserData(int userId)
  {
    var repository = ServiceLocator.Resolve<IRepository>();
    _currentUser = repository.GetUser(userId);
```

```
      }

      public void Show()
      {
        View.Show();
      }
    }
```

.
.
.

This code sample is another big step toward getting all of the business logic out of the form. In this code, we introduced a new event in the form and interface called SaveRequested. When the Save button is pressed on the form, instead of handling the save processing itself, the DataEntryForm passes the request on to the controller, which calls the save method on the repository. With this action, we remove all of the data validation out of the view and into the controller where it can be tested.

Another advantage to this structure is the ease of updating the UI. Should we decide to introduce another way of saving data (that is, a menu choice and a button), we would have to add only a click handler to the menu choice that launches the SaveRequested event. No logic has to change in the controller.

In this code, we also introduce the idea that the controller queries the user data from the database instead of the form using the repository. The form is given the User object to display but is unconcerned about where it came from, which completely removes the need for the form to work with the repository at all.

In this way, we continue moving the business logic out of the form and into the controller until the only code left in the form is UI-related and does not alter data in any way.

> **■ NOTE**
>
> All of the discussion in this chapter also applies to ViewModels. In this last section where we introduced the new event, passing the button push to the controller would have been unnecessary with a WPF-based application due to the advanced binding. However, the techniques to migrate the business logic to the view model are applicable to both view models and controllers.

Summary

If you have completed the work described in these chapters, you should now have an application that is loosely coupled. Any component can now be replaced by completely separate logic without affecting the rest of the application. Many classes can be completely removed, and the application can continue running like normal.

You should now have a much more stable application due to all of the unit tests that you have created along the way, and the road to a defect-free application is mostly behind you.

We hope this book has helped you salvage the logic and value out of your legacy application and given it a much longer life expectancy than it once had.

▪ Appendix ▪

Reengineering .NET Projects with Visual Studio 2012

By the time this book is published, Microsoft will have released its newest version of their development environment, Microsoft Visual Studio 2012. This version provides you with a range of features that make it easier to reengineer your applications. Microsoft Visual Studio 2012 with Application Lifecycle Management has a state-of-the-art source control system and also has excellent unit-testing facilities that enable you to build and execute unit tests to ensure the highest quality for your application. As you reengineer your application, you will appreciate the refactoring support from Visual Studio, especially the code clone detection that detects pieces of code that can be duplicated.

This appendix reviews the release candidate, not the final version of Microsoft Visual Studio 2012. This means that all screenshots, menu items, and procedures should work the same way in the final version; however, it is possible changes might be made before the final release.

Examining Source Control with Visual Studio 2012

Let's begin by examining the enhanced support for source control. The first thing we should do when we create a solution or project is add it to source control. With Visual Studio, this is easily done by selecting your solution, right-clicking it, and choosing Add Solution to Source Control. The Add Solution to Source Control dialog displays (see Figure A.1), prompting you to identify where you want to map your solution on the server. Pick the proper location beneath your team project and then click OK.

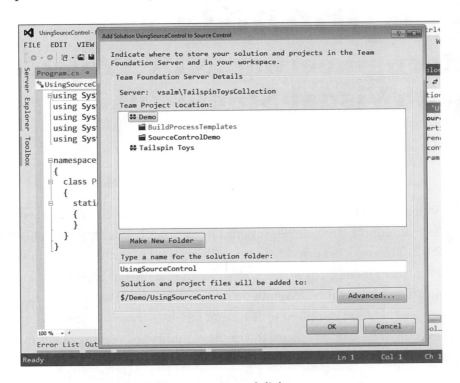

FIGURE A.1: The Add Solution to Source Control dialog

The location you selected in the previous step is called a *workspace*, and Visual Studio keeps the files contained therein synchronized with the source control server. Multiple workspaces are supported for those that develop on several machines. All code changes are saved to the workspace on the local machine, and pending changes can be viewed using the Pending Changes window. To see the Pending Changes window, go to the View menu and select Team Explorer (see Figure A.2).

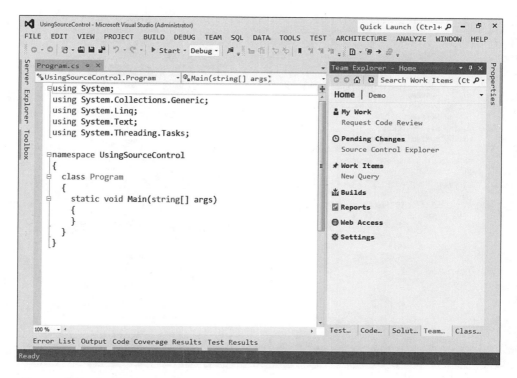

FIGURE A.2: The Team Explorer window

Here you can see the work items that have been assigned to you (the My Work link); your pending changes (the Pending Changes link); work items, reports, and so on. Clicking the Pending Changes link displays this window (see Figure A.3).

This window displays the files in the workspace that you have updated. When you check in, these files are sent to the source control server and made available to the other members of the development team. You can also see the files you have changed in the Solution Explorer window because each new or edited file has an image next to it, indicating that there is a change waiting to be checked in.

To check in your changes, type a check-in comment and click the Checkin button. Team Explorer tells you that the check-in was successful, and that it has created a new ChangeSet. Each ChangeSet has a number and is used to link all the files that were changed in that check-in. As other developers check in their changes, more ChangeSets will be created, each with a unique ChangeSet number.

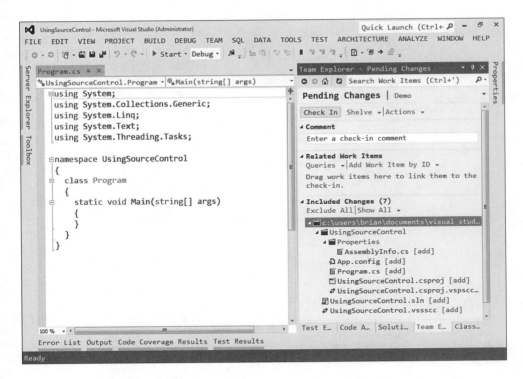

FIGURE A.3: The Pending Changes window

Managing Parallel Development

In the normal process of making code changes, multiple developers can edit the same file without interfering with each other. When two developers have made changes to the same file (each on his own machine), the first developer checks in as normal. The second developer, however, gets a warning that he (or she) needs to merge the first developer's changes. In most cases, the changes are in different parts of the file, so they don't conflict and the system can automatically merge these changes. In the case where the changes do conflict, you have to resolve the conflict manually. Visual Studio 2012 has a merge conflict tool built in that is started automatically when a conflict happens. Let's take a look at this process.

Using two different machines, open the same source code file on each machine and make a change to the same line of code. For example, if you edit the Program class, you can edit the class to look like Listing A.1 on the first machine and Listing A.2 on the second machine.

LISTING A.1: A Merge Conflict Demonstration—Edit 1

```
class Program
{
  static void Welcome()
  {
    Console.WriteLine("Hello!");
  }

  static void Main(string[] args)
  {
    Welcome();
  }
}
```

LISTING A.2: A Merge Conflict Demonstration—Edit 2

```
class Program
{
  static void Main(string[] args)
  {
    Console.WriteLine("Press any key to quit");
    Console.ReadKey();
  }
}
```

> **NOTE**
>
> Creating a new workspace for a solution with Visual Studio 2012 is easy. Open Team Explorer and click the Source Control Explorer link. Look for the solution you want to work on (the one you checked in previously) and double-click the .sln file. If there is no mapping between the server and your machine, Source Control asks you where you want to place the code. From now on, Visual Studio synchronizes this local folder to the server when you check in.

After you have made both of the previous changes (but have not checked anything in yet), open the Team Explorer window on one of the machines, click the Pending Changes link, type a comment and press the Checkin button. The check-in should succeed because this is the first change of this file sent to the server.

Now go back to the other machine and check in those changes. Visual Studio returns with an error that there are conflicting changes (see Figure A.4)

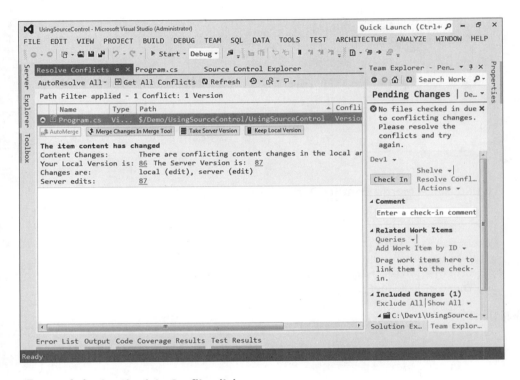

FIGURE A.4: The Check-in Conflict dialog

The Resolve Conflict window opens where you can fix the problem(s). You get four options to choose from by clicking one of the following buttons:

- **Auto Merge**: When Visual Studio sees there are no overlapping changes, this button is enabled. You click it, and all changes are merged together.
- **Merge changes in Merge Tool:** When there are overlapping changes, you need to use a merge tool (which can be different for each different language) to merge the changes by hand.

- **Take Server Version**: In this case, your changes are thrown away.
- **Take Local Version**: Throw away all changes others make.

The easiest choice is to pick the Merge Changes in Merge Tool option, but because we have made conflicting changes to the same file, this option is disabled. Clicking the Merge Changes in Merge Tool (see Figure A.5) opens the built-in merge tool.

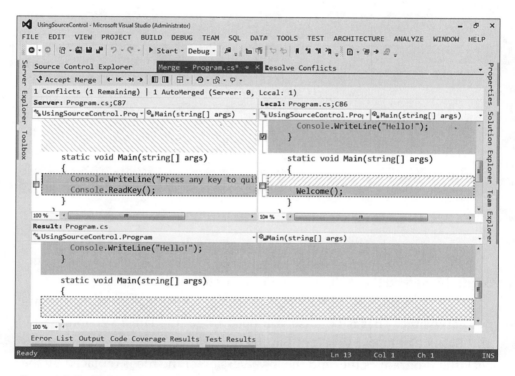

FIGURE A.5: Clicking the Merge Changes in Merge Tool

As you can see, one change (the Welcome method) has already been merged because there is no conflict with the other change. The body of the Main method we need to do manually by selecting which parts we want to keep by checking the checkboxes. We can keep either option, or both. In this case, we want both so click the checkboxes in the order we want the code to appear (see Figure A.6).

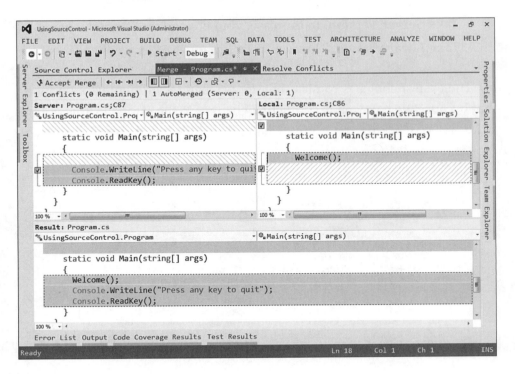

FIGURE A.6: Merge Changes window

Save your changes and close the merge window. After you have successfully merged these changes, you can try to check in again.

When you go back to the other machine, notice that your merges are not yet visible. That is because you need to get the latest version manually. Select Get Latest Version from the drop-down menu when you right-click the Program.cs file, and the local version of the file is replaced by the merged version that is now on the server.

Making Changes in Isolation

Sometimes when you refactor a solution, you need to do a lot of work that might interfere with other developers. For example, your code might not compile as long as your changes are incomplete. However, keeping these changes just on your desktop can be risky if your development machine crashes. Using multiple development machines is also a problem in this scenario because it is difficult to share code among the machines. This is where the Visual Studio Shelving function can help.

A shelf is a place on the server in source control that is separate from the main code line so it will not affect other developers. It enables you to save your changes, transfer these to other machines, and even share with other developers, but the code is always isolated from the main code line. When you are happy with your changes (and this can take several days), you check in those changes to the main code line to become available to the rest of the team.

Assume you are called away to another issue with your code in a bad state (that is, it doesn't compile). You need to work on the new problem, but you don't want to lose the changes you've already made. You can simply put this code on a shelf and then revert all the code in your workspace to get back to the current version of code that the rest of the team is working on. You fix the pressing problem and check the code in. Then, when you are ready to return to this incomplete work, you can restore your local workspace from the shelf, and you are right back to where you started.

Let's again have a look at this with another example, where you are an architect implementing a new feature. Continue with the version where we left off after the merging of conflicts and adding another method, as shown in Listing A.3.

LISTING A.3: Broken Code That Can Be Shelved

```
class Program
{
  static void Welcome()
  {
    Console.WriteLine("Hello!");
  }

  static void NewFeature()
  {
    for( int i =
  }

  static void Main(string[] args)
  {
    Welcome();
    Console.WriteLine("Press any key to quit");
    Console.ReadKey();
  }
}
```

Notice that the code snippet doesn't compile. Go to Team Explorer, click the Pending Changes link, and then click the Shelve link (see Figure A.7).

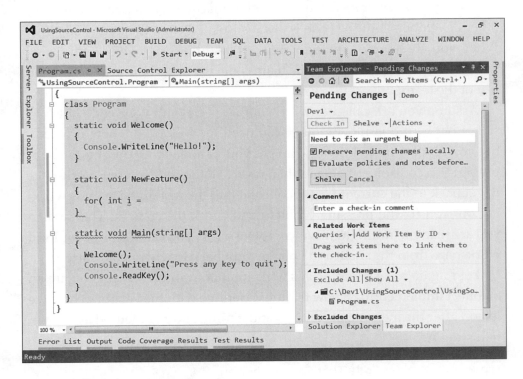

FIGURE A.7: Shelving incomplete changes

To create a shelf, type a name (for example, "halfway done implementing DialogService"). You can have your changes kept locally with the Preserve Pending Changes locally checkbox. In our case, we actually want to go back to the version before our changes, so uncheck this checkbox. The other checkbox is used if you want code-analysis tools to check your code. Because our code is incomplete, make sure it is unchecked.

Now click the Shelve button.

When you are ready to continue with the shelved work, again go to Team Explorer > Pending Changes and use the Actions link to Find Shelvesets. Look for the shelveset you created and right-click it for options. Choose Unshelve. Now you can continue to work.

Unit Testing with Visual Studio 2012

Visual Studio 2012 has improved unit test support to make it easier to increase the quality of your application. To see this new functionality in action, imagine that you have been asked to build a library with helper classes and methods. One of the methods you need to implement is a Square method, one that returns the square of an integer (see Listing A.4).

LISTING A.4: A Simple Class Needing Unit Testing

```
public class MyMath
{
  public int Square(int i)
  {
    return i;
  }
}
```

Notice this method has a bug, which we discover using the built-in unit testing framework.

The next thing we do is to create a unit test project. Visual Studio 2012 has excellent support for unit testing. It comes out of the box with Microsoft's unit test framework, but if you want to, you can install third-party or open-source unit test frameworks such as NUnit. In this example, we use the built-in framework.

Start by adding a new project to your solution, selecting the test category, and then adding the unit test project (see Figure A.8).

Creating the project also creates a framework class for a test. Rename this test class to MyMathTests.cs and choose Yes when asked if you want everything to be renamed.

After renaming, the default test class looks like Listing A.5.

LISTING A.5: A Default Test Class

```
[TestClass]
public class MyMathTests
{
  [TestMethod]
  public void TestMethcd1()
  {
  }
}
```

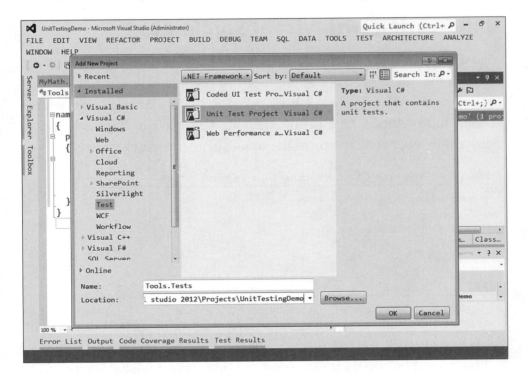

FIGURE A.8: Adding a unit test project

The first thing you should notice is the [TestClass] attribute. This is used to mark this class as a test class, which enables automated tools to locate and run all tests in a solution regardless of where they are located.

The single method is also marked with the [TestMethod] attribute. Again, this is used by the tools to recognize an individual test. Now rename the method to something more appropriate. In this test method, we test whether the Square returns the square of three correctly, so rename it Square_Three_ReturnsNine.

Writing a Unit Test Method

Following the Arrange-Act-Assert method we introduced in Chapter 3, "Unit Testing," we edit our unit test to look like Listing A.6.

LISTING A.6: Creating an Interface

```
[TestClass]
public class MyMathTests
{
  [TestMethod]
  public void Square_Three_ReturnsNine()
  {
    // Arrange
    var target = new MyMath();

    // Act
    var result = target.Square(3);

    // Assert
    Assert.AreEqual(9, result, "Square method is broken");
  }

}
```

In this method, we first create the target object to be tested. Then we invoke the Square method passing three. And finally, we see whether the result is nine. The last part is always done using one of the Assert classes, which has many helper methods that make it easy to check a result.

- The Assert class has methods to check whether the result is equal to a certain value, can check whether it is of a certain type using the IsInstanceOfType, and has a number of other utility methods.

- The StringAssert class has a range of helper methods to check whether strings start or end with a certain string or follow a certain pattern (using regular expressions).

- The CollectionAssert class enables you to check whether a collection has unique elements, whether they all are a certain type, and so on.

Running the Unit Test

To run our unit tests, we use the Test Explorer window. To open it, use the menus or search for it using the Quick Launch from Visual Studio (see Figure A.9).

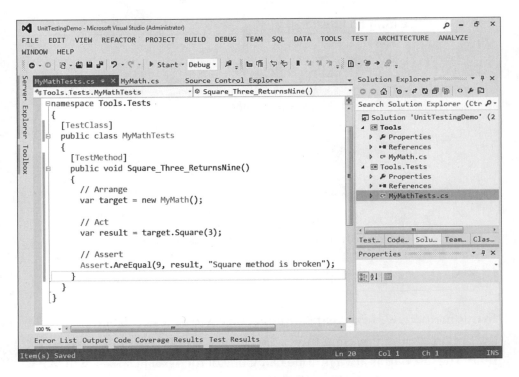

```
UnitTestingDemo - Microsoft Visual Studio (Administrator)
FILE   EDIT   VIEW   REFACTOR   PROJECT   BUILD   DEBUG   TEAM   SQL   DATA   TOOLS   TEST   ARCHITECTURE   ANALYZE
WINDOW   HELP
                                    Start ▾ Debug ▾

MyMathTests.cs ✕   MyMath.cs        Source Control Explorer                    Solution Explorer
Tools.Tests.MyMathTests                  Square_Three_ReturnsNine()
namespace Tools.Tests                                                         Search Solution Explorer (Ctr
{                                                                            Solution 'UnitTestingDemo' (2
  [TestClass]                                                                ▲  Tools
  public class MyMathTests                                                      ▷  Properties
  {                                                                             ▷  References
    [TestMethod]                                                               ▷  MyMath.cs
    public void Square_Three_ReturnsNine()                                   ▲  Tools.Tests
    {                                                                          ▷  Properties
      // Arrange                                                               ▷  References
      var target = new MyMath();                                              ▷  MyMathTests.cs

      // Act
      var result = target.Square(3);

      // Assert                                                               Test…  Code…  Solu…  Team…  Clas…
      Assert.AreEqual(9, result, "Square method is broken");                  Properties
    }
  }
}

100 %
Error List   Output   Code Coverage Results   Test Results
Item(s) Saved                                           Ln 20      Col 1       Ch 1          INS
```

FIGURE A.9: Starting the Test Explorer using Quick Launch

The Test Explorer opens. Now click the Run All hyperlink to run your tests. Visual Studio builds your project and then runs your tests. Because we have a bug in the square method, the test fails (see Figure A.10).

To see what happened, we can use the debugger to step through our code. First, set a breakpoint on the first line of the unit test by clicking the gutter (this is the area to the left of your code). A red dot should display next to the statement. Then use the TEST > Debug > All tests menu item to run your unit tests using the debugger. The debugger should stop at the breakpoint. Now you can step through the code (use the step into functionality) until you reach the body of the Square_Three_ReturnsNine method.

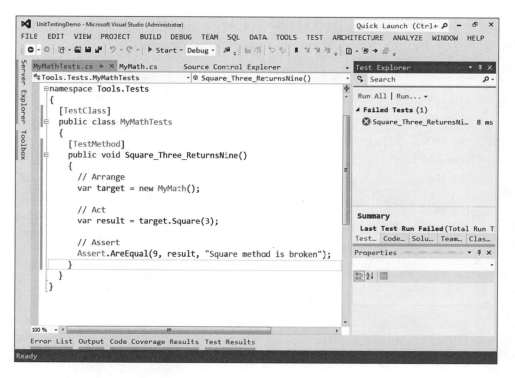

FIGURE A.10: Displaying the test's failure

Using the Edit-and-Continue Feature

Visual Studio 2012 reintroduces another nice feature: edit-and-continue. Using this feature, you can edit the code before you execute it and the debugger simply continues. So change the body of Square, as shown in Listing A.7.

LISTING A.7: Fixing the MyMath Class

```
public class MyMath
{
  public int Square(int i)
  {
    return i * i;
  }
}
```

Let's continue the execution of the code and unit test by pressing the continue (F5) button. Your test should now succeed (see Figure A.11).

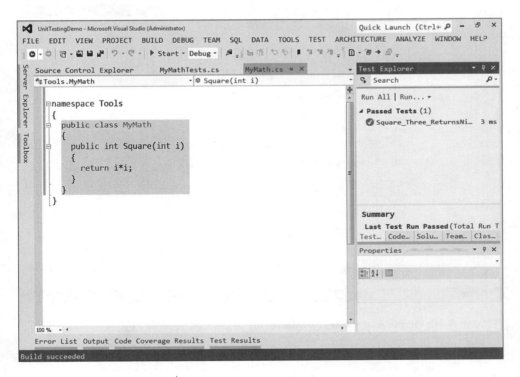

FIGURE A.11: A successful test

The unit-testing feature in Visual Studio 2012 also enables you to capture expected exceptions. By adding the ExpectedException attribute to a test, it succeeds only if that exception is thrown. You use this attribute on methods that test the edge cases that should throw exceptions.

Go back to the first unit test method, place your cursor after the test method, and then use the "testm" code snippet (simply type "testm" and then press the Tab key two times) to create a second unit test. Name this method Square_BigInt_OverflowException. This test passes only if the body throws an OverflowException. Use the ExpectedException attribute as shown in Listing A.8 to tell Visual Studio to expect this method to throw an exception; consider the test unsuccessful if no exception is thrown.

LISTING A.8: Writing a Test for an Expected Exception

```
[TestMethod]
[ExpectedException(typeof(OverflowException))]
public void Square_BigInt_OverflowException()
{
  // Arrange
  var target = new MyMath();
  // Act
  var result = target.Square(int.MaxValue);
}
```

Use the Text Explorer window to run all tests again. Unfortunately, our new test fails (see Figure A.12). We will see why this test failed and fix it in the section on Fakes.

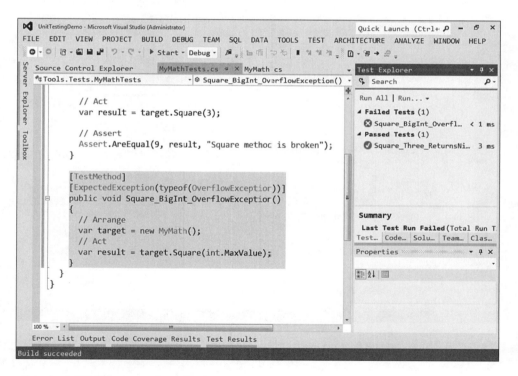

FIGURE A.12: The second test fails.

Using Continuous Test Runner

Before we examine why our second test fails, let's discuss the continuous test runner. As you develop more and more functionality, you need to make sure that your new code doesn't break older functionality. With unit testing in place, you simply run your tests each time you make changes to your code. Visual Studio 2012 makes this even easier by providing the Run tests after build feature (see Figure A.13), which automatically runs tests after each build, executing prior failed tests first. You can enable it by clicking the button to the left of the search box in the Test Explorer window.

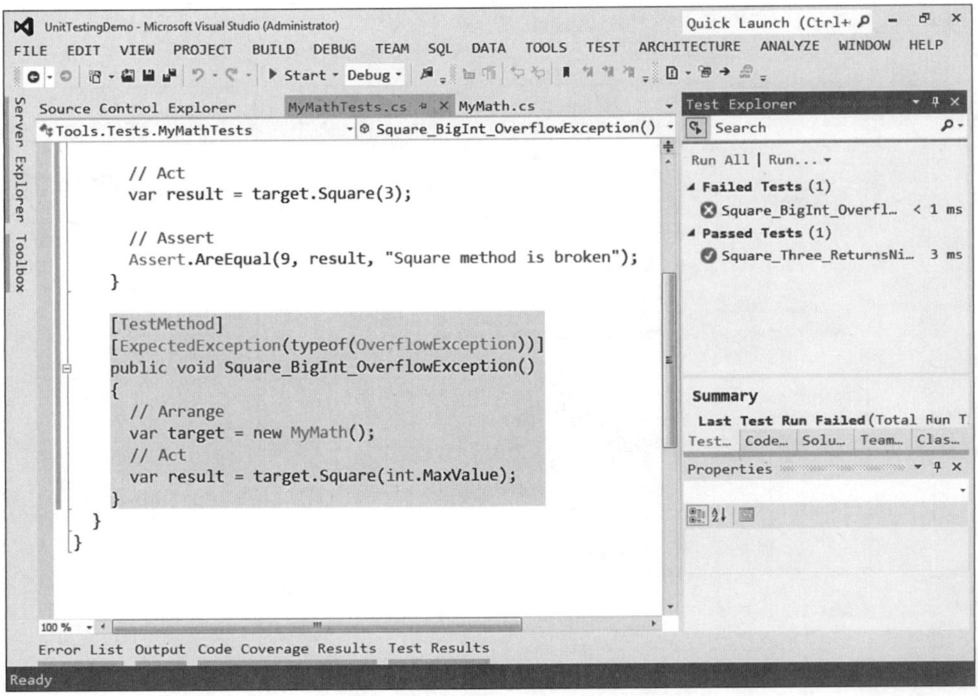

FIGURE A.13: Using the Run tests after build feature

Let's get back to our second test. This test failed because C# does not do overflow checking by default. To check the Square method's implementation for overflow, we add the checked keyword, as shown in Listing A.9.

LISTING A.9: **Square Method with Checked Keyword**

```
public class MyMath
{
  public int Square(int i)
  {
    checked
    {
      return i * i;
    }
  }

}
```

Build your solution, and Visual Studio automatically runs the tests, which now succeed (see Figure A.14)!

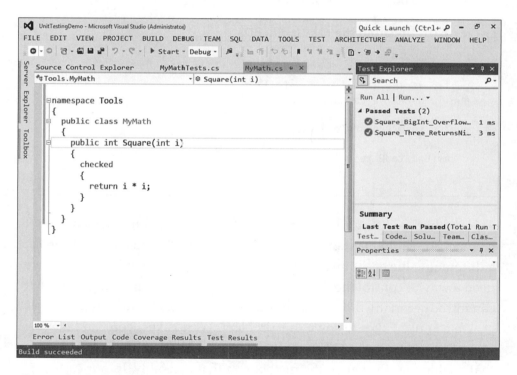

FIGURE A.14: A successful test with the check keyword

Using Fakes to Write Unit Tests for "Untestable" Code

How would you go about testing code that is untestable? I'm talking about code where the source code is missing or code built by another company (such as Microsoft)? A couple of years ago Microsoft released Moles, which was a framework built by Microsoft Research that enabled you to replace any object's method with your code. We discussed this framework in Chapter 5, "Using Test Doubles with Unit Tests." Now this framework is part of Visual Studio and has been renamed to Microsoft Fakes.

Let's see how Fakes works by replacing the result we should get from the DateTime.Now call. A typical use for a date stamp is to mark the LastUpdatedDate of a business entity, as shown in Listing A.10.

LISTING A.10: **Updating the LastUpdatedDate**

```
public class BusinessEntity
{
  public string Name { get; set; }
  public DateTime LastUpdatedDate { get; set; }

  public void PrepareToSave()
  {
    LastUpdatedDate = DateTime.Now;
  }
}
```

This method is difficult to test because it uses DateTime.Now, which cannot be mocked using our standard tools. This means that this method can set a different value each time a test is run. If we want to test this method, we need a way to control the date. We can change the machine's date, but that can introduce many other problems and is not a good way to go.

We can use Fakes to solve this problem. With Fakes, you can take any assembly and have the Microsoft Fakes framework generate helper classes that enable you to change the methods in that assembly. In our case, it is DateTime, so go back to Solution Explorer, open the References folder in your test project (make sure it is your test project!), and right-click the System assembly. Choose Add Fakes Assembly from the drop-down menu. Now you are ready to implement the test method.

Right-click the unit test project again and choose Add > Unit Test from the drop-down menu. Rename the test class `BusinessEntityTests` and rename the test method `PrepareToSave_2012_False`. Implement the method, as shown in Listing A.11.

LISTING A.11: Creating an Interface

```
[TestMethod]
public void PrepareToSave_2012_False()
{
  using (ShimsContext.Create())
  {
    var dt = DateTime.Parse('1/1/2012");
    ShimDateTime.NowGet = () => dt;
    var ent = new BusinessEntity();
    ent.PrepareToSave();
    Assert.AreEqual(dt, ent.LastUpdatedDate);
  }
}
```

In the test method, start by creating a `ShimsContext`, which enables Fakes to replace any method from faked assemblies. Next, use the `ShimDateTime` class to replace the `Now` method from `DateTime`. The `ShimDateTime` class has a property for each method from the `DateTime` class, which can be set to a delegate to replace its implementation. Properties have a getter and, or a setter, so use the `NowGet` property to replace the getter method from `DateTime` to return a date in the year 2012.

The `getter` and `setters` here are troublesome. They are adjectives describing the type of methods. Should they be in quotes?

If you execute this method in 2020, the test will still think it is in the year 2012. Next, check that the business entity is assigned the proper `LastUp-datedDate`. The test should succeed. See Figure A.15.

So with Microsoft Fakes, you can replace any method of any class, which makes this ideal for testing code that was never built with testing in mind.

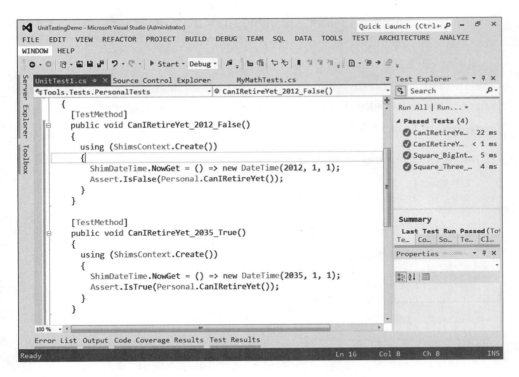

FIGURE A.15: Using Microsoft Fakes

Looking for Hard-to-Maintain Code Using Code Metrics

Visual Studio comes with a series of code analysis tools that check for possible issues in code. One such report is the Code Metrics report. It tells you which methods are hard to maintain and deserves the attention of a developer for refactoring. Simply open your solution and then open the ANALYZE > Run code metrics for the solution. Visual Studio generates the code metrics report after a while (see Figure A.16).

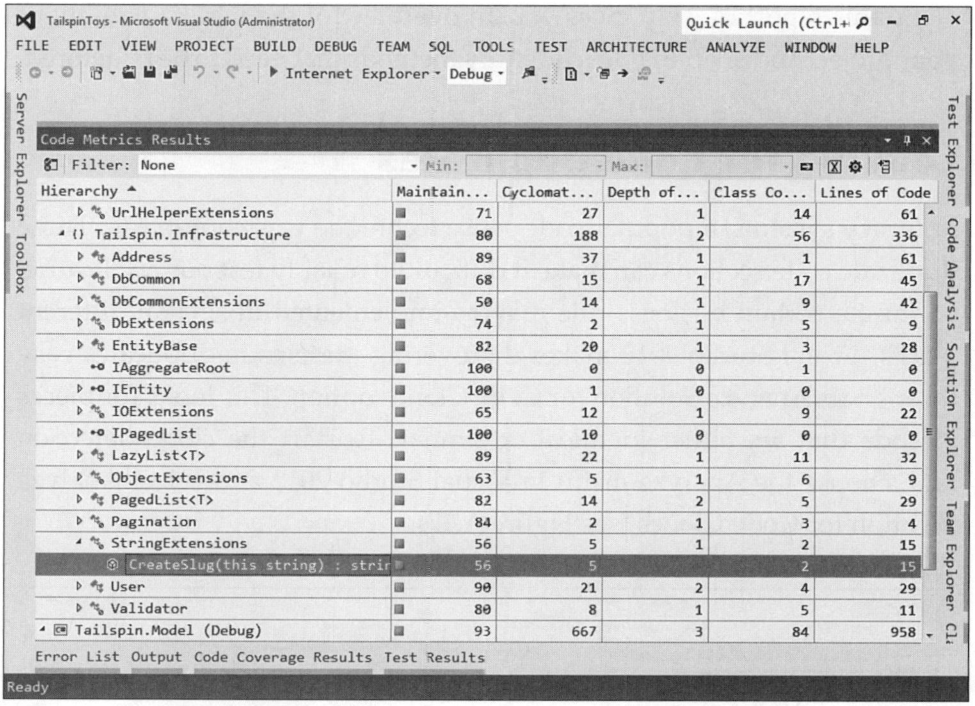

FIGURE A.16: Code metrics results

This report shows a couple of columns:

- **Maintainability Index**: This indicates the maintainability of the code with a value between 0 and 100. The highest number (100) means that this code is simple and easy to maintain. Scores below 60 generally mean that this code is hard to maintain. This score is the result of combining the other columns.

- **Cyclomatic Complexity**: This number is the possible path in the code. A single if-then-else results in a cyclomatic complexity index of 2. Lower is better.

- **Depth of Inheritance**: How many classes does this class derive from? Generally more than three overly complicates a class through inheritance.

- **Class Coupling**: How many other types are used? The more types you use in a class or method, the harder it becomes to make changes.

- **Number of lines**: How many lines of code are in this method or class?

So this report quickly gives you an overview of the maintainability of your project and enables you to identify methods that need to be refactored.

Looking for Code Duplicates

In legacy systems, a popular code-reuse technique was copy-paste. These duplicate code sections can make it difficult to reliably test our application because a certain business rule may be implemented in several different places. Visual Studio 2012 makes discovering these code duplicates easy through its Analyze Solution for Code Clones option. This looks for pieces of code that are either identical or similar. To start the clone detection tool, choose the Analyze menu in Visual Studio 2012 and select Analyze Solution for Code Clones (see Figure A.17).

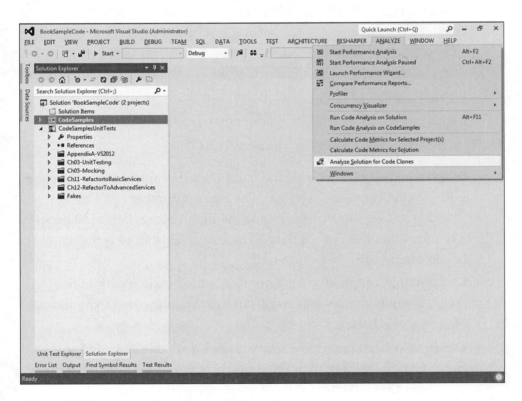

FIGURE A.17: Running the code detection tool

Running the clone detection tool against our book samples returns Exact Matches, Strong Matches, and Medium Matches (see Figure A.18).

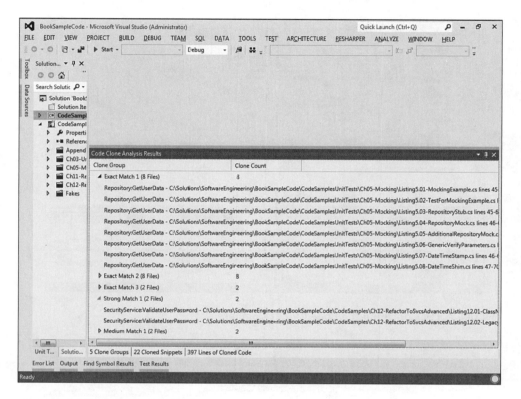

FIGURE A.18: Identified code clones

To determine how similar these code snippets are, Visual Studio 2012 has a tool to compare the two files. Select the two files that are identified as clones and right-click them to get the Compare menu (see Figure A.19).

Selecting this menu option launches the Clone Compare tool, which shows you the differences between the two code samples (see Figure A.20). Notice that it shows only the lines of code that are identified as clones, not the entire file. You can then manually reconcile any differences and write an appropriate method to replace the clones.

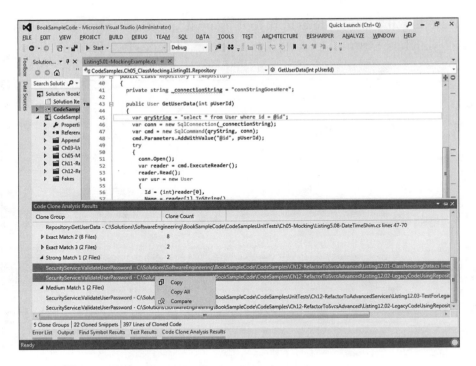

FIGURE A.19: Launching the Code Clones Compare

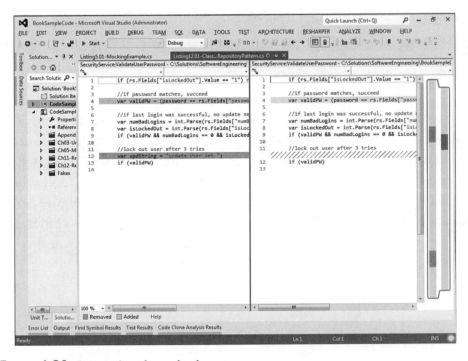

FIGURE A.20: Comparing the code clones

Summary

The new version of Microsoft's development environment, Visual Studio 2012, has many new features that can help when reengineering existing legacy code or creating new code. Of particular interest to you should be the code duplicate detection, continuous test runner, Fake framework, and code metrics. If you use these tools, your day-to-day development tasks will be easier, and they can help you quickly reengineer your legacy code.

Index

C

N–O

P

Microsoft Windows Development Series

Building Metro Applications in Windows 8 with JavaScript
Chris Sells & Brandon Satrom with Don Box

Designing Windows 8 Metro Applications with C# and XAML
Foreword by Jeff Prosise
Jeremy Likness

Visual Studio Team Foundation Server 2012 Adopting Agile Software Practices
From Backlog to Continuous Feedback
Foreword by Brian Harry, Microsoft Technical Fellow
Sam Guckenheimer & Neno Loje

Essential C# 5.0
Mark Michaelis with Eric Lippert

◆ Addison-Wesley

Visit informit.com/mswinseries for a complete list of available publications.

The Windows Development Series grew out of the award-winning Microsoft .NET Development Series established in 2002 to provide professional developers with the most comprehensive and practical coverage of the latest Windows developer technologies. The original series has been expanded to include not just .NET, but all major Windows platform technologies and tools. It is supported and developed by the leaders and experts of Microsoft development technologies, including Microsoft architects, MVPs and RDs, and leading industry luminaries. Titles and resources in this series provide a core resource of information and understanding every developer needs to write effective applications for Windows and related Microsoft developer technologies.

"This is a great resource for developers targeting Microsoft platforms. It covers all bases, from expert perspective to reference and how-to. Books in this series are essential reading for those who want to judiciously expand their knowledge and expertise."

— JOHN MONTGOMERY, Principal Director of Program Management, Microsoft

"This series is always where I go first for the best way to get up to speed on new technologies. With its expanded charter to go beyond .NET into the entire Windows platform, this series just keeps getting better and more relevant to the modern Windows developer."

— CHRIS SELLS, Vice President, Developer Tools Division, Telerik

Make sure to connect with us!
informit.com/socialconnect

Addison Wesley | informIT.com THE TRUSTED TECHNOLOGY LEARNING SOURCE | Safari Books Online

ALWAYS LEARNING

PEARSON

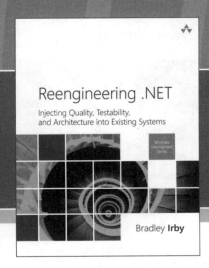

Reengineering .NET

Injecting Quality, Testability,
and Architecture into Existing Systems

Bradley **Irby**

FREE
Online Edition

Safari
Books Online

Your purchase of **Reengineering.NET** includes access to a free online edition for 45 days through the **Safari Books Online** subscription service. Nearly every Addison-Wesley Professional book is available online through **Safari Books Online**, along with thousands of books and videos from publishers such as Cisco Press, Exam Cram, IBM Press, O'Reilly Media, Prentice Hall, Que, Sams, and VMware Press.

Safari Books Online is a digital library providing searchable, on-demand access to thousands of technology, digital media, and professional development books and videos from leading publishers. With one monthly or yearly subscription price, you get unlimited access to learning tools and information on topics including mobile app and software development, tips and tricks on using your favorite gadgets, networking, project management, graphic design, and much more.

Activate your FREE Online Edition at
informit.com/safarifree

STEP 1:   Enter the coupon code: ESHYKCB.

STEP 2:   New Safari users, complete the brief registration form.
Safari subscribers, just log in.

If you have difficulty registering on Safari or accessing the online edition,
please e-mail customer-service@safaribooksonline.com